Up the Amazon Without a Paddle

Doug Lansky

Meadowbrook Press

Distributed by Simon & Schuster

New York

Library of Congress Cataloging-in-Publication Data

Lansky, Doug.
    Up the Amazon without a paddle / Doug Lansky.
        p.   cm.
    ISBN 0-88166-334-4 (MB). — ISBN 0-671-31657-5 (S&S)
    1. Travel Anecdotes.   I. Title. II. Title: Nineteen stories from
    Up the Amazon without a paddle. III. Title: Up the Amazon
    without a paddle.
    G151.L367   1999
    910.4—DC21   99-20061
                                                  CIP

Editorial Coordinator: Liya Lev Oertel
Copyeditor: Melanie Mallon
Production Manager: Joe Gagne
Production Assistant: Danielle White

© 1999 by Doug Lansky

Published by Meadowbrook Press, 5451 Smetana Drive,
Minnetonka, Minnesota 55343

www.meadowbrookpress.com

BOOK TRADE DISTRIBUTION by Simon & Schuster, a division of
Simon and Schuster, Inc., 1230 Avenue of the Americas, New York,
NY 10020

04 03 02 01 00 99   10 9 8 7 6 5 4 3 2 1

Printed in the United States of America

Dedication

for Signe

Acknowledgments

Nothing in literature is as deterring as a long acknowledgments page. I have to assume, therefore, that anyone who is reading this is doing so with the vague hope that they might find their name mentioned below.

I'd like to thank my parents, even though they both initially did everything they could to discourage me from traveling. My dad was instrumental in the completion of this book and deserves top billing. He has a keen eye for editorial detail, and he has always contributed many ideas to my writing, some of which even found their way into print. My mom has become an ardent supporter of my adventures (provided I don't tell her about them until after I've survived) in addition to keeping an eye on my quickly emptying bank account when I'm on the road. In short, the fact that I usually stay on the other side of the planet does not reflect my feelings toward my parents. I love them very much.

It's hard to sum up what Signe has done for me over the last eight years we've spent more or less together, at least without getting into sexually graphic detail. "For Signe" on the other page doesn't do her much justice either. She is an editor, photographer, frequent travel companion, and all-around great person. And I'm not just saying this because she is a doctor and financially supports me.

A big thanks to my witty editor, Melanie Mallon; overseeing editor, Liya Lev Oertel; long-time friend and input provider, Aaron Dorfman; feedback experts, Anna Ljungren and Martin Stafstrom; and everyone at Meadowbrook Press/Simon & Schuster who worked on design, promotion, and sales of this book.

Can't forget a heartfelt thanks to my two grandfathers, Grandpa David and Grandpa Arthur, both world travelers, for their inspiration and support.

Table of Contents

EPILOGUE

It's a Disney World after All!

Introduction

You're probably deciding right now that you're not going to read the rest of this introduction. And quite frankly, I don't blame you. I tend to avoid introductions myself, and when the subject comes up among friends, I've heard many of them profess to be introduction skippers as well. Naturally, this aversion also applies to prefaces, prologues, forwards, and preambles.

Fellow introduction skippers will be happy to note: you can bypass this part and not miss anything vital to your understanding of this book. It's basically about how I got started in travel writing and why I went traveling in the first place—two of the more random decisions in my life.

After two years tripping around some of the more volatile regions of the planet, I admit it was a tad embarrassing to get injured in Bangkok, a city that safely hosts about five million overweight, bicycle-short-wearing, video-camera-encumbered tourists each year. But in retrospect, I guess in terms of travel writing (and medically) you could say it was my big break.

What happened? I was crossing the street between cars waiting at a red light (jay walking) when a pickup truck surged at me for no particular reason other than it was the last Saturday of the month, which in Thailand is national Surge-a-Utility-Vehicle-at-an-Unsuspecting-Tourist Day. My quick reflexes helped me to jump out of the way, and into the path of a car that was approaching at forty-five miles per hour.

I saw the car at the last moment and dove back in the other direction. And I would have made a clean getaway if the speeding car hadn't held me back by running over my ankle.

As a seasoned traveler accustomed to handling international emergency situations, I crawled onto the sidewalk and screamed my head off. Having heard my ankle crack like a fortune cookie under the ski

1

boot of a sumo wrestler, I knew that I should get myself to the hospital, so I intermixed my yelling with the occasional "Help!" and "Help me!" and "Fuck!" I believe this translates in Thailand to "Go away!" and "Go away and never come back!" and "Fuck!" respectively.

This would explain why about seventy passing cars, including the one that hit me, failed to stop and give me a hand. It also deterred roughly fifteen pedestrians, including a Buddhist monk, from doing anything more than hovering behind me, like dogs sniffing a dead squirrel, before wandering off to more pressing business.

The police arrived after ten minutes. Upon hearing I didn't remember the car's color or license plate number, they left immediately.

Fortunately, an English-speaking man, who arrived just after the police, helped me into the back of his sports car and whisked me off to the nearest hospital after first dropping his wife off at their house about five miles in the opposite direction.

At the hospital, the nurses, following what I believe to be standard International Red Cross emergency procedures, gave me two aspirin and left me alone in a room for an hour with a motorcycle crash victim who may have been dead.

When the doctor finally arrived, I was relieved to hear that he spoke English and disappointed to hear that the only painkiller I was going to get were the two aspirin I had already swallowed. I asked if he'd heard of morphine or codeine or Jim Beam. He just shook his head and smiled as if to say he would have an easier time getting the Louvre to loan him their Renaissance collection.

They decided to put a cast on my leg and cut the cast off about five minutes later, probably so they could charge me for the procedure. I was having difficulty following their logic. I was also having difficulty remaining conscious. The agony level had reached DEFCON 2. Finally, they decided to put the cut-off cast back on my leg and fasten it with a band-aid. This had approximately the same stabilizing effect as wrapping my leg in origami paper.

The doctor returned beaming with pride at his staff's excellent work. He explained that I would require surgery within a few days but to "not worry" because it would be a "bloodless operation"— whatever that means. Would the anesthesiologist sedate me with aspirin and a toxic magic marker? Would I wake up with a cast shaped like a Japanese goldfish? I wasn't about to find out.

I decided to leave the country. I asked the doctor to call for a taxi and bring me the medical bill. The emergency room fee, doctor consultation, X-ray, aspirin, cast, removal of cast, return of removed cast, and a new set of crutches came to thirty dollars. Even for malpractice, it was a good deal.

I then picked up some Valium on the black market, went to the airport, and boarded the next plane to Europe, or in this case, Frankfurt, and took the train to Copenhagen, bus to the harbor, ferry to Sweden, and train to the house of Signe, my Swedish friend, where I collapsed from the same exhaustion and pain you would be having right now if you tried to read this sentence out loud with one breath.

My friend escorted me to a very large and clean Swedish hospital filled with doctors and nurses performing extremely socialized medicine. They didn't quite know what to do with me since they had seemingly never had to bill someone before. These Swedish hospital administrators took one look at my insurance card and gave me that same sort of dazed, confused look that American hospital administrators give you when you *don't* have insurance.

They finally admitted me . . . into the infectious wing of the hospital, probably after thinking, "Thailand, Chernobyl, whatever. This guy's a foreigner." To see me, the nurses and doctors had to don hermetically sealed spaceman suits, complete with masks and rubber gloves.

Eventually, doctors operated and gave my ankle a matching set of pins and staples. When I emerged from the anesthesia, I apparently said—loudly—a bunch of embarrassing things that everyone in the recovery room understood because most Swedes speak English better than I do. Of course, I don't remember any of this.

From what I could see—a bunch of silly drawings and naughty Swedish words decorating my cast—the operation was a success; I would be up and dodging traffic in a matter of months. This was when I started to write. By the time I was crossing streets again (now with the aid of a fluorescent orange crossing-guard vest), I had landed a job with Tribune Media Services, by conservative estimates the most brilliant newspaper syndicate on the face of the earth. Which led to some gigs for radio, magazines, books . . . an entire range of media that paid me horribly and covered none of my travel expenses. To this day, I pay for everything myself*, take no freebies, and, at the end of the year, have no money to show for any of this. Which is okay by me. I'm in it for the lifestyle.

Why I started traveling two years before this accident is another question—one I can't answer well because my rationale was nearly nonexistent. In fact, I normally devote more attention to selecting a salad dressing.

I was sitting with the rest of my college graduating class listening to the commencement speaker prepare us for life after graduation, and he had a lot of ground to cover because my liberal arts education had skirted the issue for four years. It was eighty-five degrees and the sun was beating down on my black polyester shroud and square hat—not exactly how I wanted to enter the "real world." I was just waiting for them to call my name so I could go up, collect my diploma, fold it into a paper hat, and start flipping burgers at McDonalds.

---

*I did get a little overexcited when I first got my press card and accepted three activity freebies and two $10 discounts—a total of one quarter of one percent of the more than $100,000 I've spent during the last seven years traveling. I mention these in the articles by way of repentance since freebies are not looked upon kindly in the travel writing biz, nor should they be.

Every economic forecaster had their finger pointed in a different direction and my heart wasn't pounding with the thought of a consulting job, graduate school, or slaving for a highly ethical nonprofit organization. After taking my junior year abroad, then hopping around Europe for the summer, my heart was still in my backpack.

While the speaker was rambling on about networking, my gown was turning into a sauna and I was daydreaming about canoeing up the Amazon, sailing down the Nile, crossing the desert on a camel, ski instructing in the Alps, crewing on a yacht in the Caribbean, scuba diving in the Red Sea, splashing around in the Ganges, questioning a guru in Tibet, swimming with sea lions in the Galápagos, climbing mountains in Patagonia, and white-water rafting in Zimbabwe. I know it's a lot of daydreaming. It was a long speech.

My first "real world" lesson came that evening, when I tried to convince my parents of the value of my plan. Ironically, they considered my around-the-world trip to be avoiding the "real world."

I told them I could study cultural anthropology, international relations, ecology, marine biology, geology, geography, oceanography, Eastern religions, socialism, Darwinism, social Darwinism, and numerous languages during my trip.

They didn't buy it. Fortunately, grandparents are far more receptive to harebrained schemes. Plus, I had already sold my stereo, guitar, drum set, and just about everything else I owned. Throw in a few graduation gifts and I had enough money to get started.

I had seen the Marco Polo miniseries on TV. I had read several issues of *National Geographic*. There were at least a million things to worry about on a trip like this. But if I worried about them I'd never get past my driveway. I didn't know how much money I needed, what to bring, which vaccinations to get, what kind of plane ticket to buy, where to go. Nothing. I knew only that I wanted to go—and make it back in one piece.

And I almost did.

Africa

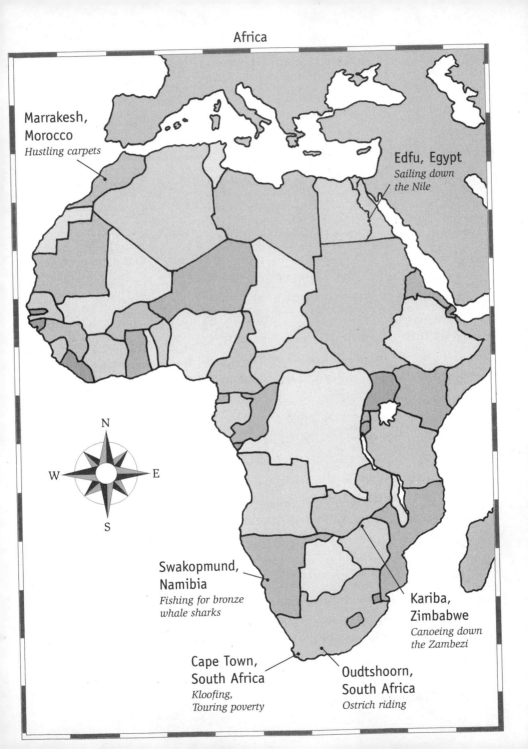

Marrakesh,
Morocco
Hustling carpets

Edfu, Egypt
*Sailing down
the Nile*

Swakopmund,
Namibia
*Fishing for bronze
whale sharks*

Kariba,
Zimbabwe
*Canoeing down
the Zambezi*

Cape Town,
South Africa
*Kloofing,
Touring poverty*

Oudtshoorn,
South Africa
Ostrich riding

AFRICA

Africa has long been called the Dark Continent, but how it got this name I have no idea. I've spent about six months in Africa, and, offhand, I cannot think of a place where I experienced more direct sunlight. My best guess is that the guy who coined this handle spent a good deal of time in my youth hostel in Harare, where the bathroom lightbulb was nonexistent. You had to carry a flashlight or candle if you had to go during the night, and even then most of the male travelers seemed to miss the toilet by more than the internationally allowable two feet. Perhaps what the guy really meant was "The Dark Incontinence."

Hungry, Hungry Hippos

Canoeing down the Zambezi

Kariba, Zimbabwe

 A canoe trip down the lower Zambezi is a bit like eating a pizza in your living room, with just a few minor differences: you are in a canoe on a murky river in Africa, no pizza is to be found within three hundred miles, and several large African animals in and around the river believe it is, in fact, their living room and you are the pizza.

Canoeing down the Zambezi, which frames the border between Zimbabwe and Zambia, is not the sort of thing you would do on your own unless large portions of your brain were missing (whereas going with a tour company only requires the absence of minor brain portions). That's why I signed up with a low-end tour company called Buffalo Safaris. Still, I had to pay $360 for a four-day canoe trip and they made me sign a waiver that basically stated they could keep the money even if I was entirely or partially eaten by one of the large animals.

I was joined by a Dutch couple, a German couple, and a Kiwi/English couple, and I can assure you we were all missing appropriate portions of brain tissue. I got to paddle in the lead canoe with the diminutive and quiet but extremely good-natured Zimbabwean guide John Mousaka (yes, he was well aware that his name is a Greek dish), while the others followed behind, two per canoe.

As a front person, my job was to paddle. The rear person was responsible for the canoe's direction. John was a fine canoeist but he didn't provide much in the way of paddling instruction for the canoeists behind us. The Kiwi/Brit team had some experience, but it was the first time for the Germans and the Dutch, who quickly fell behind with their spastic zigzag canoeing styles.

John's Zimbabwean accent (which resembled, in part, Australian, British, and mumbling), combined with the distance between the canoes, made animal identification more challenging.

"That's a stripe-necked heron," John would try to tell me in his whispered speech.

"What kind?" Chris would ask from the canoe behind.

"A hype-necked bheron!" I'd yell, unsure of my pronunciation, but unable to clarify without an animal identification book.

"It's a high-pecked baron!" I'd hear Chris tell the Dutch.

Throughout the trip, I think we inadvertently renamed nearly every animal we saw.

It took quite a while, basically the entire trip, to get used to sharing the river with hippos. Despite the fact that they look like water-logged cows, hippos are responsible for more human deaths than any other animal in Africa. Hippos are not fond of surprise visitors, and they don't treat them very hospitably.

Many hippos were floating in large groups that, from a distance, looked like partially submerged mines. Those were easy to spot and, therefore, easy to avoid. The trick was to find the ones under-water. If we didn't know where they were, there was a good chance they would surface under our canoe and bite us into anchovy-sized pieces, which John reminded us "is not a good thing." To remove the element of surprise, we used our paddles to hit the sides of our canoes continually—every thirty seconds or so—to let them know where we were. It was a bit like a courtesy knock when entering a familiar neighbor's home. The sound would travel through the water and a few hundred meters downstream hippos would pop their heads up and give us a quick glance before disappearing back into the seemingly gentle river.

Once we knew their location, we would head for the opposite side of the river, except in the smaller channels between grassy islands where the river was barely wide enough for a hippo and a canoe. In that case, we would stick to the more shallow of the two banks because—this is the Survival Rule of Canoeing with Hippos—they flee to deeper water. Unfortunately, some of the hippos had not been briefed on where they were supposed to flee, and so they ran straight at us. To be more precise, they charged at me because I was sitting at the front of the lead canoe.

There are not many ways to stop a charging hippo on the Zambezi. If John shot him with his revolver,* it would just make the hippo angry. If we bailed out of our canoes, we were crocodile bait. And if we paddled up onto land, we'd have to fend off the buffalo and elephants waiting to stomp us into Zambezi pizza toppings. So what did we do? We slapped our paddles against the water. This doesn't sound like much of a defense against a charging, angry, three-ton hippo, but it did the trick surprisingly well—although one charging hippo did get within about two yards of me before deciding he was deterred by my frenzied slapping.

Every night we camped on the banks of the river. We had plenty of company—the river banks were lined with hippos, buffalo, and elephants, as well as lions, leopards, hyenas, baboons, and tsetse flies, which were lured to the Zambezi by its fresh water and the lush grazing land that bordered it. Fortunately, we were protected by our sturdy antimalarial mosquito nets.**

---

*Which was sitting somewhere at the bottom of his waterproof bag where, in a real emergency, he could probably find it and pull it out in a little over five minutes.

**Unfortunately, they were riddled with gaping holes plenty large enough for mosquitoes, tsetse flies, and in some cases, small leopards.

We pulled our canoes over to the riverbank for some lunch, and were soon joined by a few pachyderms. I'm not sure, but I think the one on the left is mooning me.

We were not in a fenced-in camp site. We didn't even have tents. We lay on individual cots with our semipermeable mosquito nets draped over our heads. And I know for a fact that no one in our group got any sleep, including John Mousaka who, in addition to fending off any night attacks from animals, had to keep the canoes from getting stolen by the Zambians on the other side of the river, which seemed to be his biggest fear. The rest of us spent the nights listening to lions roaring and hyenas laughing (apparently, the joke was on us). This was hard to ignore because the sounds seemed to come from a distance of no more than fifteen yards away. Why didn't the animals eat us? I'm not sure. Perhaps our pungent body odors were keeping them at bay.

To compensate for our sleepless nights, we followed the animals' lead and took naps during the midday heat, which was about 110 degrees—too hot to canoe and too hot for the animals to hunt us.

Something happened on the third night that still gives me nightmares. John was fishing on the river bank for some tiger fish, a cross between a salmon and a piranha. After a few minutes without a bite, he handed the line (he had no fishing pole) over to the Kiwi, Chris. Chris followed John's lasso-style casting technique and landed the bacon-baited hook on a floating branch. While we were debating who should wade out and unsnag it, the line ran. Or, I should say, something ran and decided to take our line with it. Chris tried to hold on without burning his hands and I tried to assist by taking a fork from the bottom of the canoe and wrapping it around the speeding line. We both grabbed hold of the fork and pulled until the line snapped. One heck of a big tiger fish, . . . or so we thought.

At exactly 3:05 A.M., or maybe it was exactly 3:25 A.M.—anyway, it was early—I woke up on my mosquito-net-protected cot. I was lying on my side and I heard what I thought were feet the size of video cassettes shuffling behind me. I decided I didn't want to roll over and look, so instead, I called for John, who in theory had been trained for these situations. By the time he got up and pointed his flashlight in my direction, the critter had shuffled off.

The next morning we found the tracks of a nine-foot croc. It had passed within two feet of my bed and, not much further away, coughed up our fishing hook, recognizable because of the orange-painted tip. Apparently we had hooked one of the few crocs who observes his own catch-and-release policy.

Riding the Bird

Ostrich riding in South Africa

Oudtshoorn, South Africa

Envelope please. And the winner of the Worthless Mode of Transportation Award goes to . . . the ostrich! (Frenzied cheering by New York City subway conductors.)

Yes, you can actually ride them—ostriches, not New York City subways. And what better place to learn than Oudtshoorn, the ostrich capital of the world. I decided to visit Highgate Farm, one of three ostrich farms in this smallish town in southwestern South Africa where ostriches outnumber the residents sixteen to one.

Tours leave from Highgate's parking lot in front of the ostrich burger stand as soon as enough people have gathered, so I stood around with about twenty people and we tried to look as "gathered" as possible. Then, after fifteen minutes of coordinated gathering, Sean, the nineteen-year-old Highgate Ostrich Farm Guide, started the tour.

The first thing we learned was that Sean's real name was not Sean, but Chris, and he was only calling himself Sean because he was wearing a name tag that said "Sean" (which he had borrowed, one can only assume, from a guy named Sean). According to Sean, I mean Chris, the administration did not look highly upon hired hands who did not heed the hard-and-fast rules of Highgate, such as wearing name tags at all times.

I took the tour with a friend named Alan, who was born and raised in Oudtshoorn and knew more about ostriches than Chris and Sean put together. He had a month off from work and decided to come along just for laughs. During the rest of the year he works as the personal secretary to political diva Winnie Mandela, the estranged wife of Nelson Mandela. Remarkably, she is still one of the most popular public figures in South Africa despite the estrangement, which she seems to be wearing pretty well, usually in the form of a large hat.

Stop number one was the ostrich-feather lecture and demo. "You see," said Chris, "the high-quality male feathers are used for cabaret costumes (one pound sells for $150) and lower-quality female feathers are used for feather dusters (one pound sells for $50)." Then Chris gave us a lesson in feather dusting.

After stroking the feathers to generate static electricity, with just a few dainty dabs Chris was able to clean a small knickknack that had been covered with dust for this demonstration—this really got our adrenaline pumping.

It was off to stop number two to feed the ostriches some snack food. Just imagine the excitement of feeding live ostriches from behind a fence!

"The trick to feeding an ostrich," said Chris, "is to put the food in the palm of your hand and then hold your hand very flat so the ostrich can't bite off one of your fingers."

Alan didn't view this as any special trick. He whispered, "It's the same way you feed a duck, or a horse, or just about any other animal."

We looked at some baby ostriches, some acne-ridden teenage ostriches, and some old geezer ostriches, which can live to be eighty. But most don't live that long. The big problem with raising ostriches is that they drop dead pretty easily—if it's too hot or too cold or too just right. Forty percent die during infancy alone, but fortunately, some of the ostrich carcasses can still be salvaged. The meat tastes and looks like top-quality steak, but it's as lean as chicken. The leather is made into purses and jackets that sell for hundreds or thousands of dollars. Alan added (because Chris forgot) that their corneas are sometimes used for human transplants and their eyelashes for delicate paintbrushes and makeup brushes.

Not to be outdone, Chris bounced back with a zoological nugget: "The ostrich is, technically speaking, a reptile. And as a reptile, it is, technically speaking, in the dinosaur family." So there you have it: an ostrich is a dinosaur—or perhaps a dinosaur's great nephew by marriage, twice removed.

Whatever it is, an ostrich looks like the result of a cruel genetic experiment involving a giraffe and a turkey. Ostriches' eyes bulge out of their heads. Their necks look like bungee cords. Their ankles are where their knees should be and their feet are where their shins should be. As a result, these seven-foot-tall three-hundred-pound creatures run on two toes (at speeds up to fifty miles per hour) and can also use these toes—I'm not kidding here—to rip your chest open with a lightning-fast kick.* The best thing to do if you ever find yourself getting charged by an ostrich in the wild—something everyone should be prepared for—is to lie down on the ground. Better to have it step on you than kick you.

After sharing this little tidbit of info, Chris told us it was time to ride the ostriches. Suddenly the idea of sitting on one of these birds, I mean "dinosaurs," didn't seem so inviting anymore. But I figured the Highgate Farm people had been doing this for a while and they wouldn't let us ride ostriches if it weren't safe, right?

Actually, according to Alan, there is some controversy about ostrich riding. Animal rights activists believe it is cruel to ride ostriches, which have been known to drop dead with people on their back. I asked Chris about this. He said the danger to ostriches

---

*If only they could learn how to play football!

depends on how heavy the person is, how long the ride lasts, and how hot it is. These factors, Chris assured me, are carefully calculated. Still, it seemed to me that ostriches have enough life-threatening problems without having to worry about being ridden to death by a tourist with an enormous butt.

We entered what looked like a very small bullring, where over thirty ostriches milled around. Two ostrich wranglers (I didn't hear anyone call them birdboys or dino-busters) cornered one, grabbed it around the neck with a long hook, and pulled its head down so they could throw a lunch bag over it. Once the ostrich was blinded, the wranglers led it to a special mounting stall and secured it so several daring tourists could safely pose for photos with it.

Chris offered to let women ride first. Two volunteered for ten-second wrangler-escorted rides. Male volunteers did not get wrangler-escorted rides. And as the only male volunteer, I was unable to watch anyone else make a fool of himself first.

There are several very good reasons you don't see people riding around on ostriches, and the fact that their armpits are full of dripping gook is just one of them.

I mounted the ostrich and put my legs under its wings. I was wearing shorts so I immediately felt two things: 1) the feather quills jabbing painfully into my legs and 2) gooey brown stuff dripping down my calves. Apparently, the bird had not washed its armpits since Bill Gates was just a millionaire.

I grabbed hold of the wings and nodded like I had seen bronco riders do on TV to signal they were ready. The wranglers unhooked the mounting stall, took the lunch bag off the ostrich's head, and let go. We were off! There were no actual controls on the bird, I mean "dinosaur." No reins or stirrups. You are just supposed to hold on and go with the flow. The ostrich flowed left, then turned around and flowed back to where it started. The wranglers watched from the sidelines; they had turned into rodeo clowns, standing by to rescue me.

Suddenly, the ostrich flowed in several directions at once, bucked me off, and I crash-landed on the ground, which was cushioned with ostrich excrement. In spite of my less-than-graceful dismount, I was thankful the ostrich never got up to fifty miles per hour or tried to rip my chest open with a lightning-fast kick. The ride wasn't actually life threatening. Just painfully short.

Then the ostrich wranglers staged an ostrich race for us. The brochure showed jockeys wearing racing silks, but in real life they wore garage-mechanic jumpsuits soiled with ostrich excrement. They raced the ostriches on a twenty-meter-long simulated racetrack. And then they raced back. The whole race took about ten seconds.

That was the end of the tour. Well, almost. Alan and I decided to see who could find the tackiest souvenir in the gift shop—and it was a tough choice. I mean, beyond the standard ostrich eggs and feather dusters, there were, courtesy of the local taxidermist (who is also the pastor of Oudtshoorn), stuffed ostrich heads mounted for wall hanging and stuffed legs made into table lamps. My choice: a thousand-dollar white feather disco jacket. Alan had found a stuffed baby ostrich that pops out of its own egg when you remove the top half of the shell. It was hard to declare a clear winner, so we flipped a flat feather duster. Alan called it and won: tails.

Pulling in the Big One

Fishing for bronze whale sharks in Namibia

Swakopmund, Namibia

 Before I went beach fishing for bronze whale sharks on the Skeleton Coast of Namibia, I didn't know the first thing about fishing, other than you had to wear a vest with at least eighty pockets and be able to feign interest in a thirty-minute conversation about bait. I knew even that much thanks to an hour I once spent watching a fishing program on TV because the batteries in the remote control had died and I was too lazy to get up and turn the channel manually.

Namibia's Skeleton Coast gets its name from the scores of pre-radar ships that lie wrecked along the shore due to severe rip currents and dense fog. I'm not so sure about the etymology of the bronze whale sharks; they are neither bronze nor whale-like. They can, however, weigh up to four hundred pounds, and local fishermen swear they put up an amazing fight.

I wasn't keen on paying ninety dollars for a day of fishing with the only fishing company in town, so instead I went fishing with Connie, a man who picked me up when I was hitchhiking and gave me a lift into the colonial German town of Swakopmund. I suppose you could say he forgot to drop me off. He and his wife (both thirty-five and of German descent) insisted that I stay with them and their two baby girls, neither of whom were able to last thirty seconds without creating an eardrum-shattering noise.

In the States, fishing without beer just isn't fishing, but in Namibia, fishing also necessitates sour cream and onion potato chips. We had to stop at several supermarkets to find just the right kind, but I must admit, the chips did substantially enhance the fishing experience.

Beach fishing for bronze whale sharks requires special rigging. Connie prepared my line with a "steel lead" and "joiners." He also attached a "sinker" that I would have had trouble bench-pressing, then baited the hook with a hot dog-sized piece of mullet (a fish), which looked particularly unappetizing—and tasted even worse. I know this because Connie had reached into the bag of chips before wiping his hands.

The way casting is supposed to work is that you flip a lever that releases the "spool" and then you "fling" the rod, and the bait goes flying way out to sea. But when I tried to cast, I was nearly knocked over by a powerful incoming wave and, as a result, I flung the bait straight up in the air and then, while struggling to avoid getting hit by the dropping mullet and the bowling-ball-sized sinker, I forgot to put the brakes on the spool with my thumb, so the line got all tangled. It took Connie about twenty minutes to unravel the mess.

Once we got our lines in the water, we had to put on these thingamajigs I would prefer to leave undescribed. Let me just say that you probably wouldn't want to wear one around town, unless it was Halloween and you were going as one of the guys from the movie *Clockwork Orange*. If you haven't gotten the picture yet, it's a belt with a large and awkwardly placed mount in front that helps stabilize the fishing pole. When the pole is inserted into this holder, one can only conclude that it was definitely invented by a man. And he was a wishful thinker.

I was beginning to understand the macho appeal of this sport as I stood there, feeling quite manly, fishing in Africa for a bronze whale shark with my five-meter-long phallic extension.

I'm not trying to brag here, but in only four short hours I managed to catch several pieces of seaweed. I started out slowly with a small piece of kelp. Then a larger piece. Then I moved on to a piece of kelp about the size of a small tree. Slow, consistent improvement.

At one point I even caught a live fish: a cod. More specifically, an extremely small cod that was probably still in Montessori. It was about as challenging as hauling in Dr. Ruth with a hydraulic winch. Connie, however, snagged—and I'll have to double-check the record books on this—the world's smallest bronze whale shark. It was smaller than the bait he used to catch it.

After spending a day "fishing" with Connie, it was time to seek some professional help. I decided to hire West Coast Anglers. For a special bargain rate of fifty dollars, I was "nearly guaranteed" I would catch a huge (one- to two-hundred-pound) shark.

West Coast Anglers assigned Harmon to be my personal, professional shark-fishing guide. Harmon was a big lad. If he lived in Japan he could—if he didn't mind wearing a silk jock strap in public—make a decent living in the field of Sumo wrestling.

With massive graphite fishing poles mounted onto the front of his Land Rover, we set off down the coast. We could have gone fishing in a boat, but Harmon assured me the real sport is to catch them from the shore. Why? A shark knows where the shore is and doesn't like to go there once it has a hook in its mouth, whereas a boat is not as threatening as the shore and can actually move to help bring in the fish. Plus, he confided, you can drink more since you don't get seasick.

Harmon took me over the dunes to most of the same places that Connie had taken me. Harmon's fishing technique, however, was a bit different: he used much bigger hooks—the sort of hooks you might use to snag a fish with a mouth the size of Mick Jagger's; he baited these hooks with giant, fresh barracuda heads

("The bloodier, the better.");
and he cast it like John Daley
drives a golf ball.

Harmon got everything in
place and then we waited, chatting on the beach as naturally
as could be expected (considering we both had these plastic
rhino-tusk rod holders strapped
over our private regions). I was
no longer a fisherman. I was an
angler! Which does not mean I
had to catch fish with a pro-
tractor. "Angler" simply con-
notes a serious fisherman*.

I felt a tug on the line as I
was reeling in one of Harmon's
casts. I yanked hard, watching

*I have to be honest; this is not a
bronze whale shark. It's a 650-pound
blue marlin.*

the graphite rod bend, as I sat down and dug my feet into the sand.
This was a big one. Huge! The taut fishing line started whistling in
the wind like a boiling teapot and I cranked on the reel, but I
couldn't gain any ground. Man, this was big! Looked like I was in
for a long fight. Just me and the shark. Mano-a-fisho.

"Doug," said Harmon calmly.

"Yeah?" I grunted, beads of sweat beginning to form on my
forehead.

"I don't think you're going to pull that baby in."

"Why not?" I hissed through clenched teeth.

"Because you caught Africa."

Well, you have to admit, it was a big catch.

---

*Angler formula: If the monetary value of the fishing gear/beer ratio is
greater than 1, the person is an angler.

Free Fall from Grace

Kloofing in Cape Town

Cape Town, South Africa

As a rule of thumb, I generally try to avoid activities that sound like medical procedures, and "kloofing" sounded a bit too much like something that involved lubricant.

But in South Africa it's the Afrikaans' word for canyoning, which is exploring gorges, or, in my case, paying someone to take me into a gorge that has been previously explored and named. My kloofing tour was to take place in Suicide Gorge.

There's a reason it's called Suicide Gorge: "Exploring" it is a bit like bungee jumping without the bungee. You hike through a mountain stream and jump off the waterfalls along the way, which can be up to sixty feet high. It is, understandably, much cheaper than bungee jumping, and Suicide Gorge is now so popular it's being kloofed kommercially.

Steve, the president and CEO of Day Trippers, drove the minivan. He was also our guide. There wasn't much conversation on the hour drive out to the kloofing area because it was seven in the morning and we were still sleeping, most of us with hangovers from trying to live it up a little before attempting "Suicide."

Just before we started the three-hour walk into the canyon, we stopped at a cafe for several liters of coffee and introductions. There were eight of us: Alan from England, who had just driven overland from Cairo; Doug from London, whose first words to Steve were, "How much beer did you bring?"; David, a DJ from London with new hiking boots; Patrick, a redhead from Kentucky; Karl, a young Dutchman who didn't speak much; Colin, a Scottish guy with a strong accent who had trouble making himself understood; and Jo (also English), who had seemingly misunderstood all the warnings about being in top physical shape. That is, she wasn't.

During our walk towards the canyon I noticed I was the only one wearing sandals. Everyone else had on hefty hiking boots, including the guide. I asked Steve if I'd made a mistake. He said, "It probably won't be a problem and, besides, it's too late to turn back."

The first noteworthy part of the kloof was sliding down a thirty-foot, natural, grassy water slide into a six-foot-deep freezing pool of water. Even considering the natural elements, it wasn't your basic water slide. This one was only a water slide for the first ten feet, then it became just water. The slide part dropped out and you fell the last twenty feet, which was a bit unnerving because it was our first jump and we were all busy thinking about all the ways we could land wrong.

If your legs separate before entry, you're guaranteed an enema. Which is why I had a plastic bag stuffed down my shorts. Also, if you put your arms out to brace your fall, they'll smack the surface painfully. Entering at an angle means you'll probably have the wind knocked out of you (Steve said some former kloofers have even coughed up blood because of this). Of course, the worst would be to enter the water too straight, hit the bottom, and break your legs. The good news is that only one person has died on Suicide Gorge, and that was from cardiac arrest.

After we survived the slide without injuries and took a quick swim, we hiked downstream to Commitment Falls, thus named because once you jump, you can't turn back. It was only twenty-five feet high and, while no one chickened out, the macho talk had stopped. Patrick was always the last to jump, and it quickly became apparent that he was somewhat acrophobic*. He took his time jumping, which is about the worst thing you can do. The longer you look down, the higher it feels. After three minutes of psychological anguish, Patrick must have felt like he was kloofing the Grand Kanyon.

By most standards, this was a successful kloof. Nice flailing arm motion, proper use of gravity, and no painful enema.

Just for the record, I felt the most dangerous thing we'd done thus far was drinking the pee-colored water in the river that Steve promised us was safe. He also told us where it was deep enough (or nearly deep enough) to jump. So, we had basically put our lives in his hands, which didn't feel entirely right after having signed his extensive Kloofing Release Form. I'm pretty sure it had a clause that stated we willed our worldly possessions to Steve. But Steve was by all accounts a great guy, even though he made several jokes to the effect that he had no idea where we'd end up before he'd send us off a cliff.

Once Patrick learned I was a writer, he kept pleading with me to insert a secret code message in the story specifically for him. I told him that this book won't really be a forum for such things, but he wouldn't be put off, so here it is: kcirtaP sraeW snemoW raewrednU!

---

*Fear of acros

The subsequent jumps got progressively higher until, eventually, the words "free fall" were mentioned. The words "cardiac" and "arrest" came up once or twice as well.

At the end of Suicide Gorge is the biggie: a sixty-foot jump. From the ledge the landing pool looked the size of a toilet bowl, and just as shallow. A jump like this is not the sort of thing you can rationalize. In fact, the less thinking the better. In retrospect, I had enough time to recite Hamlet's famous soliloquy during my spastic free fall, or at least up to the part where he was talking about a sea of troubles. Which was exactly where my bare bodkin landed. I'm happy to report my mortal coil stayed intact and there was no outrageous fortune. Thank thee, plastic bag!

Colin yelled something as he leapt, David flapped his arms, English Doug landed a bit crooked, Jo made a huge splash, and Patrick stood on the edge for what seemed like an entire semester of English Lit. before jumping.

We had a two-hour hike back to the minivan, which concluded an exhausting but delightful eight-hour day. There were no serious injuries to report, just a few red arms, a red chest, sunburn, and several enormous blisters on David's feet, courtesy of his new shoes. My unprotected feet, battered by rocks and thorns, felt like they had been attacked by a Cuisinart. One surprise: my shirt was completely clean, something the dry cleaners had not been able to achieve. This, I imagine, is one of the often overlooked benefits of kloofing: stain removal.

Aparth-Tourism

Touring South Africa's poverty

Cape Town, South Africa

Cape Town is hot. And I'm not talking about the weather, which is coastal temperate. Michael Jackson might be buying a house here. Madonna, too! Rumor has it that Cher just bought a place. Rich Germans are snatching up property like it's discounted schnitzel. And people aren't just moving here, they are also visiting in droves. South Africa is one of the world's fastest-growing tourist destinations. Why all the fuss? It's a beautiful city, the exchange rate is good, and apartheid has come to an end . . . or has it?

At the Cape Town tourist bureau I found agencies offering tours of the nearby black townships. The once-oppressed blacks have become one of South Africa's hot, new tourist attractions. Cape Town has just woken up to the fact that it is sitting on an untapped wealth of poverty: several impoverished townships arranged back to back with a cumulative population of about one million.

When I got back to my youth hostel, I spoke with the reception-ist about this. As a "well-to-do" white, she had lived in Cape Town her entire life and never ventured into a township. She agreed that "poverty tourism" sounded twisted but told me about Cinga, a man from the townships who offers guided visits of his own neighbor-hood. She said some travelers had gone with him and highly recommended the unorthodox tour.

I rang Cinga and he picked me up an hour later in his reasonably new Toyota Camry. He was a young-looking forty-year-old with a bright tie, knitted sweater vest, and warm smile. Cinga had gone to college after graduating from a high school that only had enough places for one out of every fifty kids.

We drove to the neighborhood in Langa township where he grew up. In the middle of the day everyone seemed to be walking around on the street. I asked if it was some kind of parade. "No, just unemployment," Cinga explained. "Nearly 60 percent don't have jobs."

Most of the buildings were one- and two-room concrete structures, many looking as though they had been recently looted. We entered one. I shook hands with all the adults sitting around the entrance. They had seen white tourists before, but they hadn't been jaded by the experience . . . yet. Cinga asked permission, then showed me one of the rooms. It was about the size of a health-club sauna, with three single beds crammed into it.

"Three people can live in this little room?" I asked.

"No," Cinga told me, "three entire families."

On the way out, I saw a tourist minibus stopped on the road. White heads peered out of the windows, half-hidden behind their telephoto lenses. They began snapping photos of some children playing a pickup game of cricket in the street. After the cameras stopped clicking, the van drove off.

I believe many of the tourists come to the townships to help ease their apprehensions about visiting a country still divided by color. By acknowledging the poverty with their presence, they want to distinguish themselves from the white South Africans who simply ignore it. The problem is, with mass tourism, the visits end up looking like a big safari outing.

"Some of these tours," Cinga explained, "spend the whole

morning wine tasting at the nearby vineyards and then come and look at the poor people when they're drunk.

"Feel like playing cricket?" he asked me, changing the subject and motioning toward the kids in the street.

I nodded although I hadn't the slightest idea how to play. Cinga spoke with the kids and the next thing I knew I was holding a board and standing in front of a wooden crate. The kids were laughing because I was using a baseball-style stance, which was probably as funny looking to a cricket player as it was to my entire second-grade T-ball team.

The eight-year-old "bowler" took a running start and then, with a straight-armed round-house release that looked like it made his shoulder pop right out of its socket, he flung a ball towards me at roughly the speed of sound. I took a swing and missed as the ball hit a small stone in the road and ricocheted into my shin. Would I get to walk to first, wherever that was? No. Apparently, I was out. The kids high-fived the "bowler" and Cinga came over and explained in a consoling fatherly way that I had an "LBW." What? "A Leg Before Wicket," he said. I had no idea what a "wicket" was, but there was general agreement that I had put my leg before one, and God only knows what other cricket rules I may have violated. It was time to move on.

We went to a neighboring township and stopped in an area that had squatter shacks as far as I could see. Rusty beer cans, sheet metal, and cardboard were held together with staples, chewing gum, and some dirt mixed with spit. In many countries, these shacks would pass for modern art. Here, they pass for housing.

The strangest thing about the squatter-shack community, at least in the part we stopped in, were the beautiful asphalt and concrete roads, much nicer than most of the residential roads in the States. Cinga explained that the roads and electricity was partially funded by foreign aid. The aid agency didn't know how to distribute the money, so they built a road and installed electricity. Never mind the cruel irony that the people couldn't afford any cars or a single electrical appliance.

We went to a bar in the neighborhood to have a drink. There, I met Jose, a repairman. How did he feel about the tourism? First, he clarified—even though I didn't ask—he was "colored," or racially mixed. And although he works in the township, he comes from a slightly more affluent "colored" neighborhood that doesn't get tourists because it isn't poor enough.

"I don't mind if the people get off the bus and learn about our way of life," Jose told me. "If they want to spend some of their tourist dollars here, even better. But to drive by and take pictures makes us feel like animals."

We drove back to Cinga's neighborhood, and this time we stopped at Cinga's house, which was a few blocks from where we had been at the beginning. This was the wealthy part of Langa. The houses looked fundamentally the same as the other concrete structures, but these had nicer curtains and Mercedeses and BMWs parked in the driveways. Despite the in-your-face poverty, many of the black professionals who grew up here have no desire to move to the wealthy suburbs, which are generally white. There's a sense of community here, and, as Cinga said, there's no place like home.

I didn't make any sociological discoveries on this tour. I just saw a different side of Cape Town and a different way of life. This "poverty tourism" should not come as a surprise—America has the same thing. A bus tour of Harlem has been popular among visitors to New York for years. Funny how tourism can get people to do things they would never do at home.

Pulling the Rug Out

Hustling carpets in Marrakesh

Marrakesh, Morocco

Moroccan carpet salesmen can deliver a line better than Leonardo DiCaprio, are more tactical than a nuclear submarine captain, and more endearing than your own grandmother.

Ahmed, who didn't look like he possessed any of these qualities, sat across from me on the remarkably slow Marrakesh Express for five hours without uttering a word, although I could see he was reading an English magazine through his Ray-Bans. When I asked him if he spoke English, he replied, "Of course. But I figured you knew that Moroccans who initiate conversation in English are usually just trying to sell you something." I liked him immediately. Upon our arrival, I agreed to join him for *chi* in his brother's carpet shop, the biggest in town.

This was when Ahmed baited me. He simply told me how much money he and his brother, Mostefa, made selling carpets to tourists (more each day than I make in a year). The real trick, he said, was getting the tourists into the shop. Suddenly, I saw where all this was heading.

"How much commission?" I asked.

Ahmed laughed. "Typically, 6 percent."

I told him I might consider it for twelve.

"Out of the question. If you want to try it for a while, you can stay with us and earn 8 percent."

We shook hands. I was now a Moroccan carpet hustler.

The next morning the brothers sent me to the main square with Mohammed, a young man whose sole job was to help me find my way back through the maze-like market to the carpet shop. I spotted an English tour group, followed them into a restaurant, and introduced myself to a young, friendly looking couple. I told them I was a carpet hustler. Steven and Rachel laughed.

"No, really," I assured them, "I work for the biggest carpet shop in Marrakesh. My job is to guide you there and then back to your hotel when you want to leave. Mohammed here will make sure we won't get hassled along the way."

When we arrived at the carpet shop, my employers were pretty impressed. It had taken me all of fifteen minutes. Mostefa, a black belt in carpet selling, went right to work, pouring on charm like chemically flavored butter on movie popcorn. Watching Mostefa and Ahmed "push rug" was like watching Torvill and Dean ice skate, Ben and Jerry make ice cream, or Hulk Hogan and Andre the Giant perform a team slam from the third rope.

Mostefa, who speaks seven languages flawlessly, invited Steven and Rachel to join him for chi while he listened to their impressions of Marrakesh, found out what their jobs were (i.e., their credit card limits), and provided them with some interesting Moroccan insights. They discussed the weather, passport stamps, and new diet pills in Afghanistan—just about everything but carpets. Then Mostefa gave them a tour of his two-story shop, explaining the difference in quality between the carpets, the significance of the patterns, the number of knots per square inch—he even waved his lighter under some to demonstrate their fire-retardant qualities. When the tour was over, more chi was waiting for them. Not even Madeleine Albright gets treated this well on foreign visits.

"Would you like to see a few of the special carpets we don't display in the store?" Mostefa asked. How could Steven and Rachel refuse? He was practically their best friend at this point. Mostefa had noticed which style of carpets they preferred and, with the most subtle of gestures, he signaled his team of lackeys to bring them in. Carpets of various colors and sizes were flung one on top of the other, giving Steven and Rachel only five seconds to peek at one carpet before the next landed on top of it. Within a few minutes, the pile of carpets was nearly three feet thick.

When the last one had been unfurled, Mostefa confided, "Hard to take it all in, isn't it? My mother used to make so many sweets, I could never choose. What kind of sweets do you have in England?" Mostefa knew they were dying to have a second look, but he just made idle chatter until Rachel brought up the subject. Then, feigning reluctance, he swung back into action.

"Do you like this one?" he asked, gesturing to the top carpet.

"That's nice," Rachel confessed. The lackeys moved it off to the side.

"How about this one?"

"Well, not quite as much." The lackeys rolled it up and carried it away. They went through the whole pile that way, leaving Steven and Rachel with four carpets.

Now Mostefa knew he could relax for a while. Steven and Rachel got up for a closer look at the carpets they had "chosen" and began discussing which would go where in their home.

"How much is this one?" Steven asked.

"Don't worry about the price now," Mostefa told him. "First, decide which ones you want."

They decided on two carpets.

"You have developed a fine eye for carpets in such a short time," Mostefa complimented. Now it was time to bargain. "How much would you be able to give me for these carpets?" The English had no idea where to start the bidding.

"What would be a fair price?" Steven asked in return.

"Well," hesitated Mostefa, as though he'd never sold a carpet like this one before, "that carpet hanging on the wall is twice the size of *yours* and I sold that to a local man for $4,000 last week. I would certainly be willing to give that special local rate to you . . . $2,000 each. But it would pain me to see you choose, so I'll give you both for $3,800—a price you can't refuse."

Steven and Rachel swallowed audibly. Rachel managed to maintain her stiff, bleached upper lip, but Steven had suddenly developed an eye twitch.

The problem was, of course, that they were in love with these carpets and they didn't want to offend their newfound Moroccan soul mate.

"How about $3,000?" Steven countered with the conviction of Kato Kaelin.

Mostefa turned immediately serious, insulted. "I'm afraid that's completely impossible." After letting a heavy silence hang in the air, Mostefa said, "I have an idea," and went off to talk with Ahmed. They appeared to argue for several minutes and Mostefa appeared to win. "You're in luck, my friends," said Mostefa with a big smile as he walked back. "My supervisor told me I could come down to $3,500." It was brilliant. He had bargained on their behalf. The English accepted with pleasure, probably wondering if the sale of their first-born child would cover the purchase.

They shook hands, handed over their credit card, and Mohammed and I escorted them back to the market square, where I spotted an affluent German group who didn't realize they would soon be the owners of several fine Moroccan carpets.

A Current Affair

Sailing down the Nile in a felucca

Edfu, Egypt

 After two weeks in Egypt I needed a small escape from the Egyptian souvenir salesmen and the video-camera-lugging tourists.

"Take a felucca down the Nile," a South African traveler suggested. "It sounds like just what you're looking for. And the best part about traveling by felucca," he said, "is that it takes practically forever to get anywhere." I had about that long before my flight left.

A felucca is a traditional Egyptian sailboat from the Pre-*Baywatch* Period that was used by pharaohs to go places when they got sick of chariot traffic. Today feluccas carry budget travelers from Aswan to Edfu (about 150 kilometers) in three days.

Naturally, this mode of travel is popular with backpackers who are much better at spending time than money. Regular tourists sail on the Nile as well, but they tend to stick to the *botels.* A botel is a floating five-star hotel that looks a bit like the old paddle wheelers on the Mississippi, except that the botels are filled with Europeans and Americans who have all taken solemn oaths to their friends back home that they will videotape every square inch of Egypt, even if it means annoying every Egyptian and fellow tourist in the country to do it.

Renting a felucca is pretty straightforward, I was told. You just get a felucca group of five to seven people and shop around for a felucca captain. My problem was that I didn't know any felucca groups in Aswan, and moreover, I had no idea what a felucca captain was supposed to look like, so shopping for one seemed out of the question.

As it turned out, you don't need to find a felucca captain; they find you. They walk around town and beg you to come look at their felucca.

Felucca captain: "Hey, wanna see my felucca?"

Me: "No, I'm not that kind of guy."

Finding a felucca group wasn't much more challenging. At one restaurant, I noticed a few tables with travelers, so I went to the first table and, managing to keep a straight face, asked if they were a "felucca group." They said they were. What luck! An Englishman, his Dutch wife, and two young Spanish women, Maria and Anna, the pleasant-but-relentlessly-dull sisters, had met on the train to Aswan and became—perhaps this involved a ceremony—a felucca group. They were initially reluctant when I asked to join them, but after several hours of meaningless chitchat they invited me along.

They had already found a captain they liked. I asked if his name was Mohammed.

"How did you know?" Maria asked in amazement.

It was a pretty safe guess—almost three out of four Egyptian men are named Mohammed. This particular Mohammed had a large frame, a wide face, dreadlocks, and enough hashish to accommodate an entire Dead show.

We went to look at Mohammed's boat, the *Hotp*. Aside from a possible spelling error in the name and the fact that this felucca, a twenty-five-foot white-washed wooden tub with a flat cushion-covered deck and a single triangular sail, looked about as seaworthy as the Sphinx, none of us could spot anything wrong. Mohammed then introduced us to the crew: Ahmed, the first mate (one out of four Egyptian men are named Ahmed), and Mohammed, the cook. Ahmed, Mohammed, and Mohammed are the Egyptian counterparts to Larry, Daryl, and Daryl.

We set sail that afternoon. The *Hotp*, if it were piloted by Dennis Connor, could possibly approach the speed of driftwood. But Mohammed the hash dealer couldn't make it move that fast. Nor could Ahmed, who did most of the actual sailing. It would have been nice to sit back and relax while we drifted along with the current, but the wind was against us so Ahmed had to tack like crazy just to keep the boat from going backward.

We spent the day reading books, playing chess (until a bishop and two pawns fell overboard), and ignoring Captain Mohammed, who spent the better part of the journey trying to sell us hash and get us to go skinny dipping. These were his two primary objectives; apparently, his former passengers had participated in both of these shipboard pastimes. The nude swim never happened, and there was no reason to pay for the hash since Mohammed the captain, Mohammed the cook, and Ahmed were smoking enough hash to give anyone within a hundred meters a contact high.

So we just kicked back and watched the riverbanks with glazed eyes. We saw herds of water buffalo, and little boys trying to get the water buffalo out of the water, or into the water—it was hard to tell. We also saw lots of botels and tried to stay out of their way. The botels came cruising right down the middle of the river with pesky passengers waving at us from the top deck, each with a Long Island iced tea in one hand and a video camera in the other.

Tourist on the deck of the botel: "Ahoy! (to Ahmed) You in the little sailboat with the towel on your head. Yes, I'm talking to you. Can you steer your boat over here so I can get you in the picture with my wife, Barbara? Okay, now honey, wave to the people on the boat. Hey, in the boat! Can you wave to—hey, what's that smell?"

The second day, after sleeping on the boat's deck in more or less the same positions we had been lounging in, we arrived at Kom Ombo, an ancient city and our main archeological field trip. We stayed for about five minutes—long enough to catch a glimpse of the Nile-o-meter, a device that measures the Nile's height so pharaohs could tell if farmers had a good year and whether they should tax the sarcophagus out of them—and then returned to the *Hotp* because of the overpowering crowds of tourists that we were supposed to be taking a break from.

After the field trip we went swimming. Several tourists had warned us not to swim in the Nile because of parasites in the water that would supposedly permeate our skin and morph into nasty intestinal worms the size of tube socks. We took the chance. Captain Mohammed had convinced us, between puffs of smoke, that these parasites only live in standing water, not in the moving current.

Eventually we made it to Edfu. Mohammed beached the boat, helped us off, and said good-bye. We felt tanned, relaxed, and ready to brave the thirty trinket salesmen who had already spotted us.

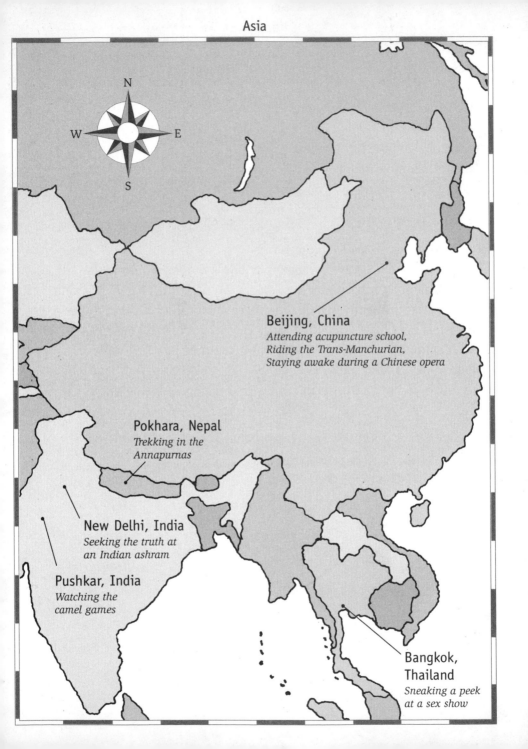

Beijing, China
Attending acupuncture school,
Riding the Trans-Manchurian,
Staying awake during a Chinese opera

Pokhara, Nepal
Trekking in the
Annapurnas

New Delhi, India
Seeking the truth at
an Indian ashram

Pushkar, India
Watching the
camel games

Bangkok,
Thailand
Sneaking a peek
at a sex show

ASIA

If you look at Asia on a map, you'll probably realize that you don't know where Asia is exactly anymore. For example, is Saudi Arabia in Asia? How about the Philippines? I always thought the Soviet Union was in Asia. But learned this is not true anymore (as of last week). When the Soviet Union split up, it seems some of the newly formed countries decided they wanted to be part of a more prosperous continent, like Europe, or Australia.

And then there's "the subcontinent," which deserves a special mention of its own, although my experience there was mostly limited to India. From the moment you set foot in India, you realize there's something different, something special in the air. Some say it's spiritual, others say it's cultural. I think it's a wicked combination of curry, cow shit, and breath-taking body odor; India has 900 million people, 200 million cows, and enough curry to turn the Pacific Ocean into a giant seafood stir-fry.

Getting the Hump of It

Watching the Pushkar Camel Games

Pushkar, India

The Pushkar Camel Fair is Rajasthan's version of a statewide used-car swap. Each year, roughly 16 trillion camels get traded in for new and improved models. Recently, however, the focus of the fair has changed somewhat. The Rajasthanis were issued a mandate from the Indian Tourism Authority to liven up the camel swapping because, apparently, the hundreds of tourists who come to the Camel Fair each year to observe this ancient tradition were starting to get bored.

The Rajasthanis needed something that would do for the Camel Fair what the greased pig has done for American county fairs. What hair spray has done for Kramer. What liposuction has done for the Academy Awards. So they got their creative juices flowing and came up with The Camel Games.

On the east side of Pushkar there's a large dirt field with a small grandstand where, during the camel fair, thousands of people, tourists and Indians alike, gather to watch these new camel-related sporting events. No one greases up a camel—at least, they didn't when I was there—but the activities are just as . . . well, interesting.

The first event was the Strongest Camel Contest. The way this was supposed to work was that a camel would sit down on its haunches and about twenty guys would pile on top and yell at it in

Hindi (the camel's native tongue) to stand up. The camel would struggle to stand and, one at a time, men would get off until the camel was able to get up. Then an official would count all the men on the standing camel and the camel supporting the most would be declared the winner. Simple enough in theory.

The problem was that after everyone climbed on, no one was sure who was supposed to get off next, so sometimes a few dismounted at once, and when the camel stood up, a few men would try to jump back on by clinging onto the poor camel's neck or tail. The official would step in and rule this illegal, and then an argument would ensue in which eight different people, each claiming to be the official official, would assert that the camel belonging to his cousin was the real winner. Clearly, instant replay was needed in this sport.

Between events, several professional advertising camels, with billboards strapped to their sides, were paraded around the field. These were, I suppose, supermodel camels: with long legs, big humps, and styled tails—if there were a *Sports Illustrated* swimsuit issue for camels, you wouldn't have to look any further.

Next came the Getting-Your-Camel-Away-from-the-Watering-Trough Event. In the West, this is known simply as "showing up at the starting line." But here, you would have been surprised how many contestants didn't make it. This is partly because they have to be there at a certain time. "Four o'clock?" some riders probably laugh, having no idea what four o'clock means. Rajasthanis seem to have derived their concept of time from a Salvador Dali painting.

This was, of course, merely a precursor to the big event: The Camel Race, Pushkar's answer to the Kentucky Derby. The race involved one lap around the large dirt field. Someone even made a white line around the perimeter for the nine camels to follow. Again, it sounded almost too simple to go right.

The camels stood at the starting line (or close to it, anyway), hoof to hoof and hump to hump. Seconds, perhaps minutes, of rigorous training had prepared them for this very moment. A gun was fired. The riders all shouted highly motivational phrases at their camels and then, when that didn't work, began whipping them with sticks. They were off.

The pack of camels was puffing away into the first turn. It looked like anyone's race. However, upon entering the second turn, the four lead camels broke off and ran toward the watering trough in that corner of the field. Their riders did everything they could to get their camels turned around, but by the time they did, the rest of the pack had taken a thirty-meter lead.

Throwing caution to the wind and, for that matter, the rules, these four riders decided to cut across the infield and catch up with the pack on the final turn. And it would have been a brilliant cheating strategy if every single person in the grandstand wasn't watching them.

As the lead pack neared the final turn, the four thirsty camels also neared it on a perpendicular course. It was going to be close. You could see the horror in the lead riders' eyes when they looked up and saw the four camels closing in on them.

Gaglerblgggghgheeeghrghh!!! The nine speeding camels collided. In one tangled, out-of-control mass of heads, humps, and hooves, they emerged on a new trajectory toward the trees to the left of the grandstand, where I happened to be standing. I was taller than most of the onlookers and managed to grab a small branch above my head, pull myself up, and leap for a second branch just as the entire pack trampled the people beneath me.

The chaos lasted about two minutes. Once the eleven injured spectators were carried away, I was surprised that the festive mood returned just as quickly as it had disappeared. No one died. Just a few cuts and bruises.

Maybe next year, they'll add a Cuts and Bruises Event.

The Malibu Guru

Seeking the truth at an Indian ashram

New Delhi, India

I woke up in the second-class compartment on an Indian train arriving in New Delhi, which was exactly where I'd hoped to be when I'd lulled myself to sleep the night before by sticking two wadded-up balls of toilet paper in my nose to avoid the pungent aroma of the laundry I was using for a pillow.

I met up with my aunt that morning at her hotel. She was in New Delhi to attend a four-day "event" at Guru Marahaj Ji's nearby *ashram* (spiritual college). This seemed like a good opportunity to take a closer look at the spirituality India is so famous for. And if I got lucky, I might even bump into an Elvis reincarnate.

That afternoon, we took a taxi to the ashram. My aunt had an event pass and I figured I could buy one at the gate. The pass checkers must have been on break, so I shrugged and walked right in.

It quickly became apparent that I was the only one in the ashram without an event pass—a very noticeable floppy disk-sized adhesive worn on one's chest. My aunt recommended I casually cover my chest with my hand. This seemed to work fine, but I felt a little stupid walking around in pledge-of-allegiance position.

We continued along through the ashram and came upon the

largest assembled group I have ever seen—oceans of Indians sitting cross-legged in neat rows on an endless flat field. On either side of the small stage was a massive color TV and a sound system that would have sufficed for the Stone's Voodoo Lounge tour.

Off in the distance I could see Guru Marahaj Ji's house. It was a cross between a gingerbread house and Caesar's Palace casino. It had more lights than the landing strip of the Bombay International Airport. My aunt told me that he spends most of his time at his house in Malibu. She added that he is an amateur pilot and owns his own plane. Marahaj Ji, it seems, is a guru of the nineties.

Ushers escorted us to the westerners' section in front of the stage, where about two hundred Americans and Europeans sat fiddling with radios. I didn't understand until my aunt pulled out a radio of her own and tuned it to the English channel. The event was being translated instantly and broadcast in several languages.

At sunset, after two hours of waiting, Marahaj Ji came out and sat center stage in what appeared to be an airplane seat. It was in the upright landing position.

Marahaj Ji had a very soothing style and spoke as you'd expect a guru to speak, but one thing distracted me immediately. He kept referring to himself in the third person. This was confusing because Marahaj Ji is also the name of his father. So I was never sure whom he was talking about or if they were the same person prematurely reincarnated.

He told some very funny stories that must not have translated well because the Indians were rolling on the ground clutching their sides while we westerners just looked on, waiting for the punch line that never came.

From what I could understand, the whole speech was centered around giving and prayer and family values. For a while, I thought I was at India's national republican convention. Then, toward the end, he told us if we "gave our love to Marahaj Ji, Marahaj Ji would return our love." Sounds nice, but come on, *The Love Connection* has stricter guidelines than that.

When Marahaj Ji finished speaking, someone cranked up the volume on the PA system and people began bobbing to the hypnotic sounds of the Indian drums. His Extreme Wealthiness just sat there in his economy-class chair nodding approvingly and lovingly at us, his face taking up the two ten-meter TV screens with the same look I saw on the face of Jim Wand, a hypnotist who once performed at my college and turned most of the audience into oak trees.

He stared at us for fifteen minutes without saying a word.

It was time to leave. On the way out we met a Dutchman. I asked why he had flown all the way to India to see Marahaj Ji.

"It's like when someone gives you complex directions and you make a right, then a left, then another left. Suddenly, the guy who gave you the directions appears and tells you you're on the right track. You need that confirmation every so often," he said.

Before we left the ashram, we stopped by the visitors' center where, to my surprise, there was a travel agency that specialized in booking flights and hotels for Marahaj Ji's "events." Nearly one hundred wealthy westerners were accompanying Marahaj Ji on his world tour. Most of these New Age followers were as exotically mismatched as Deadheads, except that they weren't selling dope or homemade hacky sacks in the parking lot to cover the travel expenses.

We got in a taxi. The driver drove us back into New Delhi. He turned left, then right, then left, then left again through the narrow and congested roads and returned us safely to the hotel.

It's always nice to have a guru behind the wheel.

The Vodka Runs through It

Riding the Trans-Manchurian

Moscow, Russia

 As I boarded the Trans-Manchurian in Beijing for my six-day train ride to Moscow, I was greeted by a mother-ly Russian train attendant who had enough facial hair to knit a pair of leg warmers.

"Welcome," she said. Welcome, it turned out, was one of two English words she knew. I asked her where my cabin was. "No," she said with a smile. That was her other word.

Mrs. Hairlipski, as I called her since I could never pronounce her Russian name to her satisfaction, was partially responsible for keeping train car #5 clean. Her jovial, rotund partner, Mrs. Buttgrabski, welcomed me by . . . well, you can guess.

For years, I had wanted to ride the Trans-Siberian, though I was never sure why. I guess, like other travelers, I liked the sound of it. Unfortunately, the actual Trans-Siberian runs from Vladivostok, sev-eral hundred miles northeast of Beijing, to Moscow. Most people either take the Trans-Mongolian or the Trans-Manchurian between Moscow and Beijing and then just tell people they took the Trans-Siberian since the only reason to go to Vladivostok is . . . well, I can't really think of a reason offhand.

In Europe, travel agents quoted me prices between $500 and $1,000 to take the train from Moscow to Beijing. This would also lock me in with a tour group, which meant that, in all likelihood, I'd be crossing Siberia and Manchuria in compartments with Europeans, which seemed to defeat the whole point of the adventure. So, I took my chances and flew one-way to China to look for a train ticket coming back the other way. With minimal legwork I purchased a second-class ticket for $180 in the lobby of Beijing's International Hotel and then a transit visa for $90 at the Russian Embassy of Extortionate Paperwork Fees.

Not long after the train rolled out of Beijing's Central Railway Station, the first passengers moved into my assigned four-person compartment: an immense, intimidating Russian man in a black leather jacket, with the eyes of an angry Ricki Lake guest, and his lanky Chinese partner. My worst fear—spending six days with Mafia hit men . . . if I lived that long.

"Sit down!" the Russian bellowed at me. I sat down across from him.

"Spaciba," I said. ("Thank you.") This was the one word of Russian I knew.

"Sit down!" he roared again. I was already sitting.

"Spaciba," I said again. Suddenly, we both realized we were using the only bit of each other's language we knew.

Then Mrs. Hairlipski popped in to see their tickets. "Welcome," she said.

"Sit down!" said the Russian.

"Spaciba," I said.

"No," chimed Mrs. Hairlipski.

What a great conversation we were having!

Instead of reaching for my phrase book, I decided to glance out the window. The view from the train? Hard to say. The windows were double paned: the outside one was filthy and in-between the two panes, condensation coated the glass. I could distinguish day and night, but not much else. To see the scenery, I had to stand in the smokers' compartments in the front or back of the train car, where the smoke was thick enough to bring on instant carcinoma.

Not that I would have missed much. In Manchuria, east of Mongolia, the entire landscape consisted of dirt fields. Not the sort of dirt that made the early American settlers drop to their knees, with tears of joy in their eyes, and start planting wheat. These fields gave no indication they could grow anything. There was not a tree, bush, or even a weed in sight—just miles of barbed-wire fences that collected blowing plastic. The Glad trash bag appears to be the tumbleweed of Manchuria.

I returned to my seat for some more stimulating conversation. After I was settled, the Russian ordered me to "sit down!" Needless to say, I had been sitting across from him for almost the entire day. He poured me a quadruple vodka, one for his Chinese pal, and one for himself. I then noticed a large bullet sticking out of his shirt pocket. Using my hands, I asked if this was for his gun. He shook his head, then removed the bullet's tip to reveal a secret knife. I swallowed hard and looked away, then spotted some boxes he had brought into our compartment. Most were stenciled with the words "Marie's Dope." I decided not to ask about them, figuring that after a night of drinking, either we'd become good friends or he'd kill me in my sleep.

When I woke up the next morning, he and his friend had left with their boxes and I was alone until that afternoon when my next guest, an Azerbaijani soldier, moved in. He had "1971" tattooed on his hand, one digit on each knuckle—either his year of birth or PIN number, I figured. He seemed like a nice enough guy. Using a phrase book, we had a pleasant conversation at the rate of one coherent sentence per hour. We were both so exhausted after establishing where we were each getting off the train, we fell asleep.

Once we crossed into Russia, the train cars were all lifted off the Chinese wheels by a crane and placed on wider Russian wheels to fit the Russian tracks while we passengers sat in the station. The decent Chinese dining car was disconnected and replaced with a Russian dining car so expensive and unappetizing, the Russian cook was able to spend his entire day making fishing nets, which he sold at our few daily ten- to twenty-minute train stops.

Other riding entrepreneurs sold shoes, jackets, and trinkets, and at times I felt like I was traveling over the continent in a giant moving garage sale. Our quick stops provided enough time to jump off and buy food from little kiosks and elderly Russian women who made what I called Babushka Happy Meals, anything from boiled potatoes to mystery pastries called *pirozhskis.* For less than three dollars you could buy all you could eat. Most of these meals were wrapped in plastic scraps sewn shut with dental floss since the plastic bags had apparently all blown to Manchuria.

While we were rolling through Siberia, the view consisted of snowy fields dotted with pastel-colored houses the size of saunas and rows of birch trees that lined the train tracks, often making it impossible to see anything beyond them. It felt vaguely like crossing Nebraska . . . about fifty times.

Trainlag didn't help matters much. No one ever knew what time it was. The moment the train left Beijing, we were officially on Moscow time, five time zones ahead. To follow the time chart for train stops, most of us kept our watches set on Moscow time, but it wasn't practical to eat and sleep on Moscow time. Both the sun and the dining car ran on local time, but nobody knew what the local time was, except the people who just got on the train at the previous stop, although most of them immediately set their watches to Moscow time. And because local time was changing daily, we couldn't rely on our internal clocks for help. So we had to look out the windows and guess. To cover our bases, most of us snacked continuously.

I spent a few hours each day chatting with the four passengers who spoke English: a fifty-something retired couple from Australia staying in a private first-class cabin and an American architect sharing a second-class cabin with an Australian girl on her first trip abroad. All four of them had purchased their train tickets from their travel agents (for at least $500 each), flown to Beijing, and hopped immediately onto the train. We all seemed to regard the train trip not as a means of transportation, but as an extended ride at an amusement park. And not a very exciting one at that!

We mostly read, napped, gazed out the window, or in my case, gazed *at* the window. It's certainly an alternative way to recover from an exhausting trip in Asia or make your way there for one, but I'd hardly call it one of the pillars of adventure tourism. Though I suppose a few parts of it were exhilarating, such as Mrs. Hairlipski's fuzzy good-bye kiss on one cheek and Mrs. Buttgrabski's hearty farewell on the other.

Wishing the Fat Lady Would Sing

Staying awake during a Chinese opera

Beijing, China

Before traveling to Beijing, my only experience with Peking Opera was limited to an Asian Theater class I attended during my senior year of college in Colorado when my roommate and I decided to take a course that challenged us academically in such a way that it wouldn't interfere with our skiing.

One of our more memorable assignments (and we were graded for this) was to make up our faces like Peking Opera characters—who were as generous with the cosmetics as Gene Simmons, the singer, or Bozo, the clown. After an hour of copying a design in painstaking detail, I let the professor grade my face painting, then I tried to wipe it off. I used soap, rubbing alcohol, turpentine, and a cloth with remarkably similar properties to sandpaper. After thirty minutes of scrubbing, the makeup, along with a few layers of skin, finally came off. And I was one of the lucky ones. Most were scrubbing away for hours. One unfortunate student was unable to remove his makeup, so we took him to the college's crackerjack health clinic where, in all likelihood, they took out his appendix.

Because it had been a while since I last "studied" the subject, I purchased the book *The Stagecraft of Peking Opera* by Pan Xiafeng and flipped through it on my way to the theater in central Beijing. Mr. Xiafeng offered numerous insights into the world of Peking Opera, such as this passage: "When the curtain rises, what the audience first spots on the stage is usually the scenery."

Traditional Peking Opera (a mix of singing, dancing, acting, acrobatics, and costumes more daring than anything in Elvis's wardrobe) may be thousands of years old, but the production I saw was staged in one of Beijing's new high-rise office buildings. I paid eight dollars for my ticket—the cheapest available—and was seated in the last row next to a group of elderly women from Wisconsin, one of whom asked me, before I was able to remove my jacket, which church group I belonged to.

"I'm not with a church group," I explained, settling down in my chair.

"Ohhh," she sighed. She didn't have any more questions for me, so I just sat back and listened to the techno music thumping out of the bar above the theater.

The curtains rose and right away I spotted—you guessed it—the scenery! Then the first opera singer, a woman wearing an elaborate costume that looked as if it were on loan from Zsa Zsa Gabor's "Divine Kitsch" collection, appeared and glided to center stage using the highly dramatic entrance device of a conveyor belt. (Yes, a conveyor belt!) She was transported to center stage like a duffel bag arriving on carousel number three, where she began to sing.

I know for a fact that millions of people (most of them in China) find this music to be among the most beautiful on Earth. I know that these singers practice, in some cases, their entire lives to develop their vocal skills, and I have the utmost respect for the artists in this profession. But I would be remiss if I did not mention—and I mean this in the most respectful way possible—that to my untrained, western ears, the singing sounded remarkably like someone playing a Chipmunks album backwards. And if the musicians had tuned their instruments since the Cultural Revolution, they hid it very well. It did not help much that whatever sounds they were producing did not blend well with the techno that was still leaking into the theater from the bar.

The first performer sang for an awfully long time, while others walked around onstage, coming and going without affecting the plot much . . . or so I thought. I turned to Mr. Xiafeng's book for help. "Differences in walking illustrate entry into large streets and small lanes. Only by knowing this can the audience be led to an understanding of what is taking place on the stage." No wonder I was confused.

Furthermore, I wasn't able to follow why the singers were occasionally singing right into their shirt sleeves. Fortunately, Mr. Xiafeng addressed this phenomenon as well: "Whenever a character is suddenly overcome by such a complex emotion that neither facial expression nor pantomime can make the meaning clear, he lifts his *shuixiu* (silk sleeves), behind which he speaks or sings his explanation, or he may quickly step to one side of the stage—these actions making it clear that the others on the stage cannot hear what is being said." Aha!

I looked at my neighbors to see if they were having any trouble interpreting the opera. The churchgoer next to me, in perhaps the most amazing feat of the whole evening, was gently snoring away despite the eardrum assault taking place both on stage and off. Several other women in the row, I noticed, were also examining the insides of their eyelids.

What did the Chinese members of the audience think? Hard to say . . . there weren't any Chinese in the audience.

As far as I could tell—and don't hold me to this—the opera was about looking at butterflies and mountain streams and making serious remarks about love and beauty. I believe this because everything was translated into English on a monitor beside the stage . . . sort of.

The translator was doing better than I could do if I had to translate an Italian opera into Chinese, but there was a typo or two in nearly every line. So most of the translations read like this: "Hurry to human wold." "Wait just a moment, I c big clam." "Takin my swordn, I stap it finally." and "The subtle melcy originates from nature."

I was impressed with the Liberace-on-acid-like costumes and the acrobatic fights, which broke out more often than at professional ice hockey games. And I was getting a good laugh from the translations. But everyone gets something different out of opera and I didn't want to provide a single-minded view, so when it ended, I turned to my just-woken Wisconsin neighbors and asked what they thought. "Lovely." "Wonderful." "Beautiful." They couldn't find enough nice things to say about it. Perhaps I had been observing the opera all wrong. Next time I'll have to try the Wisconsin method.

Nepal Bearer

Trekking in the Annapurnas

Pokhara, Nepal

 The Nepalese would no sooner trek up and down the Himalayas for fun than Americans would climb the stairs of the Empire State Building for fun. The difference is that we travel halfway around the world to trek in the Himalayas, and the Nepalese leave the Empire State Building alone, probably because they can't find any Americans to carry their bags for them.

The Nepalese may not understand our infatuation with trekking, but they've certainly learned to cater to it. When I went to Pokhara, the second largest city in Nepal, I discovered two cities with the same name located a few miles apart. One is Nepalese Pokhara and the other is "Disney" Pokhara. The first is an actual Nepalese city and the latter is an entire city built just for tourists where western trekkers outnumber locals by about ten to one.

When it comes to "Disney" Pokhara, we politically correct eco-tourists are faced with a bit of a dilemma. We detest the blatant western invasion of this beautiful culture, but we love the good restaurants that play Eric Clapton, the German bakeries that make delicious brownies, and the full range of shops that sell everything from yak sweaters and North Face sleeping bags to used Tom Clancy novels in every language. Everyone comments on how synthetic the town is, yet no one bashes it too much because we all know that if we really didn't like it, we could easily pick up and move a few miles to the real Pokhara. And who wants to do that?

I hung around "Disney" Pokhara for a few relaxing days and picked up a trekking permit, a sweater, and amebic dysentery. I then spent the next three days popping antibiotics like Raisinettes and staying not more than five meters away from the "toilet," which in Nepal is just a hole in the ground where the toilet is supposed to be. After losing almost as much weight as Oprah, I set out alone on my trek.

The trail I took to the Annapurna Base Camp, Nepal's super-highway of trekking, was fairly well marked in most places. I was glad I hadn't hired one of the guides or porters in "Disney" Pokhara who tried to convince me that if I went alone I'd get lost and end up in some little Nepalese village where no one has Coca-Cola. However, the trail was exhausting. It could have followed the winding river, but it didn't. It went straight: two or three hours up a foothill, then one or two hours back down to the river, making me think each time, "I'm gonna kill the wanker who cut this trail." And to make the trek even more pleasant, the oxygen level had significantly decreased, which I, in my not fully recuperated state, did not fully appreciate.

At one point I came around a bend and the primitive dirt trail turned into a full-sized dirt volleyball court—right on the side of the mountain! Two adorable five-year-olds were holding an authentic leather volleyball and waiting for me to play with them. I soon discovered this was a setup to get me to stop long enough for their mom to run out and sell me a Sprite, pizza, a Snickers bar, or Kodak film. She had it all. And she kept it in a shed you wouldn't think fit to store firewood, which, by the way, has been almost entirely replaced with propane since the ministry of tourism explained that if all their beautiful trees were cut down for firewood, the tourists would go trekking in Bhutan instead.

The Himalayas just look big on TV. You can see the mountain behind me is only a foot or two higher than my head.

Even though it was the winter off-season, I was running into other trekkers every hour. The city slickers looked more disheveled than most. They could be recognized by their trekking poles, which are just like ski poles, except that they make you look like a real dork when there's no snow or loose gravel or glacier, which there wasn't. An outfitter had probably sold them the poles on the premise that they would help counterbalance the additional weight of a video camera, three cartons of cigarettes, an altimeter, a water purifier, and other absolutely essential doodads that hung from their backpacks on individual carabiners like ornaments on a Christmas tree. The premise might have made sense had they actually worn their packs themselves. However, in most cases their gear was weighing down a ragged fourteen-year-old kid in flip-flops they had hired for three dollars a day.

I passed a lodging house every hour, but most of the lodges were grouped into small villages five hours apart. These small villages were popular with trekkers, who liked to stay near all the other trekkers and compare stories, or blisters. The innkeepers were friendly and some could even cook Nepalese versions of western cuisine—like yak-cheese pizza. But most trekkers were loyal to the local favorites: Snickers bars and Coca-Cola. Well, actually, the local specialty was *dal baht,* a gooey combination of white rice and mystery mush, which is supposed to be eaten with your fingers. This takes some practice and a lot of skill: You have to roll the mush into a small ball, then scoop it with your fingers and, holding it with your palm facing up, use your thumb to push the food into . . . your lap.

Socializing after dinner usually ended by 8:00 P.M. so people could go to bed and not sleep because of mild altitude sickness and aching muscles. Few stayed for more than a day or two in these lodges so the innkeepers must have gotten something of a drive-thru feeling.

The Nepalese villagers have a culture that, like the Himalayan mountain range, looks great on postcards. But they don't lead an easy life. Most attempt to grow a crop on a field that looks like a double-black-diamond mogul run. Others, usually elderly men and women, sit on the ground beating a small pile of millet with a stick. This seems to be the kind of project older villagers get if they don't have enough money to pick up and retire in Boca Raton.

After four days, I made it to base camp, which is at an altitude of 11,000 feet. The camp is surrounded by 22,000- to 24,000-foot mountains, so you get a feeling of sitting in a well with rugged, snow-capped two-mile-high walls.

I stayed for two days in a freezing, rat-infested hut called, appropriately enough, Paradise Guest House, waiting for the bulk of the cloud cover to lift. Most of my time was spent playing cards with a South African, two Kiwis, and a Frenchman. We sat huddled next to the stove eating soggy tuna pizza and trying to imagine that we were not turning into Popsicles—which is exactly what we felt like. Every so often someone would yell "There's a break in the clouds!" and we would all run out into the cold air and start snapping photos like Fuji-film shareholders.

After losing at hearts, war, and go fish, my two-day rest was over and I started my descent, taking a slightly longer route that increased my trek to eight days. My rented boots, which had given me no trouble on the climb, were beginning to turn my feet into two size-ten-and-a-half blisters.

I eventually made it down to a road at the bottom of the trail and "hitched" (for two dollars) back to Pokhara in the back of a transport truck loaded with containers of Nepalese lard. It seems like an odd way to end a long walk, but getting a lift back is one of the treks of the trade, and I hike it like that.

Taking a Stab at Acupuncture

Attending acupuncture school in Beijing

Beijing, China

Here in China they have a needle for everything. Want to lose weight? Insert a needle. Fertility problems? Just a matter of a few needles. The common cold? The Chinese have already found a cure: a needle. This was all new to me because my only first-hand experience with acupuncture was watching a 250-pound man get his nipple pierced on the street in Greenwich Village.

Does acupuncture work? I should hope so. China, a country with now over a billion citizens, has been doing it for 2,000 years—just think how many malpractice suits there would be if it didn't.

In the United States, acupuncture is known as "alternative medicine" because—as far as I can tell—pharmaceutical companies don't make much money from it yet. In China, it's just called "medicine." If you want all the fancy machines and wonderpills, you make an effort to see a "Western medicine" doctor.

Keeping a couple of needles in my first-aid kit for quick and inexpensive treatment on the road was an appealing idea, so I signed up for an abbreviated introductory course at Beijing's Academy of Traditional Chinese Medicine, one of three such schools in China, to see if it was possible to pick up a few helpful tips.

I was assigned a dormitory room with three German medical

students taking a one-month intro course. They welcomed me and, as soon as I unpacked, offered to stick some needles in my body. I was immediately reluctant.

"I'm not sick," I told them.

"Doesn't matter," they explained. "There're no side effects." I was still hesitant. "You are not afraid of needles, are you?" they taunted me.

"No, of course not," I lied. "Stick the entire sewing kit in!"

Torsten, a twenty-three-year-old with long hair and black leather pants who looked more like a back-up guitarist than a doctor, put in just one needle for starters on the crease of my elbow. The needle was the width of a prepubescent facial hair, as long as my little finger, and half of that was the grip. As the tiny needle passed through my skin, it was surprisingly painless. And I couldn't feel much as he probed around.

"What are you looking for?" I asked Torsten, then quickly had my question answered. "AAAAAAYYE," I yelped, trying to make the noise as masculine as possible as he penetrated my nerve with the needle.

"I was looking for that," he beamed. A warm tingly sensation pulsed from my fingertip to my shoulder, somewhat similar to a direct funny-bone hit. I mistook the feeling for pain at first because I had not felt anything like it before. "That's just the *qi*" (pronounced: "chee")," he told me.

I started the next morning in the clinic with two doctors: the lovely twenty-something English-speaking Dr. Wong and Dr. Wu, the chief of the clinic—a 5'5" middle-aged man who sounded like a talking fortune cookie.* He'd say things like, "A little needle manipulation goes a long way," and "We have only known each other for a short while, but I feel like we are old friends."

---

*Little tidbit: During two weeks in Beijing eating Chinese food for breakfast, lunch, and dinner, neither I—nor any traveler I met—ever encountered a single fortune cookie.

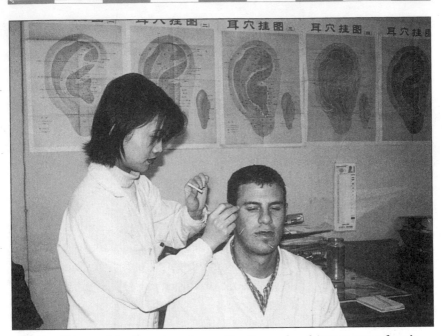

I let Dr. Wong stick about twenty needles in my head just to see what it felt like. It felt like something I do not plan to do again.

No sooner did I put on a white doctor's coat than Dr. Wu asked me to help with the next patient (I couldn't believe it either—I hadn't even opened a book yet): an eighty-year-old woman with partial facial paralysis. Aided by Dr. Wong, I asked the woman to lie down so Dr. Wu could stick about thirty needles into her face. The patient didn't seem to mind the needles even though several of them were just a few millimeters underneath her eyeball. We left her to rest with the needles protruding. So, to sum up, all I did with the first patient was tell her to "lie down," as Dr. Wong instructed me, then, because I had said this in English, Dr. Wong had to translate. Hope you're impressed.

I planned to participate more with our next patient, a man in his late twenties with lower back pain. Now, in the West, the last thing we'd want with lower back pain is to have someone jab us in the sore spots with a bunch of needles. But—you guessed it—that's exactly what the treatment is.

"Here, stick this needle in," Dr. Wu instructed via Dr. Wong's translation.

"Where?" I asked, holding the needle and hoping that the patient did not understand English. (At this point, I heard some snoring and glanced across the room. The woman with partial facial paralysis was actually sleeping with thirty needles in her face!)

"Stick one there, and another there."

I inserted them into his back with the same technique I use to jab cheese cubes on the hors d'oeuvre tray with toothpicks. I started probing and asked the patient, "Yo le mah?" (Is the qi coming?) I probed around for about a minute before he made the yelp that I recognized all too well. After the second needle was inserted, Dr. Wong and I connected some electrodes to the needles and dialed up the volts until the man's back muscles were pulsating like a conga line.

"Do you have any medical problems?" Dr. Wu asked me with translation, trying to be helpful during our short break between patients.

"I have chapped lips," I said, showing him.

He regarded me coldly. "We have no cure for that."

We admitted a new patient: an older woman with knee pain. Dr. Wong took her pulse. "It's slippery and thready," she announced. I felt her pulse as well, though I couldn't find anything slippery or thready about it. Dr. Wong had our patient stick out her tongue. "See, the white coating is very thin, and the tongue is swollen . . . yin deficiency." I couldn't see a thing, but I nodded. After asking a few questions, Dr. Wong informed me that our patient had a "liver and kidney problem." She went on to explain that this woman had endured years of poor nourishment, and now she was overweight. The diagnosis: "She's fat and her legs won't support her body, so her knee hurts." Made sense to me.

But how, you might ask, is that a liver and kidney problem? That's what the afternoon theoretical classes were for, although I admit I didn't make much progress in that area. I could understand how some needles could do wonders for some people with certain conditions, but the explanation baffled me. First, I had to learn about yin and yang, the two opposing forces in life: good and evil, light and dark, hot and cold, Ted Koppel and Jerry Springer. I could grasp the concept, just not how it applied to the body. How can you tell, for example, if someone has too much yang? And, no matter how many times the teachers explained, I couldn't understand when they'd say things like, "The spleen functions best in a dry environment and is susceptible to dampness." How does one keep the spleen dry?

I was never able to fully overcome my Western view of the body, which, now that I think about it, must sound just as odd to them. Taking pills orally to fix a headache? In Chinese medicine they put needles right into the head. This makes much more sense . . . until you hear that the headache is caused by a "qi deficiency," which stems from "wind attacking the channels," and requires a needle in a place called Gall Bladder 20, which is located at the base of the skull right next to a point called Urinary Bladder 10.

Now where'd I put that bottle of aspirin?

Demeaning of Life

Sneaking a peek at a Bangkok sex show

Bangkok, Thailand

When you get to Bangkok, avoiding a sex show isn't easy. Sex clubs are more common than McDonald's and they all hire overcaffeinated former waterbed salesmen to lure you off the street and plop you down right in the front row.

While in Bangkok, I met two female American graduate students who had been living in Asia for several months. They were interested in "checking out" one of the famous sex shows and felt they'd be more comfortable if a guy joined them. Naturally, I was not the slightest bit interested, but I felt obligated to accompany these two women for the sake of their security. It was an entirely selfless act that has not gone unnoticed by the Nobel Committee.

So we went to Patpong (Bangkok's red light district, not a Nerf version of table tennis). The whole district isn't much larger than a Kmart parking lot, but it offers at least twenty sex clubs, in addition to Go-Go bars, erotic paraphernalia shops, and more prostitutes than you can shake . . . well, you better not shake anything at them if you know what's good for you.

Patpong has become so famous, the streets are filled with more legitimate tourists than with businessmen looking for sex. European grandmothers with their grandkids in tow wander around until midnight, gawking at the famous prostitutes and shopping in the bustling street market set up by, I suppose, some government tourist commission.

Word on the street is that all the sex clubs are basically the same, so we walked up to the first one we saw and bargained with the tout over the "fixed price" of the six-dollar cover. In just a few minutes, by simply threatening to take our money to the next club down the street, we whittled the cover down to two bucks.

As we walked in, we immediately noticed three women who were dancing around naked and doing something that reminded me of Mary Poppins pulling surprisingly large objects out of her carpet bag. We had prepared ourselves for some uneasiness, but after ten seconds we were entering the first stages of traumatic shock.

The club was small and could potentially hold about fifty screaming naval pilots, but when we were there, the audience consisted of—including the three of us—three people. We were seated in the front, just below the stage.

Fifteen female waitresses, three female bartenders, and six female performers worked on this shift, and they all wore outfits that would make Hooters waitresses look Amish by comparison. Furthermore, they were all looking directly at me. I was the only guy in the bar besides the diminutive DJ, who kept interrupting the songs to make unintelligible announcements that sounded like, "Blah, blah, blah (female body part) blah, blah, blah, blah (female body part), blah (really bad word), blah blah."

The waitresses all took turns parading past me, sometimes stopping to look me in the eye or seductively drag their hands across my knee. This personal attention was a bit overwhelming. And the more embarrassed I got, the harder my two female companions laughed, to the point where I became red and they became hysterical and had difficulty breathing.

In the first feature act—and this is the whole sleazy truth—a woman, lying in a position I feel uncomfortable writing about and holding a straw in a place I'd rather not mention, blew out the candles on a cake while the DJ played Captain Kangaroo's version of "Happy Birthday." Then, this same woman, the air-compression specialist of the troupe, using the straw and a dart, did something that I'll probably never see again—which somehow popped some balloons three meters away. After this feat, she took some comfort in a relaxing cigarette, which she smoked with . . . well, you get the idea.

The next talented young lady imbibed an entire bottle of mineral water in a way that I'm afraid I can't describe here because you may have just eaten lunch.

At about this point we couldn't take any more of this entertainment and left the club with our beers mostly untouched. We were shocked and nauseated after being exposed to this degrading spectacle for five hours. Just kidding. We left after twenty minutes.

Actually, we left wishing we hadn't financially supported this abusive institution. As I later found out, thousands of young girls are taken from small villages each year and forced into this "work." Tourists who don't know about these performances may be curious and venture in. Perhaps this description—and I hope I have made myself clear—will satisfy your curiosity.

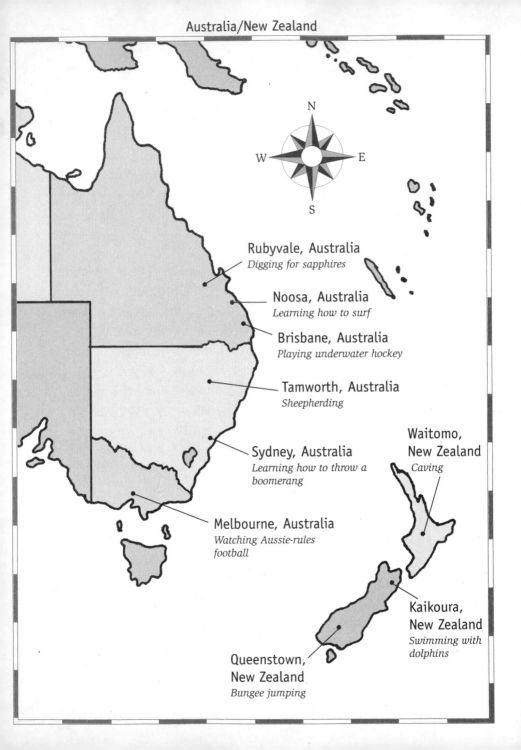

Rubyvale, Australia
Digging for sapphires

Noosa, Australia
Learning how to surf

Brisbane, Australia
Playing underwater hockey

Tamworth, Australia
Sheepherding

Waitomo, New Zealand
Caving

Sydney, Australia
Learning how to throw a boomerang

Melbourne, Australia
Watching Aussie-rules football

Kaikoura, New Zealand
Swimming with dolphins

Queenstown, New Zealand
Bungee jumping

AUSTRALIA/
NEW ZEALAND

One thing you should know about Aussies and New Zealanders (Kiwis) is that they don't like being mistaken for each other. Well, the Aussies don't mind that much, but the Kiwis—in typical little brother syndrome—hate getting mistaken for Aussies. Sometimes you can tell them apart by the expressions they use. Kiwis, for instance, say "box of birds" all the time. I realize it's hard to think of a case in which the appropriate response would be "box of birds," but you'd be surprised how often they manage to work it into conversation. Aussies, on the other hand, like to say "good on ya." ("I'm eating three jars of Vegemite every day." "Yeah? Good on ya!") Usually, though, I just ask everyone with a down-under accent if they're from New Zealand, and that way the only ones who are really bothered are the South Africans.

Live and Let Dive

Bungee jumping off the Skipper's Canyon bridge

Queenstown, New Zealand

The brochure for this South Pacific island-nation should probably read: "Come to New Zealand, visit our historical landmarks, and jump off them head first." In Queenstown in southern New Zealand, where commercial bungee jumping began, you'll be hard-pressed to find a bridge in the area without one of these giant rubber bands attached to it.

This is largely due to AJ Hackett, the PT Barnum of the adventure-tourism world. The only difference between AJ and PT is that in addition to being a talented promoter, AJ Hackett just might be a complete lunatic. The sport had its humble commercial beginnings here on the Kawarau suspension bridge (143 feet) in 1988 after Mr. Hackett bungied himself off the Eiffel Tower (illegally) the previous year. He has since bungied off many other ridiculously high ledges, often calibrating the elastic jump to touch his hand to the ground, and has now used this "science" to service over 500,000 would-be fanatics, and is currently franchising out like McDonalds.

With so many bridges to jump from in Queenstown, I finally decided to jump off the Skipper's Canyon bridge (229 feet) because, well, the marketing director at AJ Hackett's company said I could jump off for free. And I highly recommend you get AJ to pay for your bungee jump as well because the only thing that seems more outrageous than flinging yourself off a bridge is paying someone (about eighty-five dollars) to let you do it.

I knew immediately this sport wouldn't go over so well in the States when one of the AJ Hackett staffers weighed me and wrote my weight in big numbers on the back of my hand with a permanent marker. When the ten others in my group showed up, each with their weights written across the backs of their hands, it was like the first day of some sort of sadistic diet clinic. Meeting them and shaking hands felt a bit odd. "Hi, Tom, nice to meet you. I see you weigh ninety-five kilos."

Nicko, an AJ staffer, drove me and the others in a refurbished army truck over a fairly treacherous road most of the way to the bungee launch pad. We didn't drive all the way because one portion of the cliff-hugging dirt road had a huge crack down the middle and it was about to go any moment. Nicko didn't want to risk the truck but assured us it was fine to walk across, provided we do it quickly.

The first thing we did when we arrived was go to the bathroom. Everyone had to go, some more than once, since we wanted to do everything possible to avoid wetting ourselves midflight.

I was the first one to jump. Not by choice. They called out my number: "Hey, the guy who weighs eighty-two kilos is first!"

Jeremy and Spud, the outgoing bungee operators, gave me some background information while I prepared myself by taking all the loose change out of my pockets.

"We used to give free jumps to people who went naked," said Jeremy.

"Why did you stop?" I asked.

"It got boring. Everyone wanted to do it," Jeremy replied.

"But," added Spud, "we decided to call it quits after this one fat Australian guy jumped. It was just too disgusting."

The bungee may have been just a giant rubber band, but at least I could rest assured that it was being attached to my ankles

Photo by Signe Mattsson

From this angle, it sort of looks like my butt has sprouted two arms. Perhaps this is a normal Darwinian adaptation to falling off a 229-foot bridge.

with a sturdy beach towel. (Yes, a beach towel!) Of course, that's not all they used. They also secured the towel with a small piece of nylon cord about the width of masking tape. And with this advanced safety system I was supposed to jump off a bridge. What was there to possibly worry about?

To be honest, I wasn't all that worried up until this point. I had been successfully thinking about everything else but throwing myself off a suspension bridge. But when I stepped to the edge of the platform, a modern-day "walk the plank," and looked down at the river way below, I began to panic. I felt this panic first in my knees. Then it quickly moved up my legs and across my chest. After three more seconds it had found its way into my lungs, moved up my trachea, and surfaced through my mouth in the form of a sentence: "I don't think I want to jump."

"Sure ya do, mate," said Jeremy, who was a) safely fastened to the bridge with a harness and b) getting paid to help people jump off.

I weighed my natural instinct against Jeremy's advice and the embarrassment of backing out at the last moment in front of these people, then drove every rational thought from my brain and leapt off the bridge, head first.

My father had always given me a hard time about not working in "the real world," but now the real world was coming at me at 9.82 meters per second per second.* I felt the drop in my stomach. I had my mouth open but my primal yell was silent. I stretched the bungee until I was within a few yards of the river, squinting a bit to keep my eyeballs from ejecting and landing in the drink.

Then, nearly as quickly as I had come down, I started going back up. I felt the drop in my stomach, then weightlessness, then another drop in my stomach. I was completely disoriented. My views were alternating between a spinning bridge, a spinning river, and my shirt, which had come untucked from my pants and was falling over my head. I was, apparently, flashing my navel to everyone above.

After a few increasingly shorter bounces, I was lowered upside down to an awaiting jet boat. Just as I was reaching the boat, I noticed all the blood in my body had collected inside my head. I grabbed the pole Nicko extended, and he pulled me into the boat, unfastened the bungee and beach towel, and took me to shore. I stepped off the rocking boat onto rocking land, which made me realize that I was the one doing the rocking. My body was pumping enough raw adrenaline to launch Sputnik.

I watched the others bungee jump as my endorphins came back down from orbit. A few of the jumpers went tandem, a few went backwards, and several went more than once, for an additional twenty-five bucks per jump. One Danish girl went three times. She would have gone a few more times if she hadn't run out of cash.

From the time you leave the bridge until the time you touch land again is about thirty seconds. After Las Vegas, it's probably the quickest way to spend your money. But as AJ Hackett claims, it's a memory that will "be with you forever." Kind of like the pacemaker you'll need when your heart stops midjump, never realizing that you didn't die from the fall.

---

*This is not a mistake, but don't ask me to explain it.

The Dolphin Singers

Swimming with dolphins in New Zealand

Kaikoura, South Island, New Zealand

The only things I know about dolphins are 1) they are really smart, 2) the ones at Sea World can "shake hands" if you give them a dead fish, and 3) the ones that aren't in Sea World shouldn't be hanging out with tuna.

I know that dolphins are smart because I've watched hundreds of episodes of *Flipper*. Flipper, of course, was the Lassie of the ocean world—the pet of a little blond boy with cutoffs who seemed to be on permanent summer vacation. In a typical episode, Flipper would find a shipwrecked sailor and save him by swimming to shore and alerting the blond boy with a series of high-pitched screeches, which we all knew was dolphin talk for "Go get the ranger and follow me. Someone is in trouble." But it's easy to forget that Flipper is a professional actor and not all dolphins know the word "ranger."

Because of the popularity of Flipper in the United States, I suppose dolphin authorities feared that dolphin-loving Americans would go out and get dolphin pets for themselves, presumably to keep in their pee-and-chemical-saturated swimming pools, where they would be of very little assistance to shipwrecked sailors. So, to help us avoid this temptation, they have—quite reasonably—outlawed frolicking with dolphins in the wild. To swim with a wild dolphin these days, you have to leave the country, which is exactly what I did.

Even though it's quite legal in Kaikoura, I was reluctant to participate in any program that influenced dolphin behavior by teaching them Sea World tricks such as eating a dead fish from the mouth of the dolphin trainer.

I joined up with a company called Dolphin Encounter, mostly because their brochure was covered from top to bottom with names and addresses of various oceanographic protection agencies, so it seemed more credible than the recommendation my guide book offered.

I signed up for the three-hour tour because, well, it was the only tour they offered. The normal cost is about fifty-five dollars, but I paid ten dollars less because I thought the price was awfully steep for jumping into the ocean, so I told the owner I was a famous journalist and he believed me. Ha!

Before the tour began, I had to don a cold, wet wet suit in the locker room, where I met some of the other wanna-be dolphin swimmers. This was an ideal bonding experience because it invited numerous understanding looks and very sophisticated male locker-room jokes.

We then boarded the Dolphin Encounter bus, which took us to the Dolphin Encounter jet boat, and listened to Antje (we couldn't pronounce her name either), our guide, explain how to make friends with dolphins. She told us we could do certain things to make ourselves more appealing to the dolphins, so they would want to swim with us; apparently our natural charms wouldn't be sufficient.

How do you attract a dolphin? While maintaining a straight face, Antje told us that dolphins would approach us if we sang. Yes, that was really what she said. Also, we were supposed to splash around like dolphins, with our arms at our sides and our legs together. And she advised us that if a dolphin swam near us, we should imitate its motions. The basic idea, I gathered from this talk, was that we were supposed to make contact with this intelligent species by acting like a bunch of total retards.

As the Dolphin Encounter jet boat sped over the rolling swells for fifteen minutes to a place that had been located by one of their dolphin spotters that morning, I prepared myself for what I imagined would happen: I'd swim around like a singing dolphin for a few hours and a dolphin would swim next to me and sing several octaves higher and we would sort of, well, communicate. Perhaps even discuss Shirley MacLaine's book.

As we approached the dolphin swim site, the view from above the water was startling. The water was filled with gray dorsal fins as far as I could see. Antje announced that there were about 250 dolphins in this pod, but if I hadn't known better, I would have sworn I had accidentally joined the Shark Encounter tour. It was very reassuring when one of the dolphins shot out of the water for an inverse double gainer and disappeared back into the water. So many of them were throwing themselves acrobatically into the air, I began to wonder how I would imitate this maneuver if one swam by me and did it.

The sound of the captain's horn was our sign to put on our flippers and neoprene hoods and get into the water. I wasn't quite prepared for the fifty-degree temperature. It felt like jumping into a Slurpee while wearing a scrub sponge.

We must have been an amazing sight: eight tourists singing different songs and trying to swim like dolphins. And since we were all wearing snorkels, singing was not only difficult, but senseless. The snorkels simply projected our off-key wailing up into the air, where it might have attracted any low-flying birds, or more likely send them plummeting into the ocean to escape the noise.

I was butchering the words to an ABBA tune as I splashed around like a wounded sea lion, freezing my behoogies off in the process, when, suddenly, I was surrounded by about fifteen dolphins, just out of arm's reach. The five-foot-long Dusky dolphins were a bit smaller than I had imagined. And they weren't making any sounds at all, just

That might be the dorsal fin of an eighteen-foot-long great white shark circling me. Yet, I remain perfectly calm.

circling me. Following orders to imitate their every movement, I began circling in the same direction as I continued to warble through the ABBA song, in case it was my singing that had attracted them. After forty seconds, I was dizzy and completely out of breath, so I had to take the snorkel out of my mouth and recover.

At some point during this wildlife adventure, it occurred to me that we weren't checking the dolphins out as much as they were checking us out. One of the more entrepreneurial dolphins was probably running excursions called "Human Encounter" and making a fortune. My guess is that the dolphins concluded we weren't very interesting. We were lousy swimmers. We were—I think I can speak for the entire group—lousy singers.

And, with wet suits on, we weren't much good for mating.

A Wave New World

Learning how to surf in Australia

Noosa, Queensland, Australia

I've always wanted to learn how to surf, but in my mid-twenties, I feared I was too old to start learning on American beaches. "Unless you're a local's little brother," a surfer friend from Hawaii once told me, "there's a good chance of getting thrashed by locals if you ride on their waves." I heard the surfing community was a bit friendlier in Australia, so while I was traveling along the east coast of Queensland, I decided to stop in Noosa, which my Lonely Planet guidebook calls a "Surfing Mecca" (though I doubt their Saudi Arabian edition describes Mecca as a "Religious Noosa").

When I arrived in this Queensland surfing town I couldn't even figure out which Noosa the book was referring to: Noosa Heads, Noosaville, Noosa Junction, and Noosa Sound were all in a three-square-mile area. It sounded like a Dr. Seuss retirement community.

I went to rent a surfboard at a surf shop in central Noosa, and Ty, the surf bum on duty, told me it was cheaper to just get a lesson, which included surfboard rental. He handed me a surf-school brochure that listed the instructor as "Merrick Davis, 1988 World Champion." I didn't really believe it. That would be like getting a passing lesson from Joe Montana; a prayer lesson from Pope John Paul II; or a spending lesson from the U.S. Department of Defense. Ty let me use his phone to call up and make an appointment for a ninety-minute lesson with the former world champion. Only twenty bucks.

The only thing I knew about surfing prior to the lesson was that it's not just a sport, it's an entire fashion industry. And while I wasn't prepared to spend a fortune, I certainly didn't want to look like a total weenie in front of a world champion. Ty explained that I absolutely could not surf in the Patagonia shorts I was wearing. People would call me a "footie-head," which I can only assume is bad. He convinced me that I needed a pair of "surfies," nylon surfing shorts big enough to be used as a military supply tent.

"How come there's no liner?" I asked.

"Liners are lame."

"So what do you wear underneath?"

"Mate, I don't wear anything at all," Ty confided.

I paid forty dollars for a pair of maroon surfies that made Shaq's basketball shorts look like a Speedo.

When I got back to my youth hostel, I tried them on without anything underneath and it just didn't feel right, so I ended up wearing my underwear, which seemed to defeat the purpose of a swimsuit, especially a quick-drying one.

Merrick picked me up in his Ford Laser. He was a bit late because he said he'd been riding swells "a little bigger than that [two-story] house over there." I looked at the house in question and decided that the excuse seemed reasonable, especially after Merrick complimented me on my surfies. We drove to another hostel and picked up two French guys, Francois and Gerard, and an Israeli girl, Nette, who informed Merrick in the car that she was going to be "a hard case," whatever that meant. Merrick looked over at me and we both shrugged.

It struck me in the car that Merrick didn't look much like a surfer. If anything, he looked like a tennis pro. He didn't have the long stringy blond hair, saggy pants, bug-eye sunglasses, or a chemically altered vocabulary. But you didn't have to look that closely to see the collection of surfing scars on his torso. "Surfing is a macho thing," he told us.

When we arrived at the beach, Merrick lined us up on the sand and began class.

Lesson #1: Paddle Position. "Your feet should hang off the tail, hands should grip the rail, chin should go over the stringer, and eyes should face the nose." This was very confusing to all four of us, especially Nette, who practically gave up when she realized that surfing lingo was going to be involved.

Lesson #2: Standing Up. He drew an imaginary surfboard in the sand. "It's basically a high-speed push-up, springing mainly off the right big toe. Unless, of course, you're a goofy-foot, then you should spring off the left big toe." We practiced getting from the prone paddling position to our feet. During this lesson, I managed to collect a substantial part of the beach in my new shorts.

Lesson #3: Riding the Wave. "Let's not worry about that yet." (This was most unfortunate because one of my favorite dance moves—and I realize this doesn't say much for my dancing skills— is to imitate a surfer, and I was really looking forward to improving my technique.)

Merrick then handed out surfboards and gave us each a chunk of wax to rub on them. The idea was that this would improve our foot grip, should we ever achieve the standing position for more than two seconds. "It is very important," said Merrick, "to rub the wax in *small circles*." I found it hard to believe that my performance at this point in my surfing career could be hindered by a diagonal or horizontal surf-wax application. Merrick then gave us spandex surf shirts to keep our chest hairs from getting caught in the wax.

We waded awkwardly out through the small breaking waves to the larger breaking waves, which looked about eight feet tall.

Merrick said they were only three-foot waves. I said they were definitely bigger than that. Merrick informed us that surfers measure waves differently. "For example," he said, "the waves I was on earlier today (the size of that house) are called eight-foot waves. But in Hawaii, those would be called four-foot waves. There's not much logic to it."

I'm not one to make excuses, but once my surfies and underwear got wet, they must have weighed about ten pounds and were sloshing around in the surf like a broken rudder as I tried to paddle past the wave break. Also, with my Malibu (a long, round-tipped board), I couldn't duck under the swells easily so each wave picked me up and smashed me into the beach head first. This was my first taste of surfing. It was also my first taste of Noosa sand.

I figured, like Newton, that there must be a mathematical formula somewhere in this skull-shaking mishap: Perhaps the volume of the surfboard is directly proportional to the amount of water you get up your nose.

Francois, Gerard, and Nette all suffered similar fates. Merrick was always quick to the rescue and quite understanding. He suggested that we practice in the small white-water waves, which were about two feet tall by my own measurement system.

Now, I've been standing for the better part of my life. But when I finally stood up on that surfboard, it was like starting all over again. "Hey, look!" I wanted to shout, "I'm standing!" I was so caught up in the excitement of the moment that I forgot everything Merrick had taught me for twenty dollars. I stood straight up and let my arms dangle all over the place. That's why, Merrick explained later, we beginners are called "Gumbies."

Don't think for a moment that I'm making more excuses, but I'm sure I would have actually gotten the hang of surfing if it weren't for the ankle leash. The ankle leash has two purposes as far as I can tell. One is to become tangled around your legs. The other is, during a wipe out, to snap the board back into your head. It's a very challenging element of the sport.

After the lesson, Francois, Gerard, Nette, and I collapsed on the beach in exhaustion and frustration. Gerard asked Merrick what aspect of surfing he liked the most, hoping to find something about this sport to focus on. Merrick said, "I guess I like the feel of being wet." Being wet—that was the one thing I had mastered. I had one question I was burning to ask Merrick. "I don't mean to pry, but do you . . . I mean do most surfers . . . wear anything under their surfies?" Merrick confided that he wore a "sluggo" underneath. I don't know how "sluggo" sounds in French or Hebrew, but none of us asked him to elaborate.

Honk If You Love Spelunking

Caving in New Zealand

Waitomo, North Island, New Zealand

"It's like getting flushed down a toilet," offered Nick Andeef, the owner of Waitomo Adventures, as if this were a major selling point for his wet-caving expedition. The brochure for this spelunk, commercially named Haggas Honking Holes, highlighted the cave's tight passages and small enclosed spaces. Sure it sounded like an ideal trip for a gerbil, or perhaps Kate Moss, assuming she's not claustrophobic, but what about a six-foot, 185-pound travel writer who, as a child, constructed forts in the living room by pushing various pieces of furniture together and covering the whole thing with a blanket, and then pretended for hours that he was actually living in the Middle Ages in the cramped quarters of a stone fortress made of sturdy, fashionable 1970s living-room furniture?

Before Nick would let me go, he had to make sure I could fit through the cave's narrower passages. So, I had to squeeze my body through a hole in the wall of their office about the size of a cat door. It was a small miracle I managed to pull myself through without lubrication.

Dameon and Becky, a slender husband-and-wife police team from England, passed through easily. Kim, an Australian who had just gone skydiving the day before and couldn't stop talking about it, had a bit more difficulty.

After we all qualified, Jason and Mike, the two guides, brought us in a van to the cave entrance, where we changed into our "hole-honking outfits." These were almost as ridiculous looking as the name made them out to be: full wet suits, red protective overalls (to protect the wet suits, not us), hard hats with lights mounted in front, rubber boots, and climbing harnesses. My outfit was tight enough in the crotch to prevent me from lifting my arms over my head or reaching below my knees, giving me about as much flexibility as the Michelin Man. "It fits just right," said Jason.

Mike tied a rope to a tree and let us practice abseiling down a small hill. "Abseiling" is a German word adopted by New Zealanders that means paying a lot of money to slide down a rope. However, I'm more familiar with the American word "rappelling," which, at least in my case, means flashing a press pass and sliding down a rope for free and also getting a few free postcards.

After our abseiling practice session Jason asked if we had any questions.

"Why is it called Haget Jerkings Holes, or whatever?" asked Dameon, voicing the exact thought of our entire group.

Jason explained that it was derived from Mr. Haggas's name, a farmer who owns the land with the caves and collects a commission every time one of us "honks" on it. Becky explained that in England "honking" is a colloquial word for vomiting and if they were interested in attracting more visitors from the U.K., or at least ones without eating disorders, they ought to consider a new name.

The first thing we had to do was abseil down the center of a forty-foot waterfall into the cave.

"Is the cave entrance high?" asked Dameon as Mike attached his harness to the abseiling rope.

"No," he answered, "it's deep."

We lowered ourselves down through the pounding water one at

a time and tried not to let go of the wet rope and soil the bottom of the cave with our bodies. At the bottom, I saw the beginning of a tunnel cut by a subterranean river system and the bones of a sheep who hadn't been able to afford the abseil portion of the trip.

The only complaint came from Kim, who didn't realize, while putting on her wet suit, that she was going to get wet. She informed us that this definitely wasn't as good as her skydiving trip.

We abseiled down

You wouldn't know it to look at this picture, but my foot is stuck between two rocks and I'm dying to use the toilet.

Photo by Signe Mattsson

several more waterfalls until we were approximately two hundred feet underground. We were catching our breath in a small cavern when Mike trudged through the knee-deep murky water to the cavern wall, got down on his back, and disappeared underwater. After letting the silence of Mike's exit hang in the air for thirty seconds, Jason asked cheerfully, "Right, who's next?"

I timidly volunteered. Jason instructed me, "Sit'n yer bum en feel fer the hole en the wall wit yer feet, mate."

I found a hole that didn't seem much bigger than the opening of a possum's sphincter—that was the only hole.

"Okay, naw stert sliding yerself through'et feet ferst."

I squeezed my legs through the opening, but I got stuck at my waist. With my head just above water, I was beginning to joke with Jason that I had eaten too much for breakfast, when I felt two hands grab my feet on the other side and yank me underwater and through the hole.

I surfaced on the other side, with about two feet of breathing space between the water and the rock ceiling, and gasped for the breath I had forgotten to take on the other side. Mike was squatting in the water next to me with a sadistic grin on his face. "Just like poppin' out of yer mum's womb, right, mate?" I felt more like a fresh turd.

The others made it through without much effort. Kim took the opportunity to remind us that this was not as exciting as skydiving.

We continued through the tunnel, crawling much of the way, to a cavern with tremendous stalactites, giant sodium carbonate icicles that have taken several thousand years to grow; stalagmites, icicles that are just as slow but grow from the ground up; and stalagstubs, stalactites and stalagmites that have been broken off by moronic tourists looking for cheap souvenirs.

We climbed one cliff wall and took ladders up the more technical parts of others until we reached the original entrance. Kim wanted to dry off and enroll in the air force. Dameon and Becky were ready to do it again. My body was tired from fighting against my restricting hole-honking outfit for two hours and I wanted to go back to my hostel, build a fort, and take a nap in it.

A Jackaroo of All Trades

Sheepherding in Australia

Tamworth, Australia

If you were to recast the entire *City Slickers* movie (the first one) so that it involved three guys who had never met before . . . If one of the guys was an Austrian who wore a brand new cowboy outfit every day, the other was a recently discharged U.S. naval engineer who grew up in Texas without ever riding a horse, and the third guy was, well, me . . . If you replaced the herd of cattle with a herd of sheep . . . If the two ranch hands and the boss and his wife spoke Australian, not Texan . . . If you got rid of the Jack Palance character altogether as well as the supermodel who fell for the total doofus . . . Well, then you'd have the exact story of the Australian cowboy/cowgirl training school I attended, except with a totally different plot.

At first, I thought a jackaroo was a breed of kangaroo I had not yet seen. With only minimal conceit, a woman at the tourist information office in Sydney set me straight when I asked if they had one in the zoo. She then offered to find me a jackaroo course.

That's more or less how I ended up at the Echo Hills Jackaroo and Jillaroo School. Pete, the bearded Papa Smurf-like owner, picked me up at the bus station in his Land Rover, drove me out to the ranch, and offered me a few customary welcome beers that I was later billed for. Then, I met my fellow jackaroos: Tony, the

Austrian, and Dave, the naval engineer.

This "station" (farm) had cows, sheep, dogs, a ninety-year-old hermit named Doug, and kangaroos bouncing all over the place (only the kangaroos were bouncing). I had arrived during sheep-shearing season and Pete told me I would learn everything there was to know about the process. The first thing I had to learn was how to crack a whip, which looks very easy—especially when watching Indiana Jones. Let me assure you that it is anything but. I used a six-foot whip—supposedly twice as easy as the bull-whip Indiana used—but it took me over an hour to *not* get the hang of it. Will and Rob, our good-natured twenty-four-year-old jackaroo instructors, must have demonstrated roughly three thousand times before conceding defeat.

I'd circle the whip over my head, bring my arm down, snap my wrist, and the end of the whip would, at high velocity, bounce off the ground and directly into my gonads. Of course, this didn't happen every time. Sometimes I'd hit myself in the face. I wasn't the only student who flunked Whipping 101. None of us became accomplished enough with the whip to use it while riding (the sound of the whip is vital for getting sheep to move). "It would be bad," Will explained, if we whipped ourselves while on horseback, "and even worse" if we accidentally whipped our horses.

"How do we make the sheep move without a whip?" I asked.

"By whoopin' and hollerin'," Will replied.

Rob and Will had both memorized every single line from the movie *Man from Snowy River*, and they recited most of it to us line by line, which went largely unappreciated because Dave and I were the only jackaroo trainees who had seen the movie and neither of us could even remember what it was about.

My first horse, Ribbon, had everything but training wheels. What she lacked in speed she made up for in apathy and a back that sagged like a hammock. Plus, she was a little too short for me—at least I'm pretty sure my feet weren't supposed to be dragging on the ground. Still, by Echo Hills regulation, I had to wear a standard-issue hockey helmet to ride her, which had the net effect of making me look like I was trying out for the Severe-Head-Injury Riding Team. It would have taken nothing less than a ninety-gigawatt bolt of lightning in this horse's ass to make her run. After I proved myself by getting Ribbon to take three steps unassisted, I was able to transfer to Large Lucille, who was only in a partial coma.

"Lits go mustah sem woolies outtada paddock!" Will announced.

"Vas iz dat?" asked Tony so that Dave or I didn't have to.

"Herding sheep out of the field," said Rob in his best American accent.

Riding about one hundred meters apart, we walked our horses across the hilly, burr-infested, rectangular fenced terrain. Rob and Will cracked their whips. Tony yelled, "Ha!" I yelled, "Hi-ya!" and Dave occasionally muttered, "Whoop"— with the sort of unbridled enthusiasm you might expect to hear at a funeral.

I'm extremely glad they let me replace the hockey helmet with a hat for this photo. The rest of the day, I looked more like Wayne Gretzky on horseback.

Photo by Signe Mattsson

Every so often, as we crossed the paddock, a reminder that we were in Australia would pop up, in the form of a kangaroo. We'd stop and watch the roo bounce across the open terrain, then up and over one of the fences, thankful that sheep were all we would have to muster.

The sheep, who were usually milling about in small packs, would start trotting away from us before we'd even get close. By the time we reached the end of the paddock, we found upwards of a thousand sheep standing against the fence. The best way to control the flock is with a sheep dog, who will run around and stare down, bark at, or bite any sheep who even thinks about breaking away. But we didn't have a dog. We had to herd them ourselves. The key to this is keeping them together in a flock, where sheep are better behaved than a bus full of nuns on a field trip to the Vatican. If, however, one breaks off from the pack, she suddenly adopts the will of an anarchist and the athleticism of Barry Sanders, and is nearly impossible to catch, especially with my less-than-stellar riding skills.

After a few frustrating days, we eventually got the hang of mustering, and were able to herd the sheep right into the shearing shed, the heart of this station. Inside the shed, the lanolin was so heavy in the air, it cured my chapped lips.

Five shearers were at work, each holding an industrial-strength barber's clippers in one hand and a sheep in the other. Before I saw these guys in action, I was unaware that shearing sheep was considered an art. Australia actually has major competitions for shearing, and one of the shearers, a guy named Andrew, told me he makes several thousand dollars each year just in shearing-award money. Other than that, shearers get $1.50 per sheep. That's why they kept stopping every few hours to count them, an activity many claim has a history for induczzzzzzzzzzzzzzzz

Mick, one of the shearers, got a sheep started for me and then

Photo by Signe Mattsson

Now I know what it's like to be a military barber.

handed me the clippers. I would have probably had better luck with a lawnmower. This sheep got a haircut she will never forget. It would have embarrassed a Chia-Pet.

I then tried my hand as a "roustabout." Roustabouts gather the freshly shorn fleeces and toss them like picnic blankets onto the wool-classing table. Tony and Dave were instantly experts at this. When I tried it, though, I don't think I picked up the fleece just right, so the wool I tossed landed in a big clump. Peter, the shed's wool-classer, had to carefully spread out my fleece wad so he could get rid of the grungy bits around the edges and determine the grade of the wool by, as far as I could tell, just looking at it. I also tried classing wool for a while and discovered I had no talent for it.

After the wool was sorted, I helped a guy named Dutch Pete pack it into several bales (yes sir, yes sir, three bags full) with the very macho hydraulic wool-compressor. I liked this machine a lot. Unlike the other aspects of shearing, packing required minimal talent. You just loaded wool into this giant garbage compactor and pulled a lever. Finally, a task I could master!

Next, we took the naked-looking shorn sheep and marched them onto a conveyor belt. This was difficult because—and I'll bet you didn't know this—sheep have a particularly strong aversion to conveyor belts. To make them take that final step, Will showed us how to—this part is truly disgusting, but it's what real farm life is about—stick a finger up their sphincters and push them forward with our forearm. Once the sheep were on the conveyor belt, we took turns "branding" them with an Echo Hills symbol dipped in special paint; "drenching" them by forcing a sort of a water-pick filled with medicine into their mouths; and "back-lining" them by spraying their backs with bluish guck to prevent lice. Then, the sheep were ready to get mustered back into the paddock.

I didn't exactly feel qualified to seek farm work after my training, but Pete, the owner, told me, right before I left, that I was indeed a jackaroo. I suppose I had acquired a number of new skills, not to mention a riding rash that would be with me for weeks.

Mister Boomerang

Learning how to throw a boomerang

Sydney, Australia

According to local legend, fifteen thousand years ago an Aboriginal pulled the metal hook out of a wooden coat hanger, threw it at a kangaroo, missed, and it came back and hit him in the nose. Which explains why many Aborigines now prefer the Frisbee.

When I spotted Duncan MacLellan's Boomerang School, something pulled me inside. Perhaps it was the sign: "FREE LESSONS." Or maybe it was my girlfriend, Signe, yanking me by the arm.

Of course, I didn't really need the lessons. I'd spent many hours throwing a Nerf boomerang around my college dorm room, where I managed to knock over and break nearly everything in the room but the couch, which had already been broken by the previous owners.

At any rate, I'm glad I entered his one-room shop. Duncan MacLellan, at age seventy-five, is one of Australia's true folk heroes, a genuine character right down to his no-nonsense DNA.

"I'd like to enroll in your Boomerang School," I said.

"Look," he told me, "here's my card. There's a map on the back. Show up at that spot on Sunday for the lesson. Good-bye."

"Should I buy a boomerang first?" I asked, noticing what must have been over ten thousand boomerangs piled up in his tiny shop.

"Just show up on Sunday, have a throw, then you can buy a

bloody boomerang if you want to."

I was the first student to arrive on Sunday morning. Duncan was sitting on the park bench with his kangaroo-skin bag filled with boomerangs. We chatted awhile. I learned that Duncan had been in the boomerang business for over thirty-five years. He had trained under Joe Timbury, the Aboriginal champion of the 1950s. "Joe never charged me for a lesson, so why should I charge anyone? Yer not goin' to get much out of life if you don't put somethin' in."

Duncan told me about some of his famous customers, including Elton John and Arthur Frommer. "Frommer came here about twenty-three years ago when he was doin' *Australia on Five Dollars a Day*. Now it's up to about fifty dollars a day and he's probably a

Photo by Signe Mattsson

millionaire livin' in California with ten sheilas crawlin' all over him. Well, he asked if I wanted to be in his book and I told him, 'I don't care. Just pay me the bloody five bucks you owe me for that boomerang in your hand.'"

When Duncan decided it was time to start the lesson, he removed his shoes and socks and took off his pants. I asked if this was his special boomerang outfit.

I am demonstrating the correct technique for tossing a boomerang—right into Syndey harbor.

"Hell no, they're just regular shorts. And I'm afraid to bend over because there's a big hole in the crotch."

Over the last thirty-five years he's taught more people to throw the boomerang than probably anyone else in the world. Surely Duncan could teach me. I picked up a boomerang and, following his instructions, aimed it perpendicular to the ground at a forty-five-degree angle to the wind. I wound up and released it. The boomerang flew out ten yards, went straight into the ground, bounced over the guard rail and into Sydney harbor.

"Oops," he said. "That's a left-handed boomerang. You need a right-handed one."

"I'll pay for that," I said apologetically.

"Don't worry about it. These boomerangs are cheap plywood crap."

I tried with a right-hander and, much to my surprise, the thing actually came back. Which wasn't very comforting. Because it is a weapon. And it was coming right at me.

"Activate yourself and catch it!" Duncan shouted. "You might bleed a little, but you'll heal up."

"Yeah, catch it!" yelled Signe from behind a tree across the park, where she was viewing the deadly boomerang safely through a telephoto lens.

A boomerang makes a helical approach pattern as it drops. Not knowing quite how to anticipate this corkscrew descent, I could only give chase, running around—fully aware I must have looked like a world-class idiot—in ever smaller circles until the boomerang dropped just out of my reach.

Then Chris, a young German chemical engineer, showed up, followed by an American couple and a middle-aged German with his elderly father. Duncan was extremely encouraging. He'd yell "Bue-tee-full!" if we just got the boomerang in the air. If something went wrong, he'd say, "It slipped out of your hand," and if we threw it straight into the ground and it bounced up, he'd say "That's a kangaroo!"

"Is it really called a kangaroo?" I asked him.

"No, but it seems to make people feel better if I say it."

After thirty minutes Duncan had all of us throwing fairly accurate "returns." Most of us managed to catch our own throws and I managed to hit the elderly German man once and a guy sitting on the bench twice. Which probably explains why boomeranging isn't much of a spectator sport.

After the lesson I went to Duncan's office to buy a boomerang. He had several different kinds. I picked up one with an Omega-shaped curve.

"What's this one called?" I asked.

"A boomerang."

"I mean does it have a special name?"

"Sure, white people have all sorts of bloody rubbish names for them, but the Aborigines just call them boomerangs. And that's what they are. Boomerangs."

I asked Duncan what keeps him going. "I like seeing people go away with a good feeling. I give them somethin' for nothin' so long as they show up with the right attitude. Take that old German guy today; he couldn't throw for crap at the beginnin', but eventually he got it. I probably fought against that old bugger in World War II, but today I taught him how to throw the boomerang."

Through all the stories and the instruction, one thing was perfectly clear: Duncan enjoys his work. And his philosophy on life is, appropriately enough, like a boomerang. "If you put good things into the world, you will usually get good things back."

Touchdown Under

Watching Aussie-rules football

Melbourne, Australia

Australian-rules football, also called "Aussie rules" and "footie," is, according to an unemployed English actor named Barry who was staying at my youth hostel, "Australia's most popular national sport, right behind driving drunk and abusing the aborigines." Aussie rules is a bit like American football, except that, as the name implies, the rules are totally different, and they were invented by Australians. Barry told me that I had to see a game for myself to truly appreciate the difference.

I was low on cash when I arrived at the Melbourne Cricket Ground, a stadium built initially for cricket (another sport I don't understand) with a seating capacity of over 100,000, so I pulled out my press pass and walked from gate to gate, presenting it to each ticket taker until, after eight attempts, I was allowed entrance by an older man with poor eyesight who would have probably let me pass with my library card.

The first thing I did, at Barry's suggestion, was purchase a beer. He had assured me that after several beers the game would make much more sense. I also ordered a meat pie, the Aussie equivalent of a hot dog.

"What kind of meat is it?" I asked the concession attendant.

"Meat," she replied.

In this match, Carlton, a top team, was pitted against Footscray, neither a top team nor a shoe deodorant. I decided to *barrack* (root) with the Footscray fans because I like to support the underdog. I sat next to David, a farmer who drove into town specifically for this match.

The game started with an aggressive basketball-style tip-off: the umpire, standing in a designated square in the center of the field, bounced the ball (a cross between a football and a volleyball) as high as he could and let the players battle for it.

"What's that big square in the center called?" I asked David.

"The round one?" he tried to clarify. It seemed that David might not be much help.

Once the game got under way, I could see that the object of Aussie rules is, quite simply, to clobber whoever has the ball, unless you have the ball, in which case you should run like mad, remembering to bounce it every ten meters and then get rid of it, preferably by tossing or kicking it toward the opponent's end of the field, before you get clobbered.

This is not as easy as it sounds because 1) the field has no "end" as such since it is an oval, 2) it is approximately the size of a par-four golf hole, and 3) while you are holding the ball, the opposing team may use any force necessary to stop you, including—and I may need to consult the rule book on this—semi-automatic assault rifles.

And did I mention that the players were not wearing any safety equipment? Only sleeveless shirts and tight shorts, which needed constant readjusting—just like American baseball players fiddling with the motorcycle helmet they wear in their pants—which may have accounted for the large number of female fans I saw in attendance.

Those are the basics. It only took me one beer to figure them out. The technical parts, like scoring, required another beer. The strategy took a third. But I found the history of Aussie rules was the hardest to swallow. David told me it was originally played by cricketeers who wanted to stay in shape in the off-season. Translated into American, this is a bit like saying the triathlon was created for golfers to stay in shape.

I bought a *record* (program) to help me understand the game, but it wasn't very helpful because it was written in Australian. It read something like this: "Hickmont and Spalding, the roving rucker and wing middie, have converted several high marks into behinds." And it didn't help to know the players' names because all the fans referred to them by nicknames that were not listed in the program. Nor, for that matter, did it explain what a roving rucker or wing middie did. So, I put the record down and ordered another beer.

Trying to follow the action on the field wasn't easy either—too many people moving around. There were eighteen players on each side, scores of umpires, and medical trainers (or perhaps roving ruckers) running on and off the field to deliver water (or perhaps beer) to the players who, understandably, were thirsty (or as confused as I was).

I was, however, able to contribute in some small measure to the continuous exchange of impassioned opinion. Umpires most commonly miss calling the holding penalty. In Aussie rules, "holding" is not when an offensive player holds a defensive player or vice versa; it's when an offensive player continues to hold onto the ball after he has been clobbered. So it's up to the fans, some of us sitting nearly a kilometer away from the play, to spell it out for the umpire by yelling "BALL!" This sometimes motivates the umpire to see the foul and make the call, which then produces a thankful roar of "YES!" So throughout the entire game I was able to yell these two words, and by the second half (and fourth beer) I had it down pat.

A few minutes into the game, Footscray scored the first goal when the player named Ozzy, or perhaps it was Lumpy, kicked the ball between two tall posts and put six points on the board. This goal was verified by the goal umpire who, dressed like Bogart in

Casablanca, rapidly extended both index fingers at hip level as if firing two imaginary pistols. Then he picked up two white flags and started waving them as if to signal a commercial airplane over to the gate. This spectacle was by far my favorite aspect of the game.

Not much later, it looked like a fight was brewing. One of the Carlton players was about to "make a high mark" (catch the ball over his head) when a Footscray player jumped up from behind and kneed the Carlton player in the ear to prevent the catch. In the NFL, this would be called pass interference and unnecessary rough-ness and might even result in a jail sentence, but in Aussie rules this sort of activity is highly encouraged. In fact, it was the Carlton player who was asked to leave the game because of the newly instated "blood rule," which holds that a player with a huge gash in his head is not allowed to continue play.

The bleeding, ejected Carlton player was understandably upset. He started to exchange words with the Footscray player. Then sever-al other players entered this debate. But no one threw a punch. This, David explained, was because the "melee rule," also newly instated, strictly prohibits melees, which must have really gotten out of hand after the introduction of the blood rule.

When the game was over (Carlton won), David suggested I use my press pass to chat with the players in the locker room. He explained that it is the dream of every Australian man, woman, and child to meet a professional Aussie rules player, just as, I suppose, it is the dream of every American man, woman, and child to sue a rich, professional athlete, buy a large screen television, and watch *Wheel of Fortune.* So I gave it a try and, sure enough, my press pass worked. This was my first interview with a professional athlete, so I was a bit nervous, especially considering the fact that I didn't actu-ally have any questions prepared because I didn't think the pass was going to work.

I was allowed to speak with Mr. Rice, of Carlton, who seemed like a nice guy, though he wasn't overwhelmingly verbal.

Me: How would you explain this sport to an American audience?

Mr. Rice: Lot of action.

Me: Anything else?

Mr. Rice: Not really.

We shook hands, took a photo together, and I concluded this insightful interview. It was time to leave and concentrate on digesting the meat pie, which had blocked up my intestinal tract like a jack-knifed semi on the Long Island Expressway.

Octopushy

Playing underwater hockey

Brisbane, Queensland, Australia

 Underwater hockey. It sounds like a remedial phy ed class for art students. It sounds like the punch line to a stupid joke. It sounds like just about anything but an actual sport played by intelligent human beings on this planet. But that's exactly what it is. And Australian men have been the reigning world champions of underwater hockey for the last ten years.

No, I'm not kidding.

Underwater hockey, also called "octopush," has been a sport since the English—the same people who brought the world cricket—invented it in 1954, perhaps as a way for underwater basket weavers to stay in shape during the off-season.

Anyway, now underwater hockey is an actual sport, with a rule book and a governing federation and everything. And, though not as popular as its cousins ice hockey and field hockey, it is making gains. Tens or twenties or perhaps even hundreds or thousands of people currently play it.

How does one play underwater hockey? That's what I was trying to figure out when I got into a pickup game with the Underwater Hockey Club in Brisbane's Valley Pool. I've played ice hockey for years, I can snorkel, and I usually sink to the bottom when I swim. I figured I'd be a natural.

Because only six of us had shown up for practice, not the normal twelve required to make two full teams, Gene, the president of the club, decided we would play three-on-three, half-pool. She said we had to take the puck back to a designated spot (presumably like the three-point line in underwater basketball) before we could go on the offensive and try to maneuver the puck into the goal, a six-foot-wide metal tray on the bottom of the six-foot-deep pool.

Rand, an Aussie who has been playing the sport for fourteen years, let me borrow some of his backup gear: one of those cute little water polo bonnets with a number and plastic ear protection, a mask, snorkel, and fins. The stick, also called a bat, is not like your basic ice-hockey stick—not even close. It looks as though someone broke a wooden coat hanger in half, pulled out the metal hook, and attached a little wristband at one end to keep it from getting away. I wasn't sure how to hold it, but I figured at least I wouldn't have to worry about cross-checking in this game.

The last and by far most interesting piece of equipment was the protective glove worn on the bat-holding hand. All the players seemed to make their own by coating a cotton garden glove with

If you think this underwater hockey attire is odd, you should see what the cheerleaders wear.

Photo by Signe Mattsson

layers of latex. This gives it a yellow, rubbery look, which to the untrained eye looks as though someone has simply wiped their nose on the back of it about three thousand times.

Tim, the most experienced player on my team, explained the basic rules:

Offense: "Try to push the puck along the bottom until you run out of air, then pass it to one of us."

Defense: "Get the puck back."

Major "Don'ts": "Don't go for the body, just the puck."

Reassurance: "You shouldn't have any problems."

Greg, the other player on my team, normally an ultra-marathoner, told me that sometimes there is fighting.

"Underwater?" I asked.

"Yes."

I wondered if the offending players have to go to the penalty box. I couldn't see one. I just hoped it wasn't underwater.

One of the things that makes the sport so unique, other than the fact that it is an instant conversation starter at parties, is that it's the only truly three-dimensional game, which is why, Gene warned me before we started, you could "get a snorkel up your bum and have no idea which direction it came from."

When the game started, Greg and Tim let me take the puck (which is slightly larger than a regular hockey puck, about five times as heavy, coated with plastic, and sometimes called a squid) down the pool. I pushed the squid toward the oncoming defense, then stopped to contemplate my next move. Gene swam up to guard me. I looked at her and she looked at me. I figured I had about three seconds before my lungs were going to explode. With a firm wrist flick, I tried to pass the squid to Greg, but my pass went only about sixteen inches before it came to a stop. Evidently, I wouldn't have to worry about icing in this game. (In fact, a three-yard pass is practically long distance.) I sprang off the bottom toward the surface for a breath of air while Gene took the puck.

She brought the squid back to the "half-court line," passed to Rand, and he came down on offense. I swam out to stop him. Rand paused as I had done on offense. Then he kept pausing. (Rand can hold his breath for about, oh, three days.) Eventually I went up for air and he continued past me with the squid. Tim and Greg converged on him. Gene and Kerrie went to his aid. I watched from above, sucking air through my snorkel and waiting for another opening. My teammates looked like five piranha fighting for a meatball.

I spent a fair amount of time on the surface contemplating where I should swim to next, mostly because it was easier to think while I was breathing.

If you haven't gotten the picture yet, I was horrible, mainly because I couldn't hold my breath for more than fifteen seconds. I had spent the last few days scuba diving, exerting just enough energy to float along with the current and stare at fish and coral. I was totally out of shape, and, almost as frustrating, I couldn't hit my slap shot more than a few feet.

Because I spent at least half the time above the surface of the pool, I can't give you a very detailed account of the game, but to the best of my knowledge we didn't score a goal. The other team scored several.

I don't want to make any predictions about the future of underwater hockey. It may attract thousands of hyperactive snorkelers and dehydrated hockey players. Or, it may not. Either way, it's unlikely to attract a big audience. You can call underwater hockey many things, but you can't really call it a great spectator sport.

Fossicking for Sapphires

Digging for sapphires in the Outback

Rubyvale, Queensland, Australia

You know the old expression: "If it sounds too good to be true, then it's probably something you're going to try anyway." Well, that's what I did when a Swiss traveler assured me that he had just been traveling with a Danish guy who found an eighty-thousand-dollar sapphire while working for only a few days in the gem fields of Queensland. Pretty good payout, I thought. But I wasn't greedy. A twenty-thousand-dollar sapphire would be just fine.

I took a bus to the town of Emerald, where I discovered that I needed a car to get out to the gem fields. Fortunately, the gas station next to the bus terminal rented vehicles.

"You'll be wanting a UTE?"

"No, I just want the cheapest car for rent."

"Then you want a UTE," she said slowly, now realizing that I was an American, thus severely lacking in the brain department. "Fifty dollars." She pointed to a flat-bed pickup truck with roo-bars (a front-mounted steel grill to protect your car from kangaroos who can't read road signs) that must have been the UTE, and I nodded my understanding.

If you have ever driven in Australia then you know that—like the English who sent them here on prison ships—natives drive on the wrong side of the road, then try to even things out by putting the steering wheel on the wrong side of the car. I was happy to discover that the clutch, brake, and accelerator were in their regular order; the gear shift was still in the center; and the gears were located in the usual places, though the shift had to be operated with the left hand. Driving felt as natural as reading a book by holding it up to a mirror.

My biggest problem was that I kept confusing the windshield wipers with the turn signal.* In addition, I kept getting into the wrong side of the car. I'd unlock the passenger door and get in, then realize my mistake. To avoid looking like a world-class doorknob—in case anyone was watching—I'd fiddle around with the seat, then grab a map from the glove compartment before walking around to the side with the steering wheel.

I drove forty-five minutes to a town appropriately named Sapphire. Displaced piles of dirt and rock lay scattered in every direction and the entire area looked as though it had been attacked by a mob of giant gophers. Between the mounds and holes stood pop-up camper trailers, and the yards proudly displayed at least one rusted-out car with missing wheels. The most noticeable feature, though, was that every structure in this town, even those that probably did not have indoor plumbing, was selling gems.

I went first to Pat's Fossicking Center, primarily to find out what fossicking was. Pat charged me four dollars for a bucket of "sapphire rich" dirt, and her friend Ron showed me how to fossick it (or sift through it to find sapphires).

Fossicking works as follows: You dump some dirt into a metal spaghetti strainer shaped like a tambourine and shake it. The dirt falls out, leaving behind some dirty rocks. Then you soak the rocks in a barrel of water and jiggle them so the sapphires, which are heavier than regular rocks, will sink to the bottom. Then you flip the tambourine over as you would if you were taking a cake out of

---

* Hopefully, most Australians interpret this as a turn signal on rental vehicles.

a tin and—voilà!—the sapphires, if there are any, should be sitting on top. They can be any color, but normally, they look like tiny chunks of green beach glass.

I found I didn't have a natural talent for this. I kept spilling the rocks while jiggling them in the water and I couldn't spot the sapphires very well. The other amateur fossickers, including kids and grandmas, were pulling out sapphires every ten seconds. It was as though I were sitting at a broken slot machine. After sorting through two buckets (eight dollars) of dirt, I had found a few tiny bits of sapphire (or possibly petrified bird droppings). Pat examined them and said that one was good enough to be cut, which would cost me eighteen dollars. She assured me that when cut it would then have a retail value of thirty-one dollars (though she wouldn't buy it from me). The prospect of sitting on the side of the road in a folding chair, competing with all five hundred other gem shops with my zero-point-five carat phlegm-colored sapphire didn't excite me.

Now that I knew what to look for, I wanted to know where to find it. So I went to Heritage Mine (and tourist gem shop) and got a tour of this "working mine." For five dollars, Kevin, one of the owners, brought me sixty feet under ground and showed me the best rock layer for finding sapphires: the basalt. This didn't do me much good, I told Kevin, because I wasn't going to stick around long enough to dig a sixty-foot hole. So Kevin sold me a one-month fossicking license (another five dollars) and drew me a map on the back of a brochure that would lead me to "a good fossicking area." My first treasure map.

I rented a pickax, shovel, and strainer from the Capricornia Gems and Crafts Shop for three dollars (with a $120 security deposit). But when I drove out to the spot Kevin drew for me on the map, I ran into an old man who told me that I needn't dig there because there was "nothin' diggin' fer left." He gave me directions to another spot. "Jus goh along this dert roahd forabit, stick to the raight, thin take ah left over the grid. You ken ignorah the 'Noh

Trespassing Sign' cause it's awtdated. But doahn't goh down those othah roahds. If yah stert fossicking on someone's land they'll prahbably blow yer head off."

Eventually, I made it to the washpool area, where a few others were fossicking, so I figured it must be a good place. I took out my shovel and pick and started looking for a good spot to dig. The place was littered with holes. There were so many holes it was hard to find a hole-sized spot to dig in. I finally located one and struck it with my pickax, but the ground was hard and filled with billy rocks (large stones). It took me forty-five minutes to make a hole big enough to hold a basketball. So I moved on to find easier digging, but couldn't. The only thing I had to show for several hours of my efforts was what looked like a series of latrines for a Boy Scout troop.

Then I took a break and started up a conversation with Austin, a seventy-year-old man who's been fossicking since his retirement ten years ago. He had at least fifteen strainers, three barrels of water, and six buckets. He told me I was going about it all wrong. I needed water. I told him I had to get my UTE back to the rental lady soon or she'd mulch my credit card, so he let me help him with his willowby. Yes, his willowby. It's a strainer dunking device.

After working with Austin for an hour, I found a sapphire the size of a booger. It was pretty disappointing, especially after Austin showed me a ping-pong-ball-sized sapphire he pulled out of this same hole the week before, valued at about fifteen thousand dollars. I wanted to keep digging, but I had to leave.

The funny thing about fossicking is that it's addictive, like gambling, except that it's virtually free. And it's better exercise than pulling a one-armed bandit. If Jane Fonda ever does an aerobic gambling video, this would be the perfect workout.

Europe

Kiruna, Sweden
Reindeer herding

Rovaniemi, Finland
Playing ice golf

Urshult, Sweden
Moose hunting

St. Andrews, Scotland
Playing a round

Scheveningen, Netherlands
Sand sculpting

Maastricht, Netherlands
Mastering a Dutch toilet

Munich, Germany
Celebrating Oktoberfest

Spa, Belgium
Relaxing at a spa

Paris, France
Experiencing Le Moulin Rouge

Santiago de Compostela, Spain
Hiking the Camino de Santiago

Galicia, Spain
Exposing a nude beach

Bordeaux, France
Harvesting grapes

Maranello, Italy
Test-driving Ferraris

Buñol, Spain
Surviving a tomato fight

Madrid, Spain
Watching a bullfight

N
W   E
S

EUROPE

Europe, or "The Old World," is a continent rich with architecture, art, lingual diversity, and tradition. However, these countries are only united by their shared landmass, religious following of soccer, and state-approved public urination. So, you'll be hard-pressed to find people who actually call themselves Europeans. The French are French, the Germans are German, and the Swiss are French and German. Still, millions of Americans who hop across the Atlantic each year will return home after two weeks and tell friends they "Did Europe." Even if they spent just enough time in each of eighteen cities to buy a five dollar Coke with no ice.

Rudolph's Last Stand

Reindeer herding in Sweden

Kiruna, Sweden

I never managed to catch a glimpse of Rudolph the Red-Nosed Reindeer while I was above the Arctic Circle. But I may have inadvertently eaten him.

While working for Nils Nutti, a Sàmi (PC for Laplander) reindeer herder who lives thirty-five minutes by snowmobile from the nearest road, which is then over an hour by car from the nearest town, I ate what he ate: reindeer meat. Fruits and vegetables aren't easy to come by when the snow is six feet deep in most places. So, breakfast was reindeer jerky. Lunch was fried reindeer fillet. Dinner was reindeer jerky again. And I mustn't forget to mention the post-dinner coffee cheese. Yes, you heard me correctly—coffee cheese. Nils takes old, dried-out cheese and drops it in the coffee; then I guess the idea is to drink the coffee while ignoring this floating, melted blob of gook. After the coffee is gone, you're left with what looks like a wad of chewing gum at the bottom of your cup, which you are supposed to eat!

I felt weird eating reindeer. Nothing wrong with the taste. It just didn't seem right. Not only had I seen the Rudolph Christmas TV special about fifteen times, I also felt a very personal bond with Rudolph during my high-school years, when the end of my nose hosted a number of glowing zits. As you can imagine, this is just the sort of thing that high-school girls really go for.

And not only was I eating reindeer, I was lassoing them. Nils taught me how to throw a rope around a reindeer's neck and then hold on while the bounding reindeer dragged me across the snow-covered field on my stomach.

"Go get that medium-dark one with horns," Nils would tell me, pointing to a group of about forty reindeer, twenty-five of which fit this description. Nils knew each of his three hundred reindeer as though they were his own children, but only a few of them had names. Not Spot of Fluffy. Not Donner or Blitzen, either. Nils called one "Big Dark One with Broken Antlers" and another "Small White One with No Horns." His entire herd was marked in the traditional Sàmi way: with specially shaped pieces clipped from their ears. It looked like Mike Tyson had been let loose in the reindeer pen just before I arrived.

Nils, one of the nicest guys you'd ever want to meet, assured me there was a very good reason for lassoing reindeer, and explained that it didn't hurt them. We had to isolate the reindeer that weren't eating, "so they could be nursed back to health," Nils said. How nice, I thought. Then, when they regain their health, we can eat them.

Nils confines and feeds his reindeer during the winter with the help of his father, Henrick, who is seventy-eight, hard of hearing, and moves at the speed of tai chi. Normally the reindeer are on their own for food, but because there has been unusually deep snow for the last ten winters, they have had a hard time fending for themselves.

Following the Chernobyl incident, toxic vapors drifted over and contaminated some of the feeding land in Sweden. To keep the reindeer from eating the contaminated grass and moss, herders began feeding them a newly developed reindeer food, which looks a lot like dog food. Since this was not something we dropped in our coffee, I can't tell you what it tastes like.

Twice a day, my job was to tow a small trailer with reindeer food around the feeding pen with a snowmobile, then fill twenty-five separate feeding bowls with a shovel. The work went faster when Nils could take a break from trying to re-explain to his father why I was doing his job for free and give me a hand.

I was working for room and board. The board I mentioned already. The room was not much bigger than a sauna, and usually just as warm. I had to share a small reindeer-skin bed with Nils while his father snored a few feet away in his own bed. Between the beds was a table and at the foot was the wood-burning stove that made us sweat all night. No electricity. No running water. But Nils did have a cell phone, and sometimes it even worked.

To supplement his reindeer-meat income, Nils occasionally allowed tourists to visit his Arctic ranch. I witnessed two such tours during my stay. The first was a group of five Indian travel agents from New Delhi. This was the second time they had ever seen snow, and they looked perpetually vexed by it—powerless to walk in it confidently and unable to grasp the concept behind the "mysterious and beautiful" yellow snow. Upon their arrival by snowmobile, Nils welcomed them into his traditional Sàmi tent, which looks exactly like a teepee. What is a teepee doing in northern Sweden? (Get ready for an educational nugget.) Most anthropologists agree that the Sàmi, Inuit, and Native Americans came from a shared ancestry that dispersed over Arctic land bridges previously linking the continents.

Nils fried up his reindeer fillets over an open fire inside the teepee, much to the dismay of two strict vegetarians, who had to make due with second helpings of coffee cheese. Then, following lunch and story telling, Nils let the Indians try their hands at reindeer lassoing, which is extremely difficult—mainly because when you're holding a lasso, the reindeer know exactly what you want to do and they don't let you get anywhere near them. In a precious moment not captured on video, a Sikh man with a lasso chased a reindeer while wearing the fashion-forward combination of snowmobile suit and traditional turban.

The following day, there was a tour from England and Ireland. Just for fun (or perhaps crazed from one too many cups of coffee cheese) I borrowed some of Nils's reindeer boots, strapped a reindeer lasso around my chest, and Nils told the tourists I was his cousin, a professional reindeer herder who couldn't speak English. The group posed for pictures with me, saying things like, "Geoffrey, just take another photo with Nils's cousin, he doesn't care." Before the group left, Nils re-introduced me as an American and the group nearly went into catatonic shock.

I left after five days with a new understanding of the isolated life of the reindeer herder, a rekindled appreciation of fruits and vegetables, and enough reindeer jerky from Nils to prevent me from ever watching the Christmas special with a clear conscience.

Mock Speed

Test-driving Ferraris in Italy

Maranello, Italy

Maranello is not the kind of place to drive your Porsche. Or your Dodge Dart. It's the home of Ferrari, the holiest of sports cars. If you want any proof of that, in the Ferrari gift shop you can buy a picture of Pope John Paul II riding in one.

Each year, nearly 100,000 people make the pilgrimage to this town, which is located in northern Italy just outside of Modena, the elite sports car capital of the world. Lamborghini is up the street. Alfa Romeo is around the corner. The car insurance business must be thriving.

Before I arrived, the only thing I knew about Ferraris was that Magnum P.I. drove one that belonged to a guy named Robin Masters, who, against the advice of Higgins, let Magnum drive it all the time because he (Robin Masters) was always doing important things that kept him from ever appearing on the show.

But the guy giving me the factory tour must have thought I was some kind of Ferrari expert. I guess he figured America would send its most experienced automotive writer to cover such an important event as the unveiling of the all-new Formula One gearbox. At least, he figured America would send someone who knew what a Formula One gearbox was.

I spent an hour with the Ferrari tour guide, walking around the factory and making appreciative nods at what I hoped were the correct moments to illustrate that I knew exactly what I was looking at. I also threw in the occasional "Of course" and "Naturally" and "Well, that goes without saying."

Once, after he pointed out a large metal thing that had a "213.3 cubic-inch displacement 90 degree V layout," I told him, in a hushed confidence, that it looked like one of the nicest Formula One gearboxes I had ever seen.

"But it's not the gearbox," he pointed out. "It's the engine."

"Did I say gearbox? Ha ha ha."

The factory was nothing to scoff at. The floor was clean enough to perform dental surgery on—or at least make a calzone. Artisans seemed to be working on the upholstery. And an entire department consisted of people whose only job was measuring every little nut, bolt, and cog that entered the factory to make sure each was exactly the correct size. No one was rushing about, and for good reason: they only make 3,300 Ferraris per year.

The Ferrari with the Formula One gearbox (Berlinetta 355) has a top speed of 183 miles per hour, and it goes from zero to 60 in 4.6 seconds, which is quicker than my old Mazda's radio could find a station.

This is all wonderful stuff, if your driveway is the size of a race track, but what most guys want to know is how many seconds it takes to get from zero to a beautiful woman in your passenger seat.* Family drivers will want to know how much it costs to get rid of a grape-juice stain on the leather backseat. Good news for family drivers: there is no backseat.

It was only a two-minute walk to the test track, but Carlo, the always-thoughtful media relations executive, suggested we drive over in the Ferrari. No objections from me. Carlo signed for it much like you or I would check a book out of the library.

---

*According to the driver's manual, this requires three seconds of cruising.

Once at the track, Carlo took me around slowly, showing me the various features on the car. Mostly, he was teaching me how to work the Formula One gearbox: two levers on either side of the steering wheel where the windshield wiper and light switches usually are. It was a little like the "push-push" gear shift you find on some mountain bikes, and it seemed almost too easy: you just flipped the one on the right to shift up and the one on the left to shift down. No need to worry about when to use the clutch. This car had no clutch.

When it was my turn to drive, I had a big grin on my face as Carlo handed me the keys. I adjusted my seat, fastened my seat belt, and turned the key. Nothing. I had forgotten to disarm the security system. After a few minutes fiddling with the starter, I heard the engine rev . . . rather, it sang like a tenor. I flipped the lever to the right of the steering wheel and the car started . . . washing the windshield. I winked at Carlo, as if to say I knew what

From back to front: Enzo Ferrari's house. A Ferrari. A travel writer with an expired driver's license.

I was doing. But I think he may have misinterpreted my wink as a sexual pass, so I clarified: "Just getting used to the Formula One gearbox."

I pulled onto the track with a grin so wide it was becoming painful, pointed the car's nose down the runway, and stomped down on the accelerator. My body compressed against the leather seat as the car hit seventy miles per hour before the first turn—in second gear. I touched the brake, glided around the turn, and rocketed down the long back curve. I was holding back a bit because this car cost about $155,000 and I had no idea what I was doing. I wasn't even sure if my driver's license was still valid.

After a few laps, getting the car up to about one hundred miles per hour (in sixth gear) on the nine-hundred-yard straightaway, I pulled into the pit for a break. Carlo had arranged for me to drive with Dario, Ferrari's chief test driver for the last twenty years. This was Dario's backyard, and he had helped design this car. There's probably no one in the world who could get it around this track faster.

My previous experience with G-forces in a car was in junior high when my mom would drive me and some friends to soccer practice; as we rounded a turn, we would all lean to one side in an effort to crush the person sitting on the outside.

Leaning was not necessary with Dario driving. Even with a seat belt securely fastened, my head was getting mushed against the passenger window, the headrest, and the windshield—all before my neck muscles had time to react. On the nine-hundred-yard stretch, we got the Ferrari from 40 to 140 miles per hour and back down to . . . I'm not sure—I had closed my eyes at this point, thinking we were going to fly off the track. Dario managed to keep the engine above seven thousand revolutions per minute the entire time, even if it meant going into a U-turn at eighty miles per hour. It's a small miracle I was able to get out of the car with dry pants.

Want a free tour of the Ferrari factory? No problem. All you have to do is own a Ferrari. If you have $155,000 burning a hole in your pocket . . . well, now you know what to do with it. Or maybe, if you're on a budget, you could just buy a Ferrari the size of a matchbox car. They sell them in the gift shop—for only $200!

The Ferrari licensing people got a little carried away. The gift shop offered Ferrari watches ($3,000), Ferrari golf bags ($1,200), Ferrari silk neckties ($80), Ferrari red car-racing shoes ($200), Ferrari red racing jumpsuits ($200), and $100 leather Ferrari gloves to match your Ferrari's leather interior! I saw a bottle of Ferrari cologne and wondered what sort of smell they'd associate with this famous car: the evergreen car-freshener scent, Michael Schumacher's sweat, or some kind of high-viscosity oil mixture? I even saw a Ferrari steering wheel. I suppose this was for the guy who was planning to buy his Ferrari piecemeal—this year the steering wheel, next year a hand brake.

At the end of the day when it was time to leave, I realized the worst thing about driving a Ferrari is that it's hard to get back into a normal car. But I couldn't be too choosy since I was trying to hitchhike out of town.

No Truce for the Moose

Moose hunting in Sweden

Urshult, Sweden

 Moose hunting in Sweden is an extremely popular activity, and not just because Swedish men like to dress up in camouflage, sit in the woods for hours, and fiddle with their guns. These hunters are saving lives! That's right. You see, ever since the Swedish wolf population died off, moose have been mating uncontrollably, growing in numbers and—this is the important part—crossing the highway without looking both ways! Even with Swedish hunters blasting away, these thousand-pound bullwinkles still manage to cause five thousand traffic accidents and kill ten Swedish motorists every year by jaywalking.

Another reason Sweden seemed like a good place for my first hunting experience is that Sweden's gun laws are different from ours, in as much as Sweden actually has gun laws. In the United States, we just have general rules of thumb, such as "Try not to point your rocket launcher in the air if a helicopter is in the vicinity."

In Sweden, a gun license is treated similarly to a driver's license. If you want to own a shotgun or rifle for hunting, you must take a six-month (three-hundred-dollar) course and pass a written and practical test. If you want a target-shooting gun, you don't need to take a test, but you have to join a target-shooting club (fifty dollars per year plus ammo) for six months before you can buy a gun; and you can only own it as long as you remain a member of the club. Any gun, however, must be kept in your home in a large metal safe (four hundred dollars) that either weighs over three hundred pounds or is bolted to the floor. Sound strict? Lars, a gun shop owner I spoke to, said, "Yes, it hurts sales, but it makes sense. I'm sure car dealers could sell more cars if driver's licenses weren't required, but you don't see car dealers out there trying to ban driver's licenses."

So when I was invited to go moose hunting by Jan (pronounced "yawn"), an extremely handsome and kind Swedish man who also happens to be my girlfriend's father, I decided this would be an ideal time to do some "lifesaving" and, purely as a side effect, show Jan that I am a Real Man. Of course, the problem with this plan is that I have never held a gun, much less fired one, and I consider myself to be something of an animal-rights supporter.

When I say animal-rights supporter, I don't mean animals should have the right to vote or shout "fire" in a crowded theater, but I certainly support peaceful assembly. The contradiction is that I am also a meat eater—not raw meat or meat that still looks like the animal it came from, but your basic burger and Chicken McNugget variety. And, as Jan pointed out, someone had to kill these McAnimals. (As wild animals, moose technically fall under the free-range category, which means the animals do not have set exercise schedules but can just roam around totally happy and healthy and free, until, of course, someone decides to kill them and ship them off to an overpriced yuppie restaurant.)

Jan is a veterinarian, so I initially thought hunting with him would be like logging with an environmentalist, but he told me that hunting is a long-standing tradition in Sweden and that, as a nonveg-etarian, he may as well hunt the meat himself, especially considering that in Sweden prime rib costs roughly the same as a turbo Saab.

We met up with Jan's twenty-person moose-hunting party, all of whom were wearing basic green and camouflage military outfits, so, like most hunting parties, they resembled a renegade militia group. But this is not the funny part. The funny part is that moose are colorblind. So the hunters could just as easily have worn colorful ski outfits . . . like I did.

I wore my skiing attire because I didn't want to go out and spend seven hundred dollars on hunting clothes, which is what a decent outfit costs here (unless we're talking about one of those camouflage jumpsuits that makes you look like a snowmobile Storm Trooper). But the problem with wearing ski clothes is that you don't look anything like a hunter. You look like a skier with a gun, which, I suppose, could make you look like a bad guy in a James Bond film if you had on skis and were chasing Sean Connery. But I wasn't.

The way the moose hunting worked was that the group hunting leader assigned everyone to a certain spot in the woods where we could only shoot in certain directions (since rifle bullets can go a long way). We were supposed to drive to the spot in Jan's turbo Saab, sit there quietly for two hours*, and shoot any moose that happened to wander by. If we shot no moose we were to report back to the meeting place (a parking lot) and get assigned to new positions.

However, it was impossible to sit quietly because everyone had walkie-talkies to discuss moose sightings and anything else that came to mind. And the walkie-talkies made a static noise that any moose with normal hearing would have been able to detect from Norway.

Moose hunting is not just sitting in the woods with a gun and a radio waiting for a moose to appear. It also involves scanning the trees for telltale movements of birds and squirrels announcing that a moose might be headed our way, which wasn't easy, because my eyes couldn't stay focused for long. So I ended up just staring, trance-like, at a group of trees.

---

*In comfortable chairs we brought with us. Carrying them wasn't much trouble since we didn't walk more than twenty yards from the car.

Jan offered me some *snus* (the Jolt Cola of chewing tobacco) to help me stay alert. I had never tried chewing tobacco before, but I figured this was part of the moose-hunting experience so I took a smallish wad of snus and wedged it under my upper lip. The first thing I noticed was that the snus appeared to be burning a massive hole through my gums, as though my mouth had been invaded by a swarm of fire ants. This was what Jan described as a "minor tingling sensation." The second thing I noticed was that my saliva-producing glands had kicked into overdrive and I was drooling uncontrollably. A low-volume waterfall of saliva poured from my lips. And before I knew it, I had the sort of alertness one might experience after quickly ingesting a jar of Folgers crystals.

If you are beginning to form a picture of a keenly alert drooling ski bum with a crackling radio staring at trees, you have grasped the situation. Needless to say, I didn't shoot a moose. I didn't even see one. Unless you count the dead moose in the parking lot: the moose someone else shot—someone who had probably turned off his radio.

The only things I managed to hit during my entire hunting experience were a few pigeons. And they were made out of clay. Lying on the ground just a few feet away. Next to the thing that flings them into the air for target practice.

For me to actually hit a moving animal, I would need some sort of radar-guided weapon, but of course that wouldn't be fair.

A member of the hunting team actually told me this with a straight face. This provoked a discussion about which guns are "not fair" and which are "sporting," and at several points I had to restrain myself from falling to the ground and rolling around with laughter. As if twenty men with loaded rifles, radios, and a tracking dog trying to ambush an unarmed moose taking a Sunday stroll is fair. I can imagine only one way to even up the sides: issue the moose a bulletproof fur coat, assign it a secret service detail, and let it drive a Sherman tank.

Grape Expectations

Harvesting grapes in Bordeaux

Bordeaux, France

When I imagined working the grape harvest in France, I pictured myself at a château dancing barefoot in a wooden tub full of grapes with some guy named Pierre who has pronounced body odor and a large mustache. But, in reality, you can't just go up to a château and start stomping grapes, because there are big machines at the bottom of the tub that will slice your toes off.

I also didn't know that working the *vendange* (grape harvest) is tremendously popular in France. It's almost a cultural institution. So I didn't bother to apply for the job six months in advance like all the other workers. It took a series of perhaps forty long-distance phone calls, many of which involved begging, before I landed a place at Château Lagrange in the world-famous Médoc region just two weeks before the grape harvest started. As an American without a work permit, I had to agree to work without pay (normally fifty dollars per day). However, "without pay" at Château Lagrange included a place to stay, free food, and all the wine I could drink. Fine by me.

Château Lagrange makes a well-respected wine called, appropriately enough, Château Lagrange. The vineyard is run by a kind-hearted Frenchman, Marcelle Ducasse, who not only has a mustache, but an entire beard! Monsieur Ducasse, however, is not the owner. The owner is Suntory, a large Japanese whiskey manufacturer, but that's okay because the vines are not French either. A vine disease (phylloxera) swept through most French vineyards in the 1880s, and a large number of the vines had to be replaced with—and the French were not happy about this—vines from California. So, I suppose you could say I went all the way to Bordeaux to pick California grapes at a Japanese château.

Our harvesting group was quite diverse: well over a hundred of us from four different countries. More than a third of the workers came from a small village in Spain and ranged in age from seventeen to seventy. Many of the Spaniards had been working the vendange for more than ten seasons and they kept coming back because 1) they were still unemployed and 2) someone's uncle owned a bus, which provided the whole village with cheap transportation. They were a lively group and sucked down incredible quantities of cigarettes, but due to language barriers they worked separately and did not mix socially with the French-speaking group.

The French-speaking group, meanwhile, was not entirely French speaking. The majority (forty of them) were Flemish, which is not to say they had problems with their nasal discharges. Rather, they came from Belgium and spoke a mutated version of Dutch.* All forty were eighteen-year-olds on an extended field trip with their teachers. They did the sort of things you'd expect eighteen-year-olds to do, like drink too much, listen to loud music, and engage in regular grape-throwing fights while working.

The other pickers were actual French people. Some were unemployed and others had taken time off their regular jobs because they enjoyed working the vendange. There was just one wino, Fillibert. He had a crazy look and smoked about a pack of cigarettes every ten minutes, but deep down he was as good-natured as Sally Jessie Raphael pretends to be.

---

*Or maybe Dutch is a mutated version of Flemish. But who cares?

The most important thing to know about grape picking is that the grapes grow between knee and ankle level. I figure, to be a really good grape picker you should be the size of a raccoon.

I was issued a pair of rubber boots, a plastic bucket, and some garden clippers. Everyone took a row and started cutting, which basically describes the entire process: you just cut and cut and cut. Sometimes it's tricky because the grapes get all twisted around the vine and you feel as though you are untangling a fishing line. Mostly it just hurts your back. And there's nothing you can do to avoid it. One glance at us working in the vineyard would bring Swiss bank account numbers to the eyes of any chiropractor. I tried picking on my knees, sitting, and kneeling on one knee (a position I hadn't used since I posed for a photo with my second-grade soccer team). Fortunately, the locals have a simple remedy for sore backs: drinking tons of red wine in the evening.

On the second and third days, I worked as a porter, which was easier. I walked up and down the rows of vines with a large

By contributing my personal body fragrances to this batch of grapes, I hope to push Château Lagrange's wine making to new levels.

laundry basket on my back, collecting the grapes from the pickers and transporting them to a large bin at the end of the rows, where four sorters picked out stray leaves.

As a rule of thumb, about two pounds of grapes are required to make one bottle of wine. The bin, which takes sixty workers about two hours to fill and holds six thousand pounds of grapes, gets pulled off to the tub that you can't dance in, where a massive Cuisinart turns the grapes into juice. The juice then gets pumped into one of Lagrange's fifty-six missile-silo-sized metal *cuves* (vats). In these, some sulfur dioxide is added and the alcohol fermentation commences after a few days. Two weeks later, a second fermentation occurs. After that, the wine is drained into oak barrels, where it sits for eighteen months before it is transferred to bottles. All in all, it is a two-year process.

The three big decisions for Monsieur Ducasse are 1) when to start picking, 2) how to class the grapes, and 3) what wine he should drink with dinner every night. The harvest occurs at a different time every year depending on the weather, and two weeks either way can mean a big difference according to people who have hypersensitive taste buds. Besides that, the grapes' quality generally depends on the soil and the age of the vine. The vines can grow to be eighty years old and the basic rule is the older the vine, the better the wine. So châteaus tend to group their older vines together and make a premium class wine. The youngest vines are also grouped, and usually sold under a different label, which here is called "Les Fiefs de Lagrange" (The El Cheapo of Lagrange). That way they can maintain the quality brand name recognition of the main Lagrange label without wasting young vines.

The evenings at Lagrange were the most enjoyable part of the day. I dined with Monsieur Ducasse, his wife, his son, and the Japanese representative of Suntory. We ate the same six-course meals as the workers, but with better wine. It was sort of like sitting at the captain's table on the Love Boat.

I was a bit intimidated the first night because of the nine wines on the table, none were in cardboard cartons. What I'm trying to say is that I'm not, technically speaking, a wine connoisseur. I am not a beer connoisseur either, but I'm more of a beer person than a wine person. This is mostly because, at college, it would have been a tad pretentious to show up at a kegger and start asking for wine. And not just any wine. Good wine. That's another problem with being a wine person. Wine people can't drink bad wine, whereas beer people can drink septic tank water and enjoy it thoroughly.

Mr. Ducasse opened the first bottle (from a different château) and I imitated his ritual of twirling the glass, sniffing, sipping, pausing reflectively, and sipping again. Suddenly he asked me what I thought of the wine. The room went silent as everyone waited for my reply. I looked at the glass pensively, then said in my most aristocratic voice, "Interesting. . . . What do you think?"

It was, I learned, "austere" and "acidic" and "green." After commenting, Mr. Ducasse dumped his wine into a silver vase on the table, which I thought someone had forgotten to fill with flowers. The others followed his lead. I was shocked. Wasting good wine like this seemed almost criminal, so I finished the rest of my glass. We continued this way through all nine bottles, sipping, commenting, and dumping (or sometimes drinking) the glass of wine. I learned quite a bit about wine sampling, although I'm not sure I remember all of it.

To pick the 133 hectares of grapes, the entire group needs fifteen eight-hour days. I only stayed for the first five days; that was enough to get the idea: when you buy a bottle of expensive French wine, there's a chance that the grapes have been carefully picked by hungover migrant workers with ruptured discs, and the profits have gone to the Japanese.

Getting "Sauced" in Buñol

Surviving a tomato fight in Spain

Buñol, Spain

When it comes to parties, it's hard to top the creativity of the Spanish. Give them a few bulls, they run them down the street and call it a fiesta. Give them 250,000 pounds of ripe tomatoes and . . . well, you can imagine.

Or maybe you can't.

I, for one, will never again look at tomatoes the same way—those innocuous little red slices that garnish your dinner salad are actually ballistic weapons. With a few direct hits, the seeds can cause wicked eye infections, the juice can sting the inside of your nose, and that pesky skin will work its way into places where you won't find it for days.

I know this because I have attended the Tomatina, a fiesta where you can walk right up to people, shove ripe tomatoes up their noses, and, when they double over in pain, drop what's left down their pants. If you tried this, say, in New York, you'd be lucky to escape with just a few bullet wounds. But here, the victim will just pick up a tomato and do the exact same thing to . . . the person next to you. Thank God tomato juice causes blurry vision.

How did this event get started? Well, unfortunately, I barely had a minute to glance through my press kit containing all that vital information before someone ripped it away from me and tossed it

130

into the air. That's just the kind of spontaneous fun the Tomatina inspires. Fortunately, I was able to glean a few of the main details about the legend before my press kit disappeared into the crowd. About forty years ago, a tomato truck tipped over in the town plaza, an argument ensued, and was then followed by the first tomato fight. Understandably, it was the most exciting thing that had ever happened in Buñol, so they decided to do it again, even though Franco, then the dictator, strictly prohibited "fun." So, the ever-patient people of Buñol waited until Franco's Guarda Civil left, and then they went at it.

The tiny town of Buñol, located thirty miles outside of Valencia on Spain's southern coast, generally goes unnoticed (the woman at the tourist office in Barcelona couldn't even tell me where the town was while she was staring at a map of Spain).

The small medieval fortress in the center of Buñol is dwarfed by an unsightly cement factory and the town boasts of nothing else intriguing enough to coax a tourist off the train—I couldn't even find a postcard of Buñol for sale in Buñol! It seems like the sort of town that needs 250,000 pounds of tomatoes to bring it to life.

By 10 A.M. people were drinking beer and gathering in the plaza—which wasn't much of a plaza at all. It was a quarter-mile street lined with three- and four-story buildings that widened to maybe twenty yards near the center. The press was setting up their cameras in the windows of one of the taller buildings, while locals boarded up their windows and draped their walls with plastic sheets.

A few of the 30,000 participants had come prepared as well. Some wore swim goggles and gas masks. I even saw one guy who had fastened a pasta strainer to his face.

At 11 A.M. the first event—The Climb for the Ham—began. I was unable to hold onto my press kit long enough to learn the origins of this practice. Basically, a large ham had been tied to the top of a greased telephone pole in the center of the plaza and the general idea was to get it down. Young men mounted several solo and group attempts to shinny up the pole, only to topple painfully onto the heads of the climbers below. Personally, it would take a lot more than ham to get me to try to climb up a greased pole—at least in public—but the Buñolians* seemed to think this was some sort of incredible incentive.

Eventually, a lone climber succeeded and received a great roar from the crowd.

By 11:30 A.M. the crowd was packed in tight, and it was beginning to feel like the sort of mosh pit I normally prefer to avoid. From their platform, the organizers were kind enough to hose us down with cold water to keep us from overheating.

I saw someone start ripping the shirts off two young Japanese women. I was only two yards away, but because we were so tightly packed, I was unable to help . . . help rip their shirts off—one of the fine traditions of the Tomatina.

I had read about this practice before, and so had, apparently, a few Americans standing near me. I heard them say, "Shouldn't we be ripping T-shirts or something?" Mine was torn off in seconds. In less than three minutes the entire crowd was bare-chested or bra-chested. There was a moment of calm, then people began slinging the soaked T-shirt scraps in every direction.

At noon, cannon fire signaled the entrance of the first truckload of tomatoes and the beginning of the one-hour battle. The truck maneuvered through the crowds, dumping tomatoes in knee-deep piles on the street, while people riding on the trucks pitched tomatoes at the crowd.

I took my first tomato right in the ear. And the next in the chest. Someone mushed a tomato into my face. When I bent down to pick up some fallen tomatoes, they were already puréed, so I scooped up a handful and dropped the mush down the shorts of

---

*Or, perhaps they're called Buñolistas.

the American who had ripped off my shirt. Revenge is sweet. Or, in this case, piquant.

By the time the sixth truck came through, the plaza looked like the sight of a Ragu factory explosion. Tomato chunks were raining from above. Peels were pelting us from all sides. And, with everyone jumping in the ankle-deep tomato sauce, it was squirting up from below. A virtual tomato tornado.

At 1 P.M. a second cannon was fired and the tomato throwing stopped. We marched, en masse, one mile to a swimming hole that looked like a sewage treatment pond. The fact that we thought we could get clean by diving into it should provide some idea of our appearance and state of mind. We scrubbed each other's backs and dumped dishwashing fluid into each other's hair like some kind of mass bathing ceremony in the Ganges sponsored by Cascade.

Meanwhile, the town was busy shoveling, spraying, and, in some cases, repainting, so that when we returned to the plaza after just one hour, hardly a trace remained of the Tomatina. Buñol was its quaint old self.

While casually picking a few remaining seeds out of my navel on the way back to the train station, I realized I should be thankful—thankful that Buñol's pineapple truck drivers weren't quite as reckless.

Innocents Abashed

Celebrating Oktoberfest in Munich

Munich, Germany

A few weeks out of every year Germans try to atone for making overpriced cars. They do this by offering everyone who will come all the way to Munich as much good beer as they can pay for. I am referring to the Oktoberfest.

This event should not be missed, but I'm sure many people do—primarily because most of the Oktoberfest festivities are actually held in September: a trick specifically designed to befuddle American beer aficionados who make the pilgrimage.

When I heard my father was traveling to Germany on business, I suggested he fly in a few days early for some father-son quality time. He's never been much of a drinker, but he is usually game for new experiences.

We rented a car in Bratwurst—I mean Frankfurt—and drove to Munich. Our rental was a brand new Opel, which felt very fast until I took it onto the Autobahn and started getting passed by Mercedeses in second gear.

Despite its reputation as a mighty road, the Autobahn has only two lanes. The left lane is for homicidal maniacs and the right lane is for cars that cost under thirty thousand dollars.

Unlike Americans, Germans are reliable drivers. This is very important when you're pushing Mach three. They also have something that we don't have—driving etiquette. This means they will refrain from passing on the right and merging into traffic with the assistance of a semiautomatic assault rifle.

During this drive my father and I stopped for a few meals and, using a phrase book, made a serious attempt to speak German, which no one took seriously.

My father provided considerable entertainment at one eating establishment when he insisted on ordering the entire meal in German, even after our waitress explained she had spent the last seven years living in the States.

My dad: Ich vill mucher habben ein verstsnitcher.

Waitress: Sir, maybe it would be easier in English.

My dad: Nein. Ich bein habben albertschweitzer mucher ein drucker, bitter.

Me: This man and I are not related.

Waitress: But you arrived in the same car.

Me: That's purely coincidence.

When we arrived in Munich, we drove around the same block fifty times to find a place to park. In Germany, this technique doesn't work. We had to drive farther and farther away from the Oktoberfest until, eventually, we found a spot located, I believe, near the Austrian border.

Oktoberfest is like your basic American state fair, with just a few minor differences: instead of checking out farming equipment displays and pig breeding contests, everyone gets filthy drunk, dances around on the tables, and tries to avoid being photographed by my father.

Each of the approximately ten beer halls seats about ten thousand people and serves only one kind of beer, which simplified the ordering process. Even though the beer has the strength of rubbing alcohol, it still tastes better than anything brewed in the U.S., and you can't fault the amount they give you. It's served in quadruple

Big Gulp-sized glasses by robust German women the size of professional wrestlers.

A real Bavarian polka band playing mostly American cover tunes got everyone swaying back and forth, side to side, and up and down. During the singing, you drink whenever someone tells you to. And someone always does. At the beginning of the song. At least a couple of times in between, and, certainly, at the end. In fact, every song ended with the cheer, "One, two, three, drink like a barn animal." (I'm told it makes perfect sense in German.) The whole thing is like a big fraternity initiation minus the sheep.

The key issue was to get rid of the beer and make room for more. Neither of the two possible voiding methods was overlooked. For those professional drinkers who don't get nauseated from swaying, the Bavarians provide every sort of vomit-inducing carnival ride imaginable. The other, and more popular, method is to visit the *pissort*, which is exactly what it sounds like.

After testing the more popular (and very effective) method, I returned to our table and discovered that a drunk, but good-natured, Bavarian family had more or less adopted my father. He didn't seem to notice all the attention and sympathetic embraces. He was just smiling and taking pictures of his lens cap.

When the waitress came with the bill, I gave her my dad's wallet so she could rob us blind. It was hard to say how much each beer cost or how much we drank because, between my father and I, we couldn't count higher than the number three.

This brings me to my sure-fire Oktoberfest shoestring tips: Find someone to buy your drinks, find someone to pay for the rental car, and don't go in October.

Where No Sand Has Gone Before

Exposing a nude beach in Spain

Galicia, Spain

One of the most nerve-racking aspects of preparing for the beach is finding the right swimsuit to wear. Apparently this is especially difficult for women because several daytime TV talk shows have devoted entire episodes to the subject.

Some people find the prospect so disturbing they decide not to wear anything at all. And who can blame them? Unfortunately, this option is frowned upon here in America, even though it seems like a perfectly natural progression from one of the most popular swimsuit styles: the thong, a swimsuit with less surface area than a saltine cracker and that looks, if the woman is wearing it right, like she is not wearing a swimsuit at all, which would probably be far more comfortable than a thong, which, some believe, is not all it's cracked up to be.

With all the hype about nude beaches, I figured I should check one out for myself. The problem is that nude sunbathing is not a spectator sport: you have to "join the fun" if you want to take a peek.

Now, I'm not a nudist. I'm not even comfortable walking around my own house naked. In fact, I don't even have a house. During my last public appearance with less clothes on than one of Howard Stern's guests I was two years old. My mother recorded the scene on video and she still plays the cassette labeled "Baby Doug at the Beach" for every visiting friend and relative.

The whole nude beach thing was my girlfriend's idea. "It will be fun," she cajoled. She's from Sweden, a country mature enough to handle nudity; a country that—and I've seen this myself—censors the violence out of programs like *MacGyver* and leaves the nudity in. Bet you didn't even know *MacGyver* had nudity. That's because you don't get to see the European version. It's practically a porn film! (In one episode, MacGyver uses his Swiss Army knife, a stick of chewing gum, and the gravitational pull of the moon to save a brothel from financial disaster.)

Even some of the advertisements show nudity. Completely naked person in shower: "I just love to clean all my private parts with Li'l Bar of Soap. Whoops, where did it go?"

But I grew up in the puritanical United States, a country that, if you want to see naked people on TV, makes you go through all the trouble of finding an appropriate cable channel. Although I went to a liberal arts college and can discuss liberal theory, when it comes to ripping off my clothes in public, I'm far behind all the clothing-impaired people on the nude beach.

Anyway, for the sake of journalistic integrity, there I was, on a beach in Spain, walking totally naked with my totally naked girlfriend among numerous totally naked people. Thus, the concept: nude beach.

Photo by Signe Mattsson

That's the nude beach down below. I'm starting out slowly . . . by exposing myself from a distance of 300 yards.

I suppose all you guys out

there are wondering the same thing I was wondering: if you are walking around naked, watching attractive Spanish women walking around naked, aren't you afraid you might, you know, appear to be, you know, overly excited about what you are watching? I discovered that the ocean is pretty cold so you should just stay there until, you know, things change.

What surprised me about this nude beach was that it wasn't filled with people who were just working on full-body tans. These people were doing normal beach things. Things that looked extremely uncomfortable to be doing naked; for example, two guys were playing paddle ball and they were diving all over the place—not that I was watching them or anything.

Aside from making some beach sports look a tad awkward, nudity presented other problems. First of all, it gave sunburn a whole new dimension. Second, it gave sand an unfair advantage. Still, the pros—and you know what I'm talking about—seemed to outweigh the cons.

Maybe we are not yet ready for thousands of totally nude beaches here in the United States, but we could ease into it slowly, starting with, say, thousands of topless beaches. And I believe I can speak for a certain half of the U.S. population when I say we would be in favor of adopting this very sophisticated European beach fashion immediately. But topless beaches are unlikely to catch on in America because (and feel free to prove me wrong here) swimsuit lobbyists are probably throwing wads of money around Washington right now to nip this movement in the bud. After all, it would cut the bikini industry in half—literally.

Some people say that after a while the thrill of a nude beach fades away. I may have to go back to investigate this phenomenon myself.

Going Dutch

Mastering the complexities of a Dutch toilet

Maastricht, Netherlands

 It started out as an innocent excursion to Maastricht's public library to read a few periodicals. What happened was . . . when I entered the men's room to answer nature's rather abrupt call, I was confronted by three apparently empty stalls, none of which would open. And unlike most stalls in the States, there was nothing to crawl under or climb over—I tried. Each stall was its own tiny room.

Instead of handles, the doors had small slots, which I thought were for coins. So I pushed every Dutch coin I had into the hole—even a few German ones. No luck.

Finally, I went out to seek the help of the rotund library security guard on duty.

"Of course you can't get into the toilet," he told me in a booming voice that echoed across the crowded study area. "There's no handle."

About fifty heads turned towards me. I wanted to yell out and assure them, "I'm not some dopey foreigner who couldn't find his way into the toilet," but then I realized that's exactly what I was.

"Where can I get a toilet handle?" I asked. He pointed me toward the circulation desk.

I slapped my forehead. "The circulation desk. Of course!"

I walked over and noticed about six handles lying right on the counter. I reached over to grab one. "Not so fast," the librarian seemed to be saying in Dutch. I stopped cold. Now what, I wondered. Would I need a library card to check it out?

Apparently, she just wanted my assurance that I would bring it right back to her when I was done. I promised I would, then I leaned over and confided in a hushed voice that I already had one at home.

I headed back to the bathroom with renewed confidence. I inserted the handle into one of the doors*, opened it, stepped inside, and the door swung shut behind me. It was pitch black. Naturally, I couldn't find the light. I did find something that felt like a light switch, but it didn't do anything except make a clicking sound. I groped around a little more, but I didn't want to grope too much for fear of finding Paleolithic wads of chewed gum and fossilized boogers.

I reached over to open the door, but it was locked. After feeling with my hands, I realized I needed the handle to open it. And I had left the handle in the door . . . on the outside!

I banged on the door. "Help," I said in as friendly and unalarmed a voice as I could muster. A moment later I was rescued by a passing urinator.

"Thanks," I muttered, trying very hard to look natural while getting rescued from a toilet stall in the men's room.

With the door open, I searched for a light, but my visual search was no more successful than my groping had been. I opened the other two stalls (keeping a firm grasp on the handle) and couldn't find any lights there either. I even checked the main bathroom switches. Nothing. Maybe, I thought, I needed to get a light switch from the circulation desk. I went back out and reluctantly asked my favorite security guard for light-location assistance.

---

*One that wasn't jammed with coins.

This must have certified that I was the stupidest person he had ever encountered in all his years of security work. He regarded me calmly, then said in a voice so condescending it would have been psychologically damaging to a three year old, "The light is already on."

I assured him that it was definitely not on.

"Yes, it is."

"No, it's not!"

He marched me back into the restroom to show me the lights that I couldn't see. Opening one of the stalls with his master toilet handle, he pointed to a minuscule "black" micro-bulb up in the corner that gave off less light than a digital watch. "See," he said with an incredible amount of arrogance, considering we were talking about a toilet light, "IT'S ON!"

I acknowledged that the black light was indeed turned on. "But," I asserted, "you can't see anything with it."

He shrugged. "That's all we have. The black light prevents drug users from shooting up in here. They can't find their veins."

"But they can't find the toilet either," I pointed out as I pushed him hurriedly out of the stall so I could finally sit down.

After I had a few minutes to calm down and get used to the dark, I got to thinking. This no-light strategy may be successful in preventing drug users from shooting up, but it is also a great way to drive them to drink.

Last Resort

Relaxing at a spa in Belgium

Spa, Belgium

 The name is no coincidence. Spa is the home of the world's first spa, the spa all others are named for. Reportedly discovered in the Middle Ages and developed in the 1500s, Spa became the getaway for the rich and famous of the Renaissance period. Today, with European royalty tied up in divorce courts, Spa is forced to cling to its former glory. I decided this would be the perfect place to experience my first luxury resort.

I hitchhiked to the small town of Spa, located about three hours southeast of Brussels, and found the rectangular spa building, which, with its ionic columns, looked more like a college library than a resort.

The woman at the reception desk told me that a half-day treatment was not available after one o'clock, but, for seventy dollars, I could have a full-day treatment in just three hours. I swear that's what she said.

I was issued a white terry cloth robe and told to attach my program card to my lapel; the whole effect was reminiscent of nursery school, when my teacher used to pin notes to my shirt. The spa employees had an irritating tendency to walk up to everyone, read the lapel tags first, and *then* acknowledge our existence.

My first treatment was a "Massage Douche de Spa." My masseuse, Florence, escorted me into a room that looked like a Nazi medical experiment chamber. A silver box with control knobs was mounted on the wall about chest height, and a six-foot metal pole protruded from it with four nozzles attached at twelve-inch intervals and pointed downward. Florence put on a butcher's smock and instructed me to disrobe and lie facedown (naked) on the cushioned table located directly under the nozzles.

The heavy iron content in the water had, over a period of many years, turned most of the room's white tiles a deep shade of red. The darkest color surrounded the table, creating a remarkable resemblance to a well-used sacrificial altar.

The purpose of the contraption, I guess, was to provide the thrilling combination of a massage and a horizontal lukewarm shower. Unfortunately, the massage left more to the imagination than a snowmobile suit on a centerfold. Florence used a very light (almost goose-bump producing), circular "wax on, wax off" technique, and the general effect of it was that it had no general effect. Yet she kept it up for twenty minutes!

Next on my schedule was "Fitness 30," which meant I was supposed to report to the gym and work out for thirty minutes. This seemed a bit odd after a massage, but then the massage was pretty odd itself.

The fitness room was small and filled with people, most of whom had seemingly never used exercise equipment before. There were two fairly modern machines (built in the last decade or two, anyway): the Stair Master, which bucked people off every few seconds because they rode it like an escalator and reached the top rather abruptly, and a downhill ski simulator, which mainly simulated the wipe-out aspect of skiing. I think—and I'm not trying to brag here—I was the only one in the room who actually broke a sweat. Most people would lift a small weight about four times, then lose interest and wander off to another machine, apparently on the theory that merely touching the weights would produce instant muscle tone.

My next appointment was for "Douches Thermales." A bearded man named Jose approached me, read the card on my lapel, then introduced himself ("It's pronounced the French way: JO-ZAY"). He brought me into a room that looked normal enough—a single shower stall in one corner with the shower door missing—however, when he asked me to disrobe, stand in the shower stall, grab the handles mounted on either side of the stall, and brace myself, I knew something was awry.

Jose took a seat facing me on a stool about ten feet away. He then picked up a fire hose and hosed down my backside with— that's right!—lukewarm water. Standing there naked, holding onto the handles, I began to feel as though I was caught in a bad prison movie. Then Jose asked me to turn around so he could hose down my front. I can't remember if the lukewarm water blasting my body felt good because my brain was too busy repressing this event, which, I might add, lasted no less than ten minutes.

When Jose finished, he lead me into an adjacent, identical room, except that this shower—I was relieved to see—had a curtain. I stepped in and pulled the curtain as instructed. I was so overwhelmingly grateful that Jose was not in there with me, I failed to notice that this was not your ordinary shower. Activated by Jose from a remote location, twelve nozzles sprayed laser sharp shards of water, blasting me with shower-spray triangulation on four different levels. Like a soccer player obstructing the path of a penalty kick, I had to stand with my hands over my private region to prevent direct hits for the duration of the shower, which also lasted about ten minutes.

I was then ushered to my "Bain Niagara" treatment. This computer-controlled, powerful Jacuzzi bubble bath was absolutely wonderful and I didn't want to leave it, partly because I feared taking my chances with another treatment. But after twenty minutes I had to get out and go to "Bain Carbongazeux."

On my way to Bain Carbongazeux, I met two young women

from Brussels. We compared treatments. They had, in place of my firehose blasting and shower massage, taken a sauna treatment (sat in a sauna) and a solarium treatment (sat in a suntanning booth). I asked if either of these seemed new and exotic to them. "No," said

The only way to make this copper kettle of lukewarm tonic water relaxing is to add a bottle of gin and a couple of limes.

one, "I belong to a health club with a sauna." "And my family has a suntan lamp in our basement," said the other.

Bain Carbongazeux, I was told by Jose (whom I wasn't really excited to see again, though I'm sure he's a great guy when you're fully clothed and he is nowhere near a fire hose), is the specialty of the house. This treatment involved spending twenty minutes in a copper tub, which looks like an oversized French cookware pot, while lukewarm carbonated Spa waters bubbled up through a valve in the bottom. It's like sitting in a vat of Schweppes tonic. If I could have just gotten my hands on a bottle of gin and a couple of limes, I think it would have been great.

With the exception of "Bain Niagara," the treatments were only slightly more soothing than wisdom tooth extraction. However, I admit I did feel relaxed when the whole shebang was over. Perhaps this was a result of the mystical powers in this historical institution. Or maybe it was from being institutionalized.

Sand over Fist

Sand sculpting in Holland

Scheveningen, Netherlands

☼   I believe I have enough sand in my hair to start my own beach. It would be a very small beach, and probably not very popular, but a beach nonetheless. When I blow my nose . . . sand. When I clean my ears . . . sand. When I go to the toilet . . . well, forget it.

The reason? I've been competing all week in the European Sand Sculpting Championship on the northwest coast of Holland.

Before I tell you about this terribly exciting sand competition and my vital part in it, let me say that I have been sculpting sand the wrong way my entire life. I always thought you just went to the beach with a little plastic bucket and shovel and made a sand castle—recognizable by its moat—then jumped on it. How naive I was.

First, you need to bring your own sand to the beach! No, I'm not kidding. Apparently, the sand that's already at most beaches is no good for making sand castles. Beach sand is "old sand," meaning it has been ground into little round grains by the sea and by the weight of large beachgoers. For sculpting, you need river sand, which is "young sand" and is made up of little sliver-like grains that stick together better.

My team was called Team Peukie after Peukie Restaurant, our sponsor. Sounds like an unappetizing name for a restaurant? The

English-speaking owner didn't think so. (I asked him.)

Team Peukie had ten members: three who traveled around the world and did this for a living, six who had taken a sand-sculpting course, and one who was a writer who knew how to remove cat turds from a sandbox with Tonka toys.

We got 650 wheelbarrows of "young sand." We also got matching T-shirts and jackets so people who walked by could see that we meant business.

Ten teams participated in this competition. Most of the one hundred sand sculptors were Dutch art and architecture students, but there was still a pretty diverse mix of ages and nationalities, including a sixty-five-year-old physicist and a sixteen-year-old tae kwon do expert. Thanks to various sponsors, including a beer company, we were all staying for free in a four-star hotel and getting three free meals per day. It felt like a high-class overnight camp—with an open bar.

Each day at 8 A.M., the hotel operators had the Herculean chore of enticing all one hundred of us down to breakfast. Then we'd take a tram to the beach and start our eight hours of daily work.

Our first Team Peukie task was to build a giant mound of sand. This was not as easy as it sounds because you can't just pile up the sand. You need giant wooden "mulls" that look like waterbed frames. And to compact the sand into the mulls you need a "whacker." Yes, a whacker! Roughly the size and weight of a jackhammer, the whacker thumps the sand with a flat metal plate, shakes your body violently, and—most importantly—inspires endless "whacking" jokes. You also need a lot of beer. The beer, I'm told, is the key. Although, it should definitely not be wasted on the sand.

It took me and my fellow Peukies two entire days to compact five mulls into a sand lump that looked exactly like an eighteen-foot-tall waterbed, which was not our final design.

With our sand mulled and whacked, we could begin sculpting.

The way the sculpting works is that you 1) have to start at the top and work your way down, 2) keep the sand wet, 3) use special knives and trowels called "tools," and 4) must be artistic. We had pretty bad luck with the weather, so most days we sculpted in freezing drizzle, which numbed my hands and made it very hard to be artistic. At least, that was my excuse.

Once a section is complete you need to spray it with a water-and-glue mix to help the fine edges of the sculpture survive the rain and wind for a few weeks. The glue spray, however, is not the secret ingredient, as many suspected. The secret ingredient, as I said, is beer.

Our sculpture, which evolved from a sketch that didn't look anything like this, ended up as a life-sized naked male angel kissing a life-sized naked female human on top of a non-life-sized world that was being cracked open by two much-larger-than-life-sized hands. Inside the crack in the world was a utopian society, represented by a candle (which looked more like a vibrator) that lit up at certain times of the day when the sunlight passed through carefully concealed holes we had made in the world. To the right of the crack, the Pacific Ocean was pouring right off the world and onto some life-sized stairs, which, as you might imagine, caused quite a flood. In addition, hundreds of much smaller-than-life-sized disfigured, gender-neutral people (my contribution to the project) were getting caught in this flood while fighting to reach the utopian vibrator.

What our sculpture had to do with the competition theme of "Royalty" was beyond me, but it looked cool enough to win the European Sand Sculpting Championship!

At the big award ceremony, we all got bouquets of flowers, just like professional figure skaters. We also got an engraved sand-sculpting trowel and a T-shirt from our sponsor, which read, "Life is too short for cheap beer." There was even a marching band on hand, but they had nowhere to march so they just marched in place, which was still quite impressive. Then the Dutch celebrity judges, whom I didn't recognize, and several local politicians and businessmen made the sort of speeches that left me and even those who could understand Dutch counting grains of sand . . . in our hair.

The awards were followed by group photos and an impromptu international press conference during which I got interviewed by a French TV crew. "We are speaking here with Doug Lansky, a professional sand sculptor," he began. I didn't bother to correct him.

Rouge Awakening

Experiencing topless overload at Le Moulin Rouge

Paris, France

 The cabaret is an example of classic French entertainment that dates back to a time long ago when, I assume, French people were very easily entertained. It is the precursor of the Las Vegas showgirl productions, and just about every lounge lizard who visits Paris feels obliged to pay homage to this historic institution.

I decided to spend an evening (and fifty bucks) at one of France's most famous cabarets: Le Moulin Rouge, which is French for "The Red Windmill." This may explain why the front of the theater looks like a giant bag of Old Dutch potato chips. Except that it's red. And outlined in neon lights.

Now, before you start thinking I'm going to trash an icon of French culture, let me assure you—I won't. According to a few rumors (totally unsubstantiated), the people who run Le Moulin Rouge would not look kindly upon a negative review. That is to say, I would feel rather silly requiring a Salman Rushdie-type security detail, having to tell people I'm being protected from the Moulin Rouge stooges. Nor am I crazy about the idea of sitting amidst soggy croissants at the bottom of the Seine River with miniature concrete windmills strapped to my feet, if you catch my drift. So before I tell you what happened, let me just make this totally

uninfluenced statement as clearly as possible: I LOVE THE MOULIN
ROUGE! WHAT A GREAT SHOW!

I opted to skip the sixty-dollar dinner and instead purchased the
fifty-dollar budget seat at the bar, which included a free drink.
Bargain city! The bartender—*a great guy working for a great cabaret*
—pointed out a rather interesting bar policy: if I wanted an additional drink, he would have to charge me the fifty-dollar bar fee again.

"So you're saying," I tried to clarify, "if I ordered four beers
during the course of this two-hour show, I would be charged two
hundred dollars?"

"Oui," he responded.

Before I could even begin pondering how they hoped to lure
people to the bar with this policy, the show started. Understandably,
I was distracted from my mathematics when about thirty women,
most of whom were only wearing large feathers, walked out on the
stage. It looked like a beauty pageant had collided with a turkey
truck and, in the postcollision confusion, many of the women
appeared to have misplaced the top portions of their costumes.

These were the famed Doriss Girls, named after the first Doriss
Girl, whose name, I gather, was Doriss. They had exceptional pos-
ture and were very good at kicking. Over the course of the show I
noticed that, in order to keep their kicks in unison, some of the
Doriss Girls were making rhythmic, high-pitched squeals. If they
took away the music, it would have sounded like Monica Seles
playing a tie-breaker against Steffi Graf.

They danced around for a while (seemingly unaware of the
feminist movement) until they were replaced by a man and woman
in matching circus-trapeze costumes. This couple specialized in
handstands. I realize it sounds a bit absurd, but they were quite
remarkable handstanders. They could do just about everything on
their hands, including dancing the cancan for a few seconds. They
could also climb stairs on their hands and, during the pièce de

résistance, the woman did a handstand on the man while he was doing a handstand. Obviously, the crowd loved this. And who can blame them? *It's a great show!*

I don't remember hearing anyone in the Moulin Rouge speaking French except for the people on stage. And most of them were British. And Australian. The audience, I noticed, was mostly Japanese and American. I tried to ascertain the exact figures from one of the large Moulin Rouge men standing near the coat check. The conversation went like this:

Me: "What percentage would you say—"

Moulin Rouge man: "Eighty percent!"

Me: "Of the audience is American?"

Moulin Rouge man: "Eighty percent!"

Me: "And Japanese?"

Moulin Rouge man: "Eighty percent!"

The handstand act was followed by a series of topless acts. In the first act, the women were wearing yellow and green outfits with fruit baskets mounted on their heads. I couldn't tell what look they were going for—perhaps a topless fruit basket. *But a very nice topless fruit basket!*

Then came the international dancing routines: topless Scottish folk dancing, topless Japanese dancing, topless Spanish flamenco dancing, and topless Russian stomp dancing. Most of these traditional ethnic dances (including the topless Japanese) were performed by topless English women.

The audience flipped for the ballroom dance routine. The men wore tuxedos and the women wore ornate ballroom gowns. Except that some of the women (who had remembered their high heels, earrings, and tiaras) were topless. The performance didn't do much for me, except give me an idea for a T-shirt*, but, like I said, the

---

*"I Went Coed Topless Ballroom Dancing and All I Got Was This Lousy T-Shirt"

audience went bonkers, leading me to think that I had missed something—like a free round of drinks.

Then, a topless woman rode out on stage on a real white horse, which was also topless.

Among another series of topless acts (one of which involved wearing giant doilies) were three performances that deviated from the topless theme: a samurai sword-fighting act that seemed to have been thrown in for the Japanese, who loved it; a juggling drummer who played the drums, juggled some Ping-Pong balls with his mouth, and sometimes did both *at the same time*, which caused overwhelming audience appreciation; and a mime-comedian who, in my opinion, was the star of the show, largely because he invited Japanese and American tourists up on stage and then embarrassed the camcorders out of them.

The grand finale was another feather act, except that the women wore bigger feathers and more sparkles. At the end, two topless women with miniature, glowing Eiffel Towers on their heads, "floated" out over the audience in automated hanging chairs. Naturally, the audience went wild. I mean how could you not appreciate a topless woman hanging over you with a glowing Eiffel Tower on her head? *It was a great ending to a great show!*

Toward the end of the spectacle, the headwaiters who, for some reason, all walked around with small flashlights in their mouths, began to deliver the bills to their customers. Judging from the amount of champagne the audience consumed (continuously), I gathered that the bills would have a sobering effect.

By my rough calculation, the two evening performances pulled in a total of eighteen hundred people. If every patron spent about $120 and the cabaret were open 365 days per year (which it is), this French institution would gross $75 million a year. At that rate, in a few years they may be able to afford tops for the rest of the dancers.

Freezing My Links Off

Playing ice golf in Finland

Rovaniemi, Finland

I just shot a sixty-seven. And it would have been an impressive golf score if I had played a full eighteen holes; however, this was my score on nine. I could simply blame my poor golfing skills (skills I am not ashamed of), but I'd rather blame the weather. You see, I was playing in minus-forty degrees, falling snow with twenty-mile-per-hour gusts, and rarely enough visibility to see the pin from the tee on a par-three hole. Plus, I was playing on a golf course made of snow and ice that had more hazards than a Cambodian mine field.

This is a relatively new sport called "ice golf." And here in Rovaniemi, Finland, it's catching on fast. If you want to play, you should know a few things: The greens are called "whites." The fairways are groomed with a snowmobile. The game is played with an orange or yellow ball. And frozen water (*i.e.*, ice and snow) is not considered "casual water" on the fairway.

On this particular course, the clubhouse was a mini-Winnebago, the driving range was a snow cave you could hit balls into, and the only water hazard was a small hole in the ice kept open by a family, living on the shoreline of this frozen river, that enjoys taking a cold plunge after a sauna.

There were even a few new rules. I wasn't pleased to discover

Makes you wonder what the Finns will think of next: Ice diving?

that I was only permitted to use four clubs (three irons, plus a putter), because I usually avoid any club that doesn't seem to work very well. With only three irons, I might conceivably run out of clubs before I reached the first white. However, this regulation was offset by two others that I liked very much. First, teeing is allowed on the fairway. Second, if you lose a ball on the fairway, there's no penalty stroke.

When I arrived at the golf course, located adjacent to Santa's Sailing Club just outside of Rovaniemi, I noticed a sign that read "PELAAJAT! Kentää pidetään yllä talkoovoimin, joten lumituiskun jälkeen kaipaamme lumityöntekijöitä kentälle." What could this mean . . . besides the fact that their word-processing system was malfunctioning? Timo Junnunkauppi (you're on your own if you want to attempt to pronounce his last name), the golf course's head "whitekeeper," explained that it meant "Players! Please help us clear the snow off the course after big storms." Of course!

Timo offered to play a round with me to show me how to adjust my game to the Arctic Circle.

My first challenge was to come up with a new way to hold the club, since I was wearing snowmobile mittens to combat the minus-sixty windchill. I looped the tips of the mittens around the rubber handle, then locked my left thumb with my right hand. I dubbed this the Polar Bear Grip.

At the first tee, Timo showed me how to tee up my ball on the Astroturf mat. You simply find an ice cube-sized chunk of crusty snow, place it on the mat, and gently tap your ball on it until it comfortably rests on top. I hauled off with a five iron. My ball was teed up a bit high, and as a result, it went almost straight up in the air. The only forward progress it made came as a result of hitting down wind. As soon as the ball hit the fairway, it disappeared, but luckily this didn't cost me a stroke. Timo dropped a ball for me, which I teed up right on the fairway, after chopping out a ice-sized chunk of snow with my seven iron—which proved admirably suited to the job.

Once on the white, I felt a bit more at ease. The hole was twice the size of a regular golf hole, which was a big confidence booster. However, when I took my first fifteen-foot putt, the ball hit an Eskimo Pie-sized ice chunk and made a sixty-degree turn. With a good deal of luck, I managed to quadruple-bogey the first hole.

Timo, a professional greenskeeper during the summer at a nearby course, maintains the ice course with the help of two others as long as the river is frozen. It was funny watching him using his irons to chop up the fairway then make no effort to replace his latrine-sized divots. "The wind will blow new snow into the hole, and it will harden in a few hours," Timo explained. "The course is divot-free."

My hands froze the second I took off my mitts, so I decided to write down the score every other hole. When my feet froze on the fourth hole, we ducked into the Winnebago clubhouse and drank some hot chocolate out of a thermos.

After our break, the snow really started coming down. Or, more accurately, sideways. The wind whipped the snow into my eyes, making them water, and the tears streaming down my face merged with my dripping nose to form some kind of body-fluid confluence on my chin.

All of this had a rather unhealthy effect on my game. I didn't break a triple-bogey on the last five holes. And I lost a ball on nearly every drive. At least they all landed somewhere on the fairway—so there were no stroke penalties under course rules!

I must say this for ice golf: it definitely has an ecological advantage over regular golf. There's no need to graze forests or tropical vegetation. There's no need to landfill any marshes. There's no need to drain rivers to keep the grass green in a desert. And if they can just get a Zamboni to smooth out the whites, develop some Gore-Tex golfing gloves, and get Tiger Woods—who I believe is also part Eskimo—to endorse the sport, I think the game might really take off.

Bambi in the Afternoon

Watching a bullfight in Madrid

Madrid, Spain

I'm sure that a bullfight is simply loaded with symbolism that gives meaning to the act of a guy in a Baroque spandex suit and a Mouseketeer hat sticking fondue skewers into a bull that looks as lost and confused as a German tourist in the New York subway system. Unfortunately, I fell asleep while reading Hemingway's *Death in the Afternoon*, so I can't explain all the finer points. I can just tell you what happened at my first bullfight.

First, I had to find a "bunch of guys" to go with because I felt bullfighting, like baseball, was one of those sports in which the traditionally moronic male commentary would be far more entertaining than the action on the field. So that afternoon at the Prado Museum, I found Robert, a senior at the University of Colorado. He was looking for Picasso's masterpiece *Guernica* when I found him. And he might still be searching for it if I hadn't pointed out that it had been moved (against Picasso's wishes) to the Reina Sofia Museum a few years ago. He was uniquely qualified for the task at hand because not only he had never heard of *Death in the Afternoon*, but he was also completely unaware that Hemingway had even been to Spain. This, I figured, made him an unbiased observer.

Not much later we found the rest of our motley group at a cafe. Ian, a young Canadian doctor, and George, a little-known Australian television personality, were eating one of Spain's traditional meals: ham and fried-something-dipped-in-mayonnaise. And they were trying to wash this down with a shot-glass-sized Coke.

After an hour of drinking beer, the superglue of instant friendship, they decided to join us. We took the metro for ten minutes to the Plaza de las Ventas and George, in his booming Australian voice, told us (and the entire subway car full of silent commuting Spaniards) several humorous stories, all of which began, "Y'know, in Australia. . . ."

There were no tailgating parties in front of the bullring, but there was plenty of action, mostly in the form of people selling souvenirs: bullfighting hats, expensive mineral water, and custom-made posters that list your name as matador. Robert bought a poster while I picked up some mineral water; Ian and George went to the ticket counter. The bullfight was supposed to start at seven o'clock, so they figured it would be late enough to survive in cheaper seats without sombre (shade). They paid thirty-six dollars for four seats in the sixth row, plus one dollar each for seat cushions because all the Spanish people seemed to be buying them and, as Ian pointed out, they must know what they're doing.

About three seconds after we found our seats, the sun, much hotter than we expected, started baking us into Tourist McMuffins. George decided it was far too hot to be wearing socks, so he took his off. George then realized he didn't have any place to put his socks and their smell was bothering him, so he decided—and perhaps this is a tradition at Australian sporting events—to wave his rank socks over his head, which, as you can imagine, did not thrill the Spanish *hombres* in our section. We were too busy laughing to care that we were inhaling mind-numbing quantities of his toxic fumes.

Bullfighting may be an ancient traditional sport, but I noticed a few new additions: the guy sitting next to me was cutting a business deal on his cellular phone; there was a woman walking around selling Häagen-Dazs ice cream out of a cooler; and, of course, George was doing his best to popularize the sock twirl.

Trumpets announced the entrance of the first bull. The bull walked into the ring and just stood there. His name was Carabinero, but George decided to call him Bambi. Bambi the bull weighed about a thousand pounds. You have to remember that, until now, Bambi had led a luxurious life by farm animal standards. These bulls eat well, get washed, roam freely, mate regularly, and have full dental coverage and a company car. They have nothing against humans. So in order to provoke Bambi, the matador had to wear an outfit that would look extreme on Michael Jackson. He paraded around the bullring with his knee-high Day-Glo pink socks and a red cape that would send any fashion-conscious person—or bull—into convulsions. Bambi's natural good taste so shockingly offended, he charged at the matador. We cheered for Bambi as the matador ran and hid behind a wooden fence.

After a few such passes, a gate in the ring opened and out came a picador, a guy with a long spear riding a horse with special rubber armor that made the horse look like it was trapped in a giant laundry basket. The horse had to wear a blindfold because 1) Bambi would scare the bejesus out of him and 2) he would be humiliated for life if he ever saw what he was wearing.

When the bull rammed into the horse, it was the picador's job to jab the bull in the back with his spear and make a lot of blood squirt out. But not too much blood, because that would be unsportsmanlike. Apparently, the picador made this particular error, causing the crowd to boo and a Spaniard sitting near us to yell, "Learn to ride a horse!" We translated this for George who, anxious to participate, stood up and yelled it in English.

Then came the banderilleros whom Ian called the junior varsity matadors. Their job is to run up and try to stick two colorful, metal-tipped chopsticks into the bull before the bull realizes this is not an invitation to a Chinese dinner. Sometimes the banderilleros missed or got just one skewer in, which caused the audience to boo and George to twirl his socks and yell, "Learn to ride a horse!"

Now that Bambi had more wounds than Moby Dick, it was time for the matador to do his thing. He walked out and led Bambi through a series of extremely—YAWN, excuse me—dramatic passes. After five minutes the crowd began to lose interest and Bambi began his fifth cerebral hemorrhage, so the matador decided to go in for the kill.

He took his large silver sword and aimed it right at Bambi's head. Bambi, who, as Robert reminded us, had never seen a silver sword before, charged right into it. This was when Bambi was supposed to die. But he didn't. The JV team had to come out waving capes and get Bambi charging around in circles to make him dizzy, but that didn't work either. So the matador, who was now pretty pissed off at Bambi and worried that this botched effort would appear on his matador trading card, had to stab him again. Finally Bambi went down. Just to be on the safe side, the captain of the JV team ran up and stuck a knife in Bambi's head. It may not be humane, but I guess if they don't kill the bull, he will go back to the herd and give away that ancient bullfighting secret: "Don't go for the cape."

A team of horses dragged Bambi out of the stadium and into, I was told by the man with the cellular phone, a restaurant across the street. Next, for lack of a Zamboni, guys we named "sweepadors" came out and brushed the footprints out of the dirt ring.

The whole slaying and cleanup took approximately twenty minutes. There were five more bulls on the schedule of events, all of whom died, more or less, the exact same way. And I know this because I—YAWN—would have slept through the last four had the smell of George's socks not kept me awake.

Reckless Driving

Playing a round at St. Andrews

St. Andrews, Scotland

I'm the sort of golfer who can lose golf balls on the practice green. My best shot is a slice into the pond. And I've been known to outdrive my ball with a divot the size of a doormat.

In short, I had no business playing the Old Course at St. Andrews.

The Old Course is, in fact, the world's oldest course. It evolved "naturally" during the fifteenth century and is generally regarded as the Bethlehem of golf. Players from around the world make the pilgrimage here, with clubs in tow, to walk on this hallowed ground.

Not just anyone can play, I was told when I called Peter Mason, the public relations director, to make an appointment. He said I needed a documented handicap of fifteen. Conveniently enough, that's what I told Mr. Mason my handicap was. Then, possibly sensing some wavering in my voice, he warned, "If you aren't hitting like someone with a fifteen handicap, the rangers will toss you off the course."

I'm not going to tell you what my handicap really is for fear of being stabbed to death with those sharp little score-card pencils by serious golfers who don't take handicap fibbing lightly, but I will tell you that I set out to improve my game the moment I got off the phone with Mr. Mason. I did this by purchasing and then flipping through several glossy golfing magazines.

I also went to the driving range with a good golfer, who took one look at my swing and nearly wet himself laughing. The only thing I was doing correctly was holding the club by the end with the handle on it. He corrected my grip, stance, and swing, all of which resembled the technique I apply to tennis. Of course, the problem was that after these fundamental corrections, I couldn't hit the ball anymore.

This was confirmed by a Swedish golf professional during my twenty-minute private lesson (that cost me twenty bucks). "The swing looks good," she told me after I paid her, "but you're not hitting the ball."

During the next few days, I got so many blisters trying to hit the ball that I couldn't pick up a club for a week, which left me only six days to become a fifteen-handicap player. My driving-range sessions were filled with fear. After shanking five balls in a row, I imagined myself getting carted off to St. Andrews' golf-hacker prison.

When I finally arrived at St. Andrews, a small university town on the east coast of Scotland, I didn't see any locals walking around carrying golf bags or practicing their swing at bus stops . . . but the Americans were. Several of the caddies estimated that almost 90 percent of the players on the Old Course are from the United States.

The first place I went to in St. Andrews was a pro shop, where I spent about three months' wages purchasing slice-resistant golf balls, renting shoes and clubs, and buying umpteen gifts from the vast selection of items stamped with the St. Andrews insignia, an insignia that seemed to increase the item's value by as much as 300 percent. This was all before coughing up the $120 green fee to play the Old Course. It's not hard to spend money on golf here—St. Andrews has more golf shops than restaurants.

Mr. Mason paired me up with Ben MacDowel, a seven-handicap player from the marketing department, to get me and my nonexis-

tent handicap card past the starter. We were joined by—surprise!—
two Americans: Robert and Frank from Virginia.

I was understandably nervous when I approached the tee box
on "Burn," the first hole (all the holes on The Old Course have
names, as do most bunkers), since I knew full well I was capable of
sending the ball in any number of directions, maiming spectators,
or breaking handcrafted clubhouse windows. With a full gallery of
tourists, caddies, and fellow golfers watching, I smashed my first
ball—a long, wind-aided slice—just out of bounds. I declined the
provisional ball, took an extra stroke, and followed up with a shot
that landed in the tiny canal that crossed the fairway. My next hit, a
total shank, disappeared into a whin bush, a prickly monster
known to eat golf balls by the dozen. I began to wonder if I would
even be able to write about playing the Old Course, since I was
seven shots into the first hole and had not actually played it yet.
After another hit, I made it onto the green, three putted for an
eleven, and waited for the rangers to swoop down by helicopter
and arrest me.

Nothing happened. "Where are the rangers?" I asked Ben, scanning the horizon. "They're not going to chuck you off. Peter was
just winding you up." Indeed! I had been wound so tight for weeks
I probably could have cracked a golf ball with my sphincter. There
is a handicap limit, but it's twenty-eight (thirty-six for women), and
once you begin play, the rangers don't keep track of your score,
thank God!

As I walked toward the second hole and scanned the fairways
ahead, I thought the Old Course didn't look that imposing. But it
did look confusing. Other golf courses surround it, none of them
particularly well marked, so you can't tell where the next fairway
is. Nor can you tell at which flag to aim, since almost all of the
greens have two holes on them.

But it doesn't take long to discover why the Old Course has driven more than one professional golfer to heavy drinking. In addition to being dotted with the dreaded whin bushes, it has more lumps than Robert Redford's face, bunkers the size of the Gobi Desert, and other "small" bunkers deep enough to conceal the bodies of numerous golfers who refused to stop swinging away at their ball. The rough is thicker than Don King's hair, and there's usually enough wind to blow the makeup off Tammy Faye Bakker's face.

I could tell you about any of my one hundred-plus shots during the round, but the ones I choose to remember occurred on the 166-yard eighth hole, called "Short." I laid one up next to the pin with my first shot, just missed my second putt for birdie, and tapped in for par. Whereas, I'm still trying to suppress my painful experience on the fifteenth, when I deepened a bunker that—possibly affected by the gravitational pull of Jupiter—was preventing my ball from leaving. Or when, on hole eleven, with a two hundred-foot putt, I actually knocked my ball into a bunker instead of the cup. Frank's caddy had never seen someone use the putter and sand wedge in

Photo by Ben MacDowel

This is the famous "Road" bunker on the seventeenth, or maybe a racquetball court. I had a little rally against the front wall before I punched it out.

that order before.

I bogied the seventeenth, the hardest hole on the course, and hit my drive on the eighteenth over two hundred yards, missing by less than a foot two women strolling across the fairway. Other than that, I don't have much to say about my play, which went largely unblessed by the golf gods that haunt this course. I didn't think it was possible, but I may have even added a stroke or two to my real handicap, which should now be referred to as a "golf disability."

Hot on the Holy Trail

Hiking the Camino de Santiago

Santiago de Compostela, Spain

Before the age of high-speed trains, jet planes, and eco-tours, tourism used to be different. You had to have a good reason to go somewhere because traveling was a real pain in the ass. Today, videotaping the pigeons of Venice seems to be reason enough.

Santiago de Compostela, because of the holy remains of Saint James and the cathedral built over them, was Europe's most popular tourist destination in the twelfth century. More popular, in fact, than Jerusalem or the Vatican. To really get a feel for Santiago, many tourists don't just visit, but replicate the ancient pilgrimage there as well. Amazingly, forty thousand people still make the journey on foot or bike every year. You can start anywhere along the trail. Some start walking in Holland, others simply walk the last twenty meters from their tour bus and up the steps of the cathedral. But the most popular starting point is on the French border; this 950-kilometer trek takes around thirty days to complete on foot.

With only five days to spare, a small part of a pilgrimage seemed better than nothing. My girlfriend, Signe, and I started from a town 160 kilometers away and the first thing we did was get lost. We were looking for a Catholic version of the Yellow Brick Road and couldn't find one until, finally, a Swedish man named Arne pointed us in the right direction. Why had it eluded us? We were looking for a well-marked trail, but at this point, El Camino was simply the unmarked shoulder of a highway.

We could see a few other *peregrinos* (pilgrims) ahead and behind, but when El Camino left the highway and became a narrow trail, the many curves hid the others. And El Camino continued to change frequently and dramatically. One minute it followed a dirt road through beautiful farm land, the next it cut through an industrial parking lot or someone's backyard. It crossed highways and passed through the centers of towns. How did we follow this convoluted trail? Spray-painted yellow arrows on trees, fences, and walls indicated the direction; cement markers every kilometer told us the remaining distance to Santiago; and occasional memorials were erected where former peregrinos had dropped dead en route.

We arrived at one of the many *refugios* (free lodging for all peregrinos) in the afternoon. Other walkers and bikers began swarming in and claiming vacant beds. I could sense a definite rift between the two groups. The late-arriving walkers would snarl and curse the bikers who had "taken their beds." Arne explained that the walkers think the bikers are lazy, faux pilgrims; and the bikers think the walkers are snobs. This ongoing tiff had all the depth of "less filling" vs. "tastes great." It was hard for me to take either side seriously.

The first order of business was to get a stamp in our *credencial* (pilgrim passport). But we had forgotten to get credencials. "It's important to collect stamps from all the refugios," we were berated, "to prove that you are following the route of the ancient peregrinos and are not just some wandering idiots." Personally, I couldn't see the difference, but good fortune prevailed and the refugio manager located one for each of us.

The first activity of the evening involved gathering around the lounge area with twenty other peregrinos to compare blisters. We had only walked thirty kilometers, but this was enough for me to get at least three blisters the size of kiwi fruit on each foot. Sympathy points were awarded for big ones, new ones, and infected ones. Athlete's foot did not count.

After dinner Signe and I found a group of musical peregrinos: Frenchmen who had grown up in Ireland. They had a violin, flute, and a bottle of vodka and they were singing a mixture of French folk songs, Irish drinking songs, and Metallica. Believe me—you haven't experienced heavy metal until you've heard it performed in French with a flute and violin.

Our bunk beds were in a room with a middle-aged Spanish couple. Lights out was at 11:00 P.M. By 11:02, the Spanish guy was snoring so loudly I thought he had a weedwhacker lodged in his throat. I put my head under my pillow, then dragged my mattress into the hallway. After three hours, I marched into the room and told him that no one in this room, or even in this part of the country, was getting any sleep.

The couple left the next morning without saying a word. They just glared at me. After one day as a peregrino, I already had enemies on the trail.

We began walking and met Stephan, a lieutenant in the French army. He was walking El Camino to honor the memory of his grandfather and to clear his head from two tours with the UN as target practice for the Bosnian-Serbs. He wore a scallop shell, the badge of the peregrino, around his neck, and carried a wooden staff, the other traditional symbol, which is most practical for fending off local dogs.

We passed the Spanish couple just before lunch and they glared at me again. Like many other European peregrinos, they maintained their smoking habits in spite of five to eight hours of daily aerobic activity. "Geez," we'd hear some say, "that hill was tough. I need a cigarette." In the afternoon, we passed two Americans on the trail: a Spanish teacher at an East Coast prep school and a thirty-five-year-old house painter from San Francisco, who was making progress with two attractive nineteen-year-old Spanish peregrinos.

The following day we walked thirty kilometers, then forty the day after that, when we met a young woman from Toronto. I asked her why she was making the pilgrimage. She replied, "I just turned twenty-five, and that's an important year, you know, so I wanted to do some thinking." She was easily the slowest peregrino we had met. She told us she had been walking for eighty-nine days. I asked if she had started in Toronto.

We had sixty kilometers remaining until Santiago—normally, a two-day walk—but because we hadn't experienced the same kind of suffering as "real" peregrinos of years ago (who didn't have Nikes, sport tape, sunglasses, polypropylene, or Gore-Tex), we decided to make up for it by completing this journey in one day.

We started at six in the morning. By noon, Signe was feeling her old knee injury; the sun was cooking our brains; our feet were covered with blisters; and—worst of all—I couldn't get that "Achy Breaky Heart" song out of my head. By half past nine that evening we had walked fifty-one kilometers and were moving at the speed of long division. Then my head started to hurt. I got dizzy and sat down on the trail. I had a fever. I couldn't get back up. Signe had to perform the first-aid procedure of going to a nearby road, flagging down a car, and getting me to a hotel.

We started our fifth day with only nine kilometers left. "Ultreia!" we exclaimed as we reached the cathedral. This is the traditional thing you're supposed to say if you're still alive when you get there. It's Latin for "Miller Time!"

Antigua, Guatamala
Studying Spanish, Hiking a volcano

Tulcan, Ecuador
Riding a horse to Colombia

Leticia, Colombia
Blowgun hunting

La Paz, Bolivia
Getting to the world's highest ski slope

Potosí, Bolivia
Venturing into a mine

San Pedro de Atacama, Chile
Searching for the full-moon party

Pucon, Chile
River rafting

Buenos Aires, Argentina
Attending tango school

SOUTH AMERICA

If you are American, the most important thing to know when you go to South America is not to say you're American. This has nothing to do with your personal security, but much to do with offending South Americans. If you want to tell people where you're from, you have to remember to say "North America," or as I prefer, "Yankeelandia." South Americans are understandably upset that Americans are trying to steal exclusive rights to the name of their continent. "Yes," many will tell you when you say you're American, "we are also American." Of course, this "North American" business may upset the Canadian travelers, who will do just about anything to distinguish themselves from American travelers, even if it means covering themselves from head to toe with little red maple-leaf patches. And we should really be careful not to upset Canada. After all, it's our biggest suburb.

Cable Manners

Getting to the top of the world's highest ski slope

La Paz, Bolivia

Aspen may be the most pretentious ski resort in the world, France's Val d'Isere may be one of the biggest, but Bolivia's Chacaltaya can safely lay claim to being the most absurd. At 17,229 feet, this resort's summit is the world's highest; a breathtaking experience to say the least. As an avid skier, I figured a day on the slopes here would be not so much a challenge as a high-altitude experiment—perhaps one that should be tested on lab rats first.

Club Andino, the only ski club in La Paz, owns the resort and runs most of the transportation to the mountain. I waited with a few other curious skiers—three Americans, three Swiss, two Germans (one of whom was a dead ringer for Ozzy Osbourne), and an Israeli (who has only seen snow twice in his life)—for Club Andino's off-road vehicle, which was an hour late. Furthermore, it was not an off-road vehicle at all but an Isuzu minivan that looked like it would have trouble traversing a speed bump.

The ski resort was located an hour out of La Paz on a dirt road. En route, Mike, a traveler from Seattle, sat in the front seat next to the driver and spoke to him nonstop, not put off in the slightest by the fact that the driver didn't understand a word of English. The Swiss were speaking Swiss-German with each other. And the rest of us had our eyes closed and were trying to get some sleep.

174

Once we started going up Mount Chacaltaya, the scenery was impossible to ignore—for fear that we might soon become part of it. We were on a cliff-side road the width of a queen-size mattress and we quickly learned to lean toward the

When they said four-wheel drive vehicle, I guess they meant it was a driving vehicle that had four wheels.

Photo by Signe Mattsson

mountain when passing over bumps to keep the narrow-based, top-heavy minivan from tipping over and bouncing down the mountain. In addition, we had to get out and push the minivan up the steeper parts of the road, which was the only time I actually felt safe.

Miraculously, we arrived at the world's highest ski lodge after just two hours: one hour riding in the minivan and one hour pushing it. The lodge was not exactly a four-star accommodation: the wood was decaying, the windows broken, and it looked like it might have formerly belonged to the Addams Family but had since fallen into disrepair. I thought it curious that this lodge wasn't located at the bottom of the hill, like at most resorts I've seen, but halfway up it. Although this is not saying much, since the run—and this resort had only one run—was four hundred meters long.

Anders, a middle-aged man wearing a white baseball cap, was running the show. He charged fourteen dollars for equipment rental plus a lift ticket. His conditions: no refunds, no ski patrol, no first aid, and no lawsuits. But he did allow sharing. To save money, everyone found a partner with a common shoe size, figuring correctly we wouldn't be able to ski very long without oxygen. It was

Photo by Signe Mattsson

That's the cozy ski lodge behind me.

the first time I had ever sought someone out based only on the size of their foot. And it will be the last. I ended up sharing my skis, boots, poles, and lift ticket with Rolfe, a Swiss guy with stinky feet.

The equipment wasn't as bad as I expected—manufactured in this millennium, anyway. I must say I looked dashing in my gear and ski outfit: khakis with long underwear and a knitted hat and mittens that cost me a buck at a local Bolivian market. Not the sort of thing you'd see anyone sporting on the slopes of Aspen without risk of a fashion citation from the ski patrol.

I knew I had made the right decision to share when I began hyperventilating while using just enough energy to tighten the ski boots. To fill my lungs with enough air to ski, I wondered if I would have to open my mouth wide and point my skis straight down the hill.

The trick to breathing, according to Anders, is coca leaves. He suggested that we all gnaw on huge wads of them, which we had been instructed to bring with us from La Paz, where they are sold legally for next to nothing in giant buckets on many street corners. This sounded like a very Bolivian thing to do, so we all jumped at the idea. Unlike their chemically altered white powder cousin, coca leaves don't cause any mind-altering effects. Supposedly, they just open the air passages a tad, but I couldn't really feel any breathing difference, though my tongue felt numb. In addition, this treat tasted as though I had pulled a handful of leaves off the nearest tree and shoved them into my mouth. More than anything, the huge wad just triggered my gag reflex.

Before I hit the slope with a mouth full of coca leaves, Anders gave me a four-foot rope with a metal hook attached to one end and a rolling-pin-sized piece of wood to the other. This was for grabbing the rope tow, which was not a rope at all, but a cable that, Anders claimed, would immediately tear my hands to shreds if I tried to grab it. (Uncle Fester would love this!) The idea, Anders continued, was to place the hook on the moving metal cable, put the wooden bar between your legs, and go. He demonstrated on a piece of garden hose until we all nodded our heads in what he thought was understanding.

The run had no official difficulty rating but I figured it was intermediate, or advanced-intermediate considering the conditions: an inch of crusty snow covering the icy glacier and lousy visibility due to the cloud that had parked itself on the mountain. Surprisingly, I skied down to the bottom without much difficulty, although I nearly choked on my wad of coca leaves. The real trick was getting back up. The slope might have been intermediate, but the rope tow was experts only.

It was like lassoing a freight train with a bent sewing needle. I spent ten minutes trying to get the metal hook to catch on the cable. When I finally did, it pulled me along for about ten meters before the cable surged and bounced my hook off, sending me sliding backwards down the hill to where I started. After another ten freezing and frustrating minutes, I got the hang of it. Sort of. I got a good grip with the hook, went five meters, then the cable stopped. I waited several minutes, perfectly poised in my newfound towing position, which looked remarkably like the position I used in college to get reception out of my antique black-and-white television. After several minutes of cramped twitching muscles, I began to stand erect. The tow operator must have noticed this, because this is exactly when the cable restarted, knocking me over and dragging me up the hill until I managed to shake the hook loose.

Eventually, I hooked in again. The cable stopped, started, stopped, went backwards for ten meters, then started pulling me up the hill. The tow operator was having a field day with me. In theory, this cable was supposed to rest chest-high on metal wheels, but it had fallen off two of them and was now half-buried in the snow. I had to crouch in the fetal position to stay attached.

When I came to the first metal wheel, I was a bit nervous because Anders had told us that the day before a tourist had gotten his arm painfully pinned between it and the cable. As I tried to steer a few feet away, I pulled the cable off the wheel and it fell on me and ripped my pants. The cable stopped.

My fingers were numb. My legs were wet and freezing. And I was gagging on my coagulated wad of coca leaves. I decided to quit before things could get any worse. I had made it two-thirds up the four-hundred-meter slope, so I took off my skis and walked across the hill to the lodge.

My experience was about average for our group. Sean, the highly persistent American from Woodstock, held the record with six runs. The Israeli carried his skis at least twice as far as he skied on them. And the Ozzy Osbourne twin took one look at us on the slope and decided he had had enough. It was hard to blame him. I guess we all could have skied more, but without air, it just didn't feel worth the effort. At most resorts, I can at least count on the ride up the hill for some time to relax. At Chacaltaya, it's where the work begins.

The Wrong Place at the Right Time

Searching for the full-moon party in Chile

San Pedro de Atacama, Chile

 "You can't miss the full-moon party in San Pedro," a Swiss traveler told me. Just outside this oasis town in the middle of the world's driest desert in northern Chile, "they transform a moon-like valley into a raging party, and the *luna llena* lights up the minerals like a disco ball."

"Do they have one every month?" I asked.

"Normally, yes. But the only way to know for sure is to go."

So I went.

When I arrived in San Pedro I set about the task of trying to ascertain whether the full-moon party was going to happen. Most locals didn't know. One said he always avoids the full-moon parties because that is the time for his "private meditation," stressing the word "private" in case I was thinking of joining him. I learned from another that the party would not come to pass because the guy with the lights and sound system was in Santiago for the week. Still another insisted that it would definitely happen, though this person was also the owner of Hostel Puri and was benefiting from the five dollars per night I was spending to stay there.

My room was made of mud. The entire hostel was made of

mud. In fact, every building in the whole town was made of mud. As you can imagine, this makes for a booming development industry because anyone with a shovel, some water, and a bucket of dirt can build a house in about two days.

San Pedro looks like a dusty ghost town that has been reinhabited by budget travelers. Full-moon party or not, there's still plenty to do. Adventure-tour companies run jeep trips, horseback-riding trips, and rent mountain bikes so we can do all the things that the indigenous people supposedly used to do before they gave up their culture to sell postcards and T-shirts.

But what people here do most is sleep. The whole town seems to be affected by narcolepsy. In three days, I couldn't work up the energy to make it past the "lobby" of Puri, which was just fine because there were a lot more interesting things going on inside the hostel. For example, a traveling five-star Swedish chef named Martin worked in the mud-kitchen. And aiding Martin in the mud-restaurant was Don Roberto, a German opera singer who left his lover in Santiago for a San Pedro man; however, it seemed a visiting transvestite was now complicating things. Occasionally, Don Roberto would break into arias and dance across the room while serving food.

Also, there was a little legal battle going on. Apparently, someone from the competing mud-hostel across the street had stolen some of the cassettes from behind Puri's mud-bar. The thieves, of course, denied that they had taken the tapes, but every afternoon, they would play the tapes loud enough for us to hear them. This made Carlos, the bartender with dyed red hair and a three-inch-long goatee, furious. Much to my surprise, Carlos was a lawyer, which explained why he spent most of his time talking about how he was going to formally press charges. Carlos amused the hell out of Martin, who was really just hanging out until his latest girlfriend, a French woman, arrived from Santiago so they could go to Lima together.

The morning of the full moon, I received an absolute confirmation that the guy with the sound system was in Santiago. But Carlos assured me that something would happen. "At three o'clock you won't know, at six o'clock you won't know, at nine o'clock you'll have three choices, and by ten o'clock there will only be one choice. Just relax."

Naturally, I figured the full-moon party, if it happened, would be in the Valley of the Moon. I then discovered that the Valley of the Moon is sixteen kilometers out of town and, using mathematical calculations, I determined that the four-hour hike back to San Pedro would be a serious buzz-kill at five o'clock in the morning. In case something was going to happen, I wanted to be ready, so I looked into some transportation. One of the tour company operators told me that if I got a group of ten, we could go in his van for three dollars each.

So I went back to the hotel and asked the other travelers if they were interested in taking a van, should the party happen. About twenty people, most of whom had also heard of this party, claimed interest, so I went back and reserved two vans. Here I had come to this town to observe the full-moon party, and now I was arranging it.

Early that evening a few clouds began to form and, wouldn't you know it, it started to drizzle. Everyone went into shock. It looked as if the party plans were about to be ruined by, according to my guidebook, the first rain shower in over three hundred years. Fortunately, the drizzle stopped after three minutes. Martin wanted to bet everyone that this wouldn't count in the record books.

At ten in the evening the vans showed up at Hostel Puri and, as I was doing a final head count, the driver pulled me aside and asked me, "What do you want to go to the Valley of the Moon for? Usually the party is in the Valley of Death (three kilometers away) so everyone can walk." I don't know why he had forgotten to mention this before, but it seemed a bit late to change plans. Now, not only was I arranging the event, I was doing it wrong.

I decided not to say anything about the Valley of Death because I had put too much energy into getting this Valley of the Moon stuff organized. And besides, who would know the difference? We all stocked up on beer, wine, and, the local favorite, Pisco. Pisco is Chile's answer to Greece's ouzo or, perhaps, kerosene. It's best consumed with lemon and egg white, but that takes preparation and we were pretty lazy, so we just mixed it with ginger ale, which somehow gave the ginger ale a bathroom cleanser taste.

The Valley of the Moon was as quiet as an Iraqi souvenir shop. We took a seat and started looking at the moon. "So when is everyone showing up?" people began to ask me, as if I was in charge of the whole event. Imagine my surprise and delight when other people did start showing up. Word had gotten out. By midnight, there were almost a hundred people and thirty stray dogs in the Valley of the Moon. About fifty people came in cars. Another fifty rode bikes. And the ten that walked had been followed by the dogs.

All in all I'd say my full-moon party turned out pretty well. People played guitars, bongos and, in lieu of a sound system, several car owners decided to crank up their radios—with different songs, of course. The dogs ran around pissing on car tires and curling up next to comatose partiers.

I heard locals walking around saying to each other, "This is great, but why are we having the party here?" I didn't bother to tell them.

¿Habla Margarita?

Studying Spanish in Guatemala

Antigua, Guatemala

After four years of French in high school, the only thing I was qualified to do was order a croissant at Denny's. I figured if I actually wanted to learn a language, I would have to go someplace where people speak it. I heard Antigua, Guatemala, had a decent language program and I liked the idea of being isolated in a third-world country—nothing to do but speak Spanish . . . and avoid death squads.

I stepped off the plane in Guatemala City without a guide book, not knowing where to begin looking for a Spanish course. A man named Gorge (pronounced HOR-hay) walked right up to me at the baggage carousel and asked if I wanted to learn Spanish. Who would expect to find a language instructor at the baggage carousel? When he told me he was working for the best language school in Antigua, I was immediately suspicious. I mean, when I pick up my luggage in the Boston airport, I am never greeted by an admissions recruiter from Harvard. But, for lack of any better lead, I followed him.

At the bus station, I noticed the buses didn't have numbers— the bus drivers just stuck their heads out the door and yelled where they were planning to go. Our bus to Antigua had been painted by someone from the esteemed "We're-Out-of-Blue-so-Let's-Start-Using-Green" school of bus design. The interior decorating theme was centered around a large Jesus figurine on the dashboard, better known as the Latin American emergency brake. The consoles and floor around the driver were nowhere to be seen. If he missed the gas, brake, or clutch, his foot would end up in the engine. The upside was that the driver could conceivably solve any mechanical problem from inside the bus.

There was barely enough leg room to slide a magazine between my seat and the one in front of it. I smushed in with two other adults in a seat designed to hold two growth-stunted six-year-olds. Amazingly, two people stood in the aisle between each seat, and somehow more kept getting on. I'll never know how the bus driver's assistant (every bus driver has an assistant) managed to climb over everyone and collect our bus fare: roughly twenty cents.

All of the windows were jammed shut, probably with thirty-year-old chewing gum left by junior-high-school baby boomers in Nebraska before the bus was sold to the Guatemalans. But the local passengers seemed less concerned with the critically low levels of oxygen than they were with their belongings. Most were busy lifting things—things like this year's harvest—onto the roof of the bus. That's why there was a guy riding up there, loading and unloading at every stop. (In Guatemala it's a full-time job since no one seems to travel with less than five metric tons of crap.)

My favorite part of the bus trip was when the driver yelled to the people standing in the aisle to duck down as we drove past the police checkpoint because, evidently, the government has regulations about cramming four times the legal amount of passengers onto a bus. It was too crowded to duck, so people just bent their heads a little. The police gave them credit for trying and let us pass.

When we arrived in Antigua, I decided to do a little comparison shopping before committing to Gorge's school. Strolling through town, I saw a similar language school every fifty meters or so—the whole town was packed with them. It seemed to be the town's cottage industry. To open up a "school," apparently all you needed were a few chairs and tables and a hand-painted sign outside the door. I went back to Gorge and told him to sign me up because I figured he should receive something for his efforts. For the standard rate of fifteen dollars a day, I got four hours of one-on-one tutoring, a private room, and three home-cooked meals with a family that didn't speak English.

Gorge took me to meet my family—a good-natured, robust woman with a thirty-year-old daughter. A German named Horst stayed in the room across the hall. He introduced himself when I arrived and never said much after that.

I learned my first words of Spanish that evening: *No papel de hygienetico en el servicio* (Don't put toilet paper in the toilet). I found out the hard way when I put the "toilet paper," actually strips of newspaper hanging from the wall on a nail, into the toilet* and flooded the entire house.

I learned my next words, *tenga cuidado* (be careful), the next morning after I almost electrocuted myself in the shower. Many Latin American shower heaters are small electrical devices that are attached right to the showerhead. There are live wires all over the place, so everyone is supposed to wear rubber sandals while showering. Apparently, my hostess had tried to warn me.

After recovering from the morning's electroshock therapy, I began my lessons at the school. My teacher sat across a small table from me and tried to pretend she didn't know a word of English so I would be forced to speak to her in Spanish. But it soon became obvious that she knew almost as much English as I did, maybe more.

Hundreds of young Westerners studied Spanish in Antigua. And that was the problem. There really wasn't any isolation at all. The social scene was hopping. The guacamole was abundant. And I

---

*In most of Latin America, used toilet paper, even the regular kind, goes into a trash bin next to the toilet.

didn't find a single margarita I didn't like. I was having so much fun that I lost interest in my studies. Sort of like at college. Except that El Gallo beer is half the price of Coors.

The other problem was sleep, or lack thereof. Nearly every morning, a few hundred people would set off firecrackers to celebrate something—a saint's birthday, their own birthdays, or sometimes just for practice. And the few days they weren't blasting away, men drove around at six in the morning making political statements through PA systems attached to the roof of a car. It sounded as though Che Guevara had commandeered a Good Humor truck.

I left Antigua after three weeks with a marginal grasp of Spanish and a thorough addiction to guacamole. I was just about qualified for a trip to Taco Bell.

Sightseeing for Sadists

Venturing into a Bolivian mine

Potosí, Bolivia

Move over, eco-tourism. Suffer-tourism is here. Yes, step right up and pay money to watch people suffer. No joke. It's happening in the Bolivian mining town of Potosí right now. And what better place? Over the last few hundred years over 8 million men working in the silver, copper, and zinc mines have died from a combination of cave-ins, explosions, and lung disease. Potosí is a far cry from Club Med, but somehow it has managed to become one of Bolivia's most popular tourist attractions.

When I arrived in Potosí tour operators fought over me in the street. For five dollars I allowed myself to be crammed into a Koala Tours minivan with about twenty other young (Swiss, German, Australian, and English) travelers. We were driven to the other end of town to pick up our mining gear: a hard hat, rubber boots, and rain jacket. They could have just as easily hung "El Dorko" signs around our necks.

Jaime (pronounced: HI-may), our guide, strongly recommended we pop around the corner and pick up some gifts for the miners before we entered the mines. Just what sort of gifts would they want? Jaime, who used to be a miner himself, told us we couldn't go wrong with sticks of dynamite, fuses, blasting caps, coca leaves, and unfiltered cigarettes. I didn't quite believe it, but not to be the first to disappoint the miners, I headed off down the street in my junior varsity fireman outfit with a shopping list that would get me arrested in most American supermarkets.

Much to my surprise, every little convenience store on the street carried these items. It was like a Hezbollah flea market. I could just walk up and purchase a stick of dynamite as easily as a candy bar —and the dynamite cost less! Blasting caps and fuses were even cheaper. A dozen unfiltered cigarettes cost a dime, a lunch bag full of coca leaves cost about twenty cents. (I half expected to see the sign: If it doesn't blow up, catch fire, or put you in an altered state, we don't sell it!)

Everyone in my group went a bit overboard. I spent three dollars and got a few sticks of dynamite and a couple of blasting caps with fuses. The others bought at least twice as much. Shopping was fun, but when we reboarded the minivan I realized I was rather uncomfortable surrounded by enough explosives to blow up several minivans and perhaps a few full-sized vans. It was especially worrisome because the dynamite sticks were not in the possession of the military or even trained terrorists, but tourists who, myself included, were handing them around and comparing them like Eiffel Tower refrigerator magnets.

As we walked to the mine, I couldn't help noticing a number of miners sitting around eating—this is not an exaggeration—a pound of coca leaves each. Their mouths were stuffed to bursting capacity, and several of the older miners had stretched cheek bulges that would put Dizzy Gillespie to shame. Jaime explained that this is their "meal" for the day, or rather it suppresses their hunger so they can work without eating. He introduced us to a few of the men and they held out their hands; we dutifully gave them some of our gifts. ("Here's a stick of dynamite for you. And a blasting cap for you.") It felt like Halloween . . . in Afghanistan.

Jaime lit our lanterns and led us into the mine, which he said was being "rented from the devil." (Comforting thought.) We walked hunched over through the dark, narrow four-foot-tall tunnel that went, more or less, straight into the hillside, pausing occasionally to let a few miners scurry past us with eighty-pound bags of rock debris on their backs. Safety standards? Don't be ridiculous. The whole idea was that we experience the same horrid conditions that existed three hundred years ago.

The air I was trying to breathe had already been sucked free of oxygen by at least five hundred people and replaced with a memorable mixture of asbestos, soot, and body odor. Support beams were almost nonexistent, though I do remember one in particular. Jaime pointed out a huge crack in it and said "that one's about to go," then tapped it and some loose rocks fell on my head. Suddenly, I was afraid that the whole mine could cave in at any moment. And it wouldn't have been the first time this happened.

We stopped to chat with a sweaty twenty-two-year-old who was pounding a rod into a rock with a hammer; he seemed to be progressing at the rate of one millimeter per decade. Presumably, he was going to insert a stick of dynamite into the hole and cave in the entire mine. Through Jaime's translation, he explained that 95 percent of the miners are making three to five dollars per day in small collective work groups and the other 5 percent, who have discovered mineral-rich veins, own several Mercedeses each. Never mind that there isn't a decent road in the country on which to drive them.

Jaime then introduced us to the Devil of the Mine (affectionately called "El Tio," or The Uncle), a clay figure about as scary looking as Mr. Potato Head. It was adorned with cheap jewelry and a used hair piece, part of which had been cut off and fitted as a goatee. Flasks of alcohol and unfiltered cigarettes had been left as "sacrifices" by miners. With such a high death rate (most miners die of lung disease by age forty, if not before), making a sacrifice to "El Tio" is regarded as a practical safety measure.

After an hour, the tunnels all looked the same to me. I was beginning to feel the effects of the nearly oxygen-free air and I felt like I was pushing my luck by staying in the mine. My head felt like it couldn't take another ten minutes, but we still had two hours to go. On the walk back out, we stopped occasionally to chat with a miner and shorten his life by giving him a couple of unfiltered cigarettes. But I could understand the addiction. With the poor ventilation, an unfiltered cigarette must seem like a breath of fresh air.

I got so excited when I saw the light at the end of the tunnel (literally!), I smacked my head on the rock ceiling and got knocked backwards into a mud puddle. I struggled to my feet and hurried to daylight, where I gulped in fresh air like it was free beer.

The three-hour subterranean tour felt like an entire week. And there's nothing quite like seeing people slaving in a mine for a few dollars a day to put my own problems into perspective. Obviously we shouldn't be turning a blind eye on this and other human hardships. On the other hand, it just doesn't seem right that tour operators are profiting from this suffering. The problem for the tour operators is that if they helped these miners get a safe, breathable, well-lit working environment, the suffer-tourism would likely come to an end. Potosí does have a few modern mines, but tours are not led through them because, Jaime claimed, "there's nothing special to see."

After getting a glimpse of the mine, not to mention a splitting headache, a hacking cough, and a supply of soot particles that would undoubtedly be oozing from my nose for the next week, I confess I still can't understand its appeal. I mean, people are not exactly popping off to sweatshops in Bangladesh to see eight-year-olds make carpets or heading to Somalia to watch farmers try to grow food without water, but I suppose if Potosí's success continues, these "attractions" could be just around the corner.

Tango in Tevas

Attending tango school in Argentina

Buenos Aires, Argentina

I suppose I could describe myself as rhythmically challenged. So when my girlfriend, Signe, spotted "Volver," a tango school, while we were walking around Buenos Aires, I wasn't thrilled by the prospect. "C'mon," she insisted, "this is where it all started." I checked the guide book. Sure enough, she was right. Moreover, it said that tango, "the dance of love," was invented in a brothel, so I figured it might be worth investigating after all.

Eduardo and Sylvia were the instructors advertised on the front door, though when we walked upstairs to the dance studio, we found out that it was now Eduardo and Veronica, so, naturally, we asked for a discount. The receptionist, who was also the bartender, explained that the cost was ten dollars per person for ninety minutes and fifteen dollars for three hours—with no discount for the absence of Sylvia.

I asked how many lessons we would need to make it around the floor of a tango club without looking like we were trying out for the Special Olympics Greco-Roman wrestling team. She wasn't sure what Greco-Roman wrestling was so she went and got Eduardo, a kindly man in his early sixties who, with his slicked black hair, black polo shirt, and black baggy pants, looked more like a professional bowler. He was followed by Veronica who, wearing black shoes, black stockings, a black high-cut tango skirt, black leotard, and black earrings that matched her black hair, looked like one of David Copperfield's assistants.*

Eduardo told us that we could get the basics in three hours if we were quick learners.

"What if we aren't quick?" I asked.

"Then," he said with exaggerated patience, "it will take longer."

Eduardo invited us to take the lesson that was about to begin. "But we don't have the right shoes or clothes," Signe protested. Eduardo looked at our Teva sandals, pants, and T-shirts (none of which were black) and shrugged, indicating they were fine. The other tango students weren't wearing classic tango clothes either, so after meeting them, we didn't feel quite as self-conscious. They were, however, wearing real shoes—something we didn't have with us, even at the youth hostel. We decided to take one lesson anyway and see how it went.

Most of our fellow students were Dutch and had come to Buenos Aires specifically to learn the tango. One of the Dutch students, Sebastian, was by his own confession, the worst dancer in the group. He was particularly glad that we were taking that position from him.

First things first: rhythm. Eduardo lined us up on one end of the dance floor and started the music. He took his position in front of us and began marching in place: *"Derecha, izqierda, derecha, izqierda . . ."* (right, left). After several minutes of stationary marching, we actually crossed the dance floor. *"Uno, dos, tres, (pause),"* Eduardo counted. We crisscrossed the floor for half an hour, sometimes even going backwards. This was the wax on, wax off, sand the floor, paint the fence of tango.

Then I had to learn how to hold my partner: shoulders back, head up, one hand on her spine, the other in her hand, rigid, yet relaxed, firm, yet gentle. "Derecha, izqierda, derecha, izqierda,"

---

*Maybe she made Sylvia disappear.

Eduardo got us going. *"Ahora!"* We were off. "Uno, dos, tres, (pause), uno, dos, tres," I counted, much to the disturbance of Signe, who thought I was taking the romance out of it. We managed about seven steps before our first accident. Our Tevas, which had been designed to climb mountains, ford rivers, and cross deserts, could not handle the rigors of tango. The Velcro straps came undone and connected with each other, tripping both of us. We dismissed it as a fluke, but after two more such incidences, we taped our Tevas into place.

This complex tango position is about as far as I got. Signe was at the hospital getting her crushed toes examined.

Once we got the hang of the marching and the holding, Eduardo got us all going counter-clockwise around the floor. It reminded me of "Couples-Only Period" at my junior-high roller rink.

The next day, during our second lesson, we learned how to turn, sort of. Signe got the hang of it before I did, so she began leading me through the maneuver. This was fine, but she sometimes forgot to give the lead back to me, which became more than a little confusing and often entangling.

On the last day, we got those kinks worked out and learned *ochos,* or eight-count steps. This required minimal work on my part (walking backward) and maximum effort on Signe's part (turning gracefully on every step while walking forward, juggling burning torches, and whistling the anthem of the former Soviet Union—or so she felt). At the end of the lesson we were more confused than when we started and Signe had two massive blisters.

Eduardo said that we had the basics and we could, if we wanted, go to a tango club. The whole class was going to one that night, so we decided to join them.

When we arrived at the club, the dance floor was filled with people, so we took a seat to watch. The atmosphere was very intimidating. You couldn't just disappear in the center of a dark dance floor. The whole place was well-lit and the dance floor was almost like a theater-in-the-round, with balcony and ground-level seats overlooking the entire dance floor.

We decided to, well, do it. We got into the ready position. The music started. "Derecha, izqierda," I whispered. "Shhhhhh!" Signe whispered back. I started forward with my left foot. Signe moved back with her right, but not quickly enough. Our Velcro meshed midstep. Without missing the beat, we yanked our feet apart and kept going. On every step our Velcro would catch slightly, just enough so we could hear the ripping sound of pulling them apart.

We maneuvered over to the side for a pit stop, fixed our sandals, and merged back into the counter-clockwise traffic. We were doing the tango! However, we only knew how to tango on the move. We couldn't tango in one spot, which is what all of the other people were doing. They would move a little, then tango in one spot, then move on. We would move a little, then ram into everyone who stopped to tango in one spot, then move on to ram the next couple. We made contact with everyone on the dance floor by the end of the first song and lapped them twice.

Eduardo and Veronica had joined our classmates, who were nearly rolling on the floor after our performance. We went up to greet them. Eduardo seemed particularly slow to acknowledge our presence, for fear that we would ruin his reputation. Which, I suppose, is exactly what we did.

Hoofing It

Buying a horse and riding it to Colombia

Tulcan, Ecuador

If they ever start handing out awards for ill-conceived travel plans, this one might take the grand prize, or at least get an honorable mention. After traveling for four weeks in Ecuador, I got an idea—possibly from a combination of South American beer and overexposure to the equator's harsh sun rays—that I could buy a horse, ride it to Colombia, and sell it for a higher price. I figured it would be a nice little adventure. Plus, I could make some money. And this might have been a perfectly decent plan if I 1) knew how to ride a horse, 2) had a map, 3) had a tent, and 4) knew the going price of horses in Colombia. The whole thing makes *City Slickers* look plausible by comparison.

A fellow traveler, Anita, wanted to come along and see if I was actually going to go through with this plan. The first step was to find a horse. We went to Otavello, the largest market in South America, figuring if there was a horse for sale in Ecuador, I could buy it there. But when we arrived at eight in the morning we learned we had already missed the early morning horse market. A man working at the Otavello Pie Shop advised us to try a town called Ibarra.

In Ibarra we asked around the town square until we found a farmer with two horses—a golden one named Tequila and a brown one named Dollar. The farmer gave us permission to inspect them. I had barely survived two trail rides at a dude ranch so I was about as qualified to inspect horses as I was to pilot the Space Shuttle. I gave each horse a pat on the back and rubbed its forehead—the equestrian equivalent of kicking the tires. The horses looked fine to me. The farmer, surprised that I didn't inspect the horses' teeth, opened Tequila's mouth and showed me what was inside. I didn't know what I was supposed to be looking for. The teeth were yellow and crooked and speckled with grass. It was obvious to me that this horse didn't know the first thing about oral hygiene.

The farmer would only sell both horses together for one price: one thousand dollars. Anita had never been on a horse before but announced she was up for the ride. I offered him four hundred. He laughed and said "Nine hundred." We started walking to the taxi. "Eight hundred!" he shouted. We kept walking. The price came down every five steps. By the time we reached the taxi, we agreed on seven hundred including two saddles. We then signed an illegible contract handwritten in Spanish, stating, I suppose, that we were total idiots to pay seven hundred dollars for those horses.

All things considered, the first twenty minutes of our ride went fairly smoothly. My horse, Tequila, immediately wandered off into the bushes. Then Dollar spooked and galloped down the street with Anita screaming her head off. I wanted to come to her rescue, but I couldn't pull Tequila away from the roadside vegetation. With the help of several locals, we eventually got things under control and started our ride north out of Ibarra on the shoulder of the Pan American Highway.

On the Pan American Highway it would be about eighty miles to the Colombian border, which I figured would take us four days. If we took back roads it would take longer—much longer because our hand-drawn map was as vague as the one Columbus used when he accidentally discovered the New World. The problem with the Pan American Highway was that the driver of every single car, truck, and bus felt the urge to honk when they passed us. This spooked the horses. After four or five hours of honking, our horses were going into traumatic shock. We had to detour onto the less-frequented, winding dirt road, which took us through picturesque grassy meadows surrounded by snowcapped peaks.

Anita recommended that we stop at a small roadside market to buy the horses some food. We picked up some sugar cubes and a few carrots. After that, we let them eat the grass on the side of the road. It was cheaper and they seemed to like it just as much. Not that I was any good at gauging equine facial expressions.

By four o'clock we began to wonder where we were going to spend the night. I had a vague idea of sleeping in a barn, if we could find one. However, that plan never materialized. After questioning a few villagers for sleeping suggestions, we were directed to a hacienda in the area. When we rode up the driveway, we found two thirty-year-old men in a pickup truck. I told them, in Spanish, that we were looking for a place to stay for the night. They replied in perfect English, "Sure, we have a room in the back you can use." They had both graduated from Texas A&M with degrees in agriculture.

This became our plan: stopping at haciendas. Everyone was so surprised to see two lost, inept riders so far off the gringo trail that they welcomed us wholeheartedly. Some places had better facilities than others, but they all served us homemade Ecuadorian cuisine for free. Some of our hosts even had their servants take care of our horses while we slept in beautiful guest houses.

On the morning of our seventh day, a few miles from the previous night's hacienda, my horse stopped. I kicked him. He wouldn't move. He had apparently gone on strike. Anita and I didn't really want to go any farther either—we had only made it halfway to Colombia and we were both so sore we couldn't sit down in the evenings. So I did what any urban cowboy would do—I turned the horse around to face the sparse traffic, stuck out my thumb, and started hitchhiking from my saddle. Sure enough, a car stopped. It was a Toyota hatchback. The driver offered to go back into town, get his brother's truck, and take us wherever we wanted in return for my broken guitar. It was an offer I couldn't refuse.

In one hour we were in Tulcan, an Ecuadorian town a few miles from the Colombian border, where we found out that the famous Colombian horse market had been quarantined for forty days. Suddenly Colombia didn't seem all that appealing. We decided to sell the horses as soon as we could.

Anita thought we should ride around with *se vende* (for sale) signs painted on our horses' rear bumpers. I suggested we first try our luck at the nearest hacienda. After a few hours we managed to find one potential customer. Unfortunately, he looked like Pancho Villa's surly brother, complete with eye patch, black cape, gold tooth, and a small posse of similarly dressed men. He went straight to the horses and began inspecting them. He would look at some part of the horse and say "Ha!" then, on cue, all his men would laugh "Ha! Ha! Ha!" This continued for about fifteen minutes to convey the idea that our horses were totally pathetic and we would be lucky if they took them from us for free and made them into glue.

We sold the horses for five hundred dollars. Anita and I were both a little disappointed, but I tried to look at the bright side. We had each spent one hundred dollars for seven days of room and board and an interesting adventure. We had discovered a great way to travel off the beaten path.

"No," Anita said, "we just paid a hundred dollars to go fifty miles."

Up the Amazon without a Paddle

Blowgun hunting in the Amazon

Leticia, Colombia

There are certain things in life you only do once: eat yellow snow, brush your teeth with hair gel, and wander deep into the Amazon to hang out with headhunters who toss around machetes like Congress tosses around lucrative defense contracts.

Looking for some jungle adventure, I arrived in the small town of Leticia, where Brazil, Colombia, and Peru intersect. A local tour guide explained that he wouldn't take me deep into the jungle because he makes more money schlepping wealthy adventure tourists to Monkey Island, a tiny isle a few hours up the Amazon with a jungle lodge that has every modern convenience short of a garage-door opener. He told me that Monkey Island natives will shed their T-shirts and Reeboks for traditional costumes and let the adventure tourists take their picture for a five-dollar per-person fee. It didn't sound like quite the adventure I was after.

I wanted to rent a boat and head up the Amazon myself, but the gas alone for a week-long trip would be almost four hundred dollars, which was out of my price range. And it required at least that much gas to get well past the Monkey Island tourist attraction and into virgin jungle. Peter, from Denmark, and Claudia, from

Germany, the only other travelers in town, decided (after several hours of persuasion) to join me and split the cost.

After considerable bargaining, we landed a week's boat rental and gas for five hundred bucks. The boat owner insisted that a driver come along for security—not ours, the boat's—and to fix the motor if things went wrong. He then gave us a map that looked like a used McDonald's place mat and pointed to a few spots on it where he told us we might run into ketchup and mustard stains—I mean, Jaguar Indians and possibly some headhunters. He wished us luck and walked away, leaving us to rethink the wisdom of our trip.

After eight hours motoring up the Amazon in our wide-body dugout canoe powered by a fifty-horse Johnson engine, we made a right turn onto a tributary, the Ataquari, and stopped at a village where we were greeted by a swarm of natives wearing not only T-shirts, but entire Umbro soccer outfits. The name of the village was "7th of October," the date of a revolution that no one seemed to remember. From what I could tell, the 7th of Octoberian men played soccer all day while the women farmed, cooked, and took care of the children. You might think the men got off easy, but don't worry, playing soccer wasn't all they did. They also played volleyball!

While Claudia helped the women prepare yucca, which tastes like it sounds, Peter and I—both a head taller than their tallest person—set a new 7th of October record for volleyball spikes.

That night we slept in hammocks under a thatched shelter. Large black widow spiders dropped from the ceiling onto our mosquito nets at night and walked just a few inches from our faces. This was not dangerous, provided the nets held up, but it freaked Claudia out. She used her net as a catapult to launch them into the air and, if they landed on Peter or me, we launched them right back.

The following day, some Octoberians took us on a jungle hike in exchange for a bag of rice. This was a great opportunity for me to try out the machete I had purchased. At first I thought the object was to take a swing at every branch I passed. After thirty minutes, however, my arm was too tired to cut anything, so I just ducked under the branches like the Octoberians, who had figured this out long ago. They were also wearing snake-proof boots. We weren't. Every step through the field of chest-high grass we had to cross was like playing a round of Russian Roulette—we would surely die from any snake bite before we could get back to the hospital in Leticia.

Before we left for the next village, we gave the Octoberians several bags of salt (an inexpensive, but useful item we were assured they already had, so it would not disrupt their culture) as a token of our thanks. You would have thought we were handling out free hacky sacks at a Dead show. They fought over every grain and then said a tearful good-bye to their departing volleyball heroes and requested that we come back soon. Be wary of the headhunters up the river, they warned.

Our driver guided us as far up the river as our petrol would get us—to the village of El Sol (The Sun) where we were greeted by people who were, for the most part, naked. Well, they didn't exactly greet us. They just stood there and stared as if we were space aliens from the planet Dipstick. We didn't really know what to say. "Hey, you must be the headhunters!" wasn't quite appropriate. We just began handing over bags of salt and rice until the chief, the only man at this village who knew Spanish, stepped forward and offered us a shelter for the night.

Except for the chief, the Solians only spoke Cetchua. At first, the chief thought we were spies, then missionaries. He couldn't understand why we would go all the way up to El Sol for no apparent reason. He wasn't the chief for nothing.

He told us we were the first whites to visit their village, which explained why the villagers were always watching us. I mean, *always*. A small crowd watched us eat, sleep, and even followed us into the "toilet," which in the rain forest is anywhere you please. They kept asking us, via the chief, to tell them about the Amazon village we were from. We told them that in our village we have buildings many times taller than their tallest tree, the most popular activity is sitting in front of a box, and some people eat sour cream and onion yucca until they are too big for their hammocks. Explaining the moon landing, TV shopping, and Michael Jackson having a baby seemed a bit too advanced.

The following day, after catching some piranha in the river with a simple fishing pole, we jumped in the same river to swim with the village children. Although I had been sweating myself to sleep for four days and smelled like a barn animal, I was extremely apprehensive about sharing my bathtub with piranha. But the chief promised as long as I wasn't bleeding or thrashing about, I didn't have much to worry about—unless, of course, there was a crocodile in the vicinity. Comforting.

On the fifth day, the chief assigned a man to take us hunting—with five-foot-long blowguns and darts laced with lethal poison. We put on all available clothing to protect us from the wilds of the jungle. Our guide, however, wearing a loincloth and a tattered, pre-*Love Boat*-era sky-blue

After a full day of blowgun hunting with poisonous darts deep in the rainforest, I managed to hit (and possibly wound) two trees.

jacket that somehow made it up this tributary, did not appear to feel underdressed. Before we started, he cut up some red tree roots and, using his saliva, made it into—no metaphors come to mind— reddish saliva, which he smeared on our cheeks and foreheads. There were no mirrors around, but I believe we looked like fierce jungle warriors. Or Washington Redskins fans.

We cut our way through the dense jungle for several hours. Despite all efforts, we made too much noise to get within the same zip code as any wild animal, but my third-grade spitball skills proved useful—I believe I wounded three yucca plants.

That evening, the chief held a party for us, complete with drums and a handmade flute. Peter ran out of cigarettes and was in a bad mood. Everyone else got drunk on *cheecha,* fermented corn juice that tastes worse than beer sucked out of a sponge left in a fraternity sink. One of the villagers had a bit too much cheecha and, at three in the morning, he decided to play what I could only guess was a really funny Amazon-headhunter joke. He woke me up by touching the blade of his machete to my nose and screaming like a pig passing a kidney stone. As you can imagine, this is not an ideal way to wake up.* I nearly pissed my pants. After screaming for about five minutes, he wandered off and, hopefully, fell into the river and was eaten by a crocodile.

We left for Leticia the next morning with our heads still firmly attached. The chief had never mentioned anything about headhunting and we never got up the nerve to ask.

During our ride back, we were quite frank about our accomplishments; in six days we had achieved in the field of social anthropology what Anna Nicole Smith has achieved in the field of rocket science. However, we had succeeded in seeing some untouched rain forest, experiencing Amazon cultures, and giving out more salt than the Culligan Man.

---

*Even compared with some early morning DJs.

Lure of the Lava

Hiking a volcano in Guatemala

Antigua, Guatemala

The most popular day trip from Antigua is a visit to Pacaya, an active volcano a few hours away. And the trip would be even more popular if there weren't reports of banditos and guerrillas in the surrounding area.

I was advised to go with a tour company for protection. Many such companies posted handwritten advertisements in the entrance of a popular restaurant. After a few minutes of deliberation, I chose the one with the least spelling errors.

The following afternoon, I met up with my group. Like several other volcano-tour companies in Antigua, this company's sole possession was one unmarked van and some "defensive weapons." For fifteen dollars, I was packed in with thirteen others and we set off on the two-hour ride to the volcano.

Our guides parked the van in a small village at the foot of the volcano. I looked at the locals and thought that anyone who makes a village at the base of an active volcano is asking for trouble. They looked at me and probably thought that anyone who shells out fifteen dollars to walk up an active volcano has no right to call us stupid.

When we began our hike, I noticed that our two young tour guides were each carrying Little League baseball bats, the so-called "defensive weapons" that were supposed to protect us from the banditos and guerrillas. I'm sure those hillside warriors were shaking in their munitions belts when they saw us coming—fourteen tourists being led by two 5' 3" teenagers who probably couldn't hit a softball if my grandma pitched one right over the plate.

Bandito 1: Let's move in on that group of tourists.

Bandito 2: Wait, the leader is carrying a Little League baseball bat. We don't stand a chance with our machetes and semiautomatic weapons.

Bandito 3: I want to be Bandito number 2.

Bandito 2: I was Bandito number 2 first.

Bandito 1: And you two idiots wonder why we haven't taken control of the country yet.

Bandito 3: You're just saying that because you always get to be Bandito number 1.

We took a snack and potty break after an hour of walking. "Men's toilet here," the guide said and pointed to the woods on one side of the trail. "Women's toilet here." He pointed to the woods on the other side of the trail.

We then hiked across a volcanic field and scurried up a steep, loose gravel trail. A cloud enveloped us during this last ascent and we couldn't see more than a few meters in any direction. The next thing I knew I had reached the top. The lead guide and a few others were lying on their stomachs peering over the lip of the volcano, so I crawled up next to them and looked down. At the bottom of the crater was a Jacuzzi-sized tub of gurgling orange lava. It was mesmerizing.

After a few minutes of staring at the lava, the guides led us along a ridge to a "better viewing point." I was a bit confused. How much better view could you get?

The cloud cover cleared when we were forty yards from the lip, just in time to watch Pacaya erupt. The lava shot a few hundred feet into the air, some of it landing on the lip where we had just been not one minute before. I dubbed it a near death experience.

I asked one of the guides how often it actually erupts. "Depends on the day," he said. "Sometimes every five or ten minutes." I wondered how many tourists had been killed here. I mean, if the banditos don't get you, the volcano will.

We watched a beautiful sunset, then stayed a few more hours and cheered the volcano's eruptions. It was spectacular. Nature's free fireworks. We sat on the ridge and drank cheap Guatemalan wine and ate Guatemalan crackers with Guatemalan pâté (road kill, probably), then headed down with flashlights at about ten o'clock.

The banditos and guerrillas must have been busy plotting an insurrection, for we couldn't have been a much better target—tipsy tourists laughing and waving flashlights.

It's amazing the kind of opportunities tourism can bring to a country. Marching people up to the lip of an active volcano has become a cottage industry in Guatemala, possible only because these guys don't have to pay insurance premiums. Obviously, Guatemala doesn't have enough lawyers yet.

Having the Last Raft

Rafting the wild Biobio

Pucon, Chile

"Raft the Biobio now so you can tell your children about it" read the sign on Chando's rafting company in southern Chile's wanna-be glitzy Lake District town of Pucon. Apparently, a nearly completed hydro-electric dam was about to put an end to one of the world's most famous stretches of Class V white water. Never mind that I didn't have any children to tell and that my only rafting experience entailed applying sunscreen and floating belly up on a lake in Minnesota—I figured I couldn't pass up the opportunity.

In Pucon, there's no shortage of companies who want to take you down the Biobio, which cuts a path through the nearby Andes. They all publicize themselves in a curious way: they display ongoing videos of an athletic, enthusiastic group going down the Biobio, flipping the raft, getting rammed against rocks, getting sucked underwater, and screaming their collective heads off all the while— as though those were major selling points. Then they assure you that you don't need any prior experience and that the whole thing is perfectly safe.

Judging from the videos, even if I did live to tell my future children about it, I would probably be doing it from a wheelchair, slurring my speech.

I decided to throw caution, and my wallet, to the wind. At $250, Chando had the best deal in town, but it was still a bit steep for a three-day trip. I decided this would be an ideal time to try out my new, full-color press ID card, which is supposed to work in the world of tourism something like James Bond's license to kill works in the world of international intrigue.*

Chando, a forty-something Peruvian who was covered from head to toe in Patagonia clothing, stared at my card, then at me, then at the card, and after several strained minutes of examination he said, "Okay, you can have fifty dollars off and you can borrow a sleeping bag. I'd give you more, but this is the last trip down the Biobio." Fair enough, I thought.

The itinerary said that we would leave early in the morning, drive eight hours to the put-in spot, inflate the boats, and raft for two hours. The second and third days we would raft all day on class IV and V rapids then drive back late at night.

The first day turned out to be driving to the put-in spot and then not rafting, but swimming in a nearby lake until we all got too cold to perform normal bodily functions—like moving our lips. To defrost, we went to a nearby thermal hot spring, where the four Chilean businessmen on the trip, all naked, took turns singing various Chilean songs that even I could discern as out of tune. Tom, a nineteen-year-old Canadian traveler and the youngest member of our group, seemed very uncomfortable with nudity and spent much of the time sneaking from boulder to boulder, going to tremendous lengths to keep his Canadian Mounty out of view.

The second day, we put in our four-raft flotilla. Chando handed

---

*Although I can't remember ever watching a James Bond film in which 007 actually had to present this license to some small-town cop to justify a homicide. "See, I have this license—the double-zero means 'I am allowed to kill anyone I want,' and the seven means 'even in your country'."
"Oh, you have one of those—okay, then, you can go."

out wet suits, life jackets, and helmets and gave us a safety speech. The funny thing about rafting, according to Chando, is that an empty raft can, nine times out of ten, float down a river just fine on its own. "When you put humans in it and let them busy themselves with paddling, you get trouble." The funny thing about Chando's safety speech is "Hold your breath before you get sucked underwater." No duh.

Aside from Chando, we had three other guides, all in their early twenties. I started out paddling in the front of a raft guided by Christian, a Chilean guide who could, without any help from us, navigate his way down the Biobio backwards with his paddle and possibly both arms tied behind his back. But the rapids didn't seem that dangerous so, to find a bit more excitement, I transferred over to a raft guided by Willy.

Willy was, in rafting terms, a psychopath. So was Florian, a German traveler who shared Willy's thirst for constant danger. He joined me at the front of this raft, which wasn't much bigger than

Now that I'm wearing dry clothes and sitting on land, I don't mind admitting that my paddling was rather ineffective.

an inner tube. We never tipped, but we did manage to submerge the raft in every rapid. Over the next hour, I learned that Florian—who did not possess a full-color press ID card—also got fifty dollars off.

After three hours of our "full day of rafting," Chando pulled over and told us we were done for the day, despite our protests. Chando, who'd had more positive energy than a cheerleading squad on Vivarin when he sold me my ticket, had hardly grunted a word since we got on the river. People had been shuffling in and out of his raft all day because nobody, save the four Chilean businessmen, could stand riding with him. Chando always took the easiest route down a rapid, he never said a word, and no one saw him crack a smile.

The third day, we backtracked with the bus and put the rafts in much farther up the river to hit the big stuff. I decided to switch back to Christian's raft to improve my chances of living.

After we navigated the rapids "Jug Buster" (someone broke a bottle of wine there once) and "Milky Way" (numerous rocks), we came to "Lost Yak." Lost Yak is short for "Lost a Kayak," which is river-speak for "We Lost a Kayak While a Guy Was Still in It," which means—in case you're still not with me—the guy died. It seems that a name like Lost Yak could be open to such interpretations as "A Guy Puked Here, but It Washed Away," which would explain why several kayakers have wandered into this same rapid and been washed away permanently. To avoid future deadly misinterpretation, this rapid is in dire need of a new name like, perhaps, "Cemetery."

Because of the low-volume water flow, Chando determined that there was too great a chance that we could fall out of the boat and get sucked under the same rock as the kayakers—so we walked around this one.

Next up was "Lava South"—the best rapid on the trip, though it had the dopiest name. It was, roughly speaking, a thirty-foot flume followed by a ten-foot-high standing wave followed by a boat-smashing rock wall. We didn't tip, no one got injured, but, a few minutes later, several of us realized that Tom had peed in his wet suit (he suddenly volunteered to take a quick swim between the next rapids).

We finished the day exhausted and sunburnt but happy. I was glad to be on the last ride down the Biobio, I told Chando.

"Well," he said, in a controlled, almost rehearsed way, "we have one more trip next week. But that one will be the last for sure."

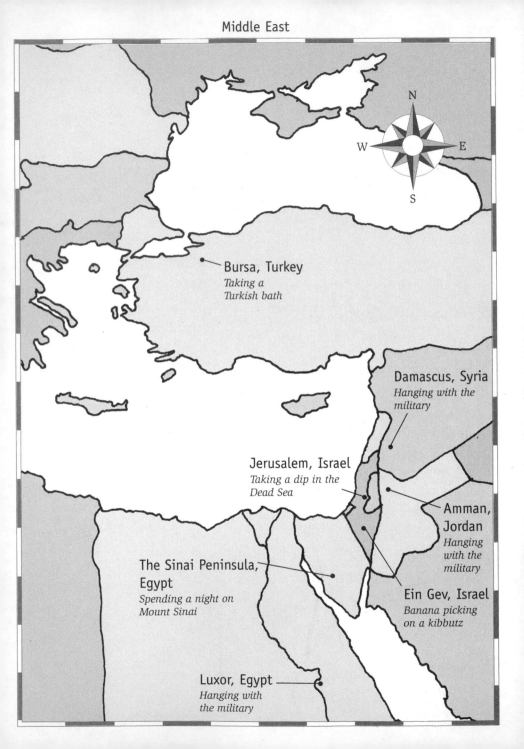

Middle East

Bursa, Turkey
*Taking a
Turkish bath*

Damascus, Syria
*Hanging with the
military*

Jerusalem, Israel
*Taking a dip in the
Dead Sea*

Amman,
Jordan
*Hanging
with the
military*

The Sinai Peninsula,
Egypt
*Spending a night on
Mount Sinai*

Ein Gev, Israel
*Banana picking
on a kibbutz*

Luxor, Egypt
*Hanging with
the military*

MIDDLE EAST

The Middle East is a vast cultural and well-oiled region that does not happen to include Egypt, which is technically part of Africa. However, in this section you will find a story about Egypt. Why? Well, first, United States' Middle East policy lumps them together; second, Egypt felt to me much more Middle Eastern than African; and third—perhaps most important of all—the Middle East section of this book was looking a little on the thin side. So, with a few key strokes, the book's production manager (check inside front cover to see the name of the person who deserves credit for this) evened things out a little. Besides, the Middle East is facing several more-daunting problems than having Egypt dropped into their section of the book.

Dead Sea Stroll

Taking a dip with Mom in the Dead Sea

Jerusalem, Israel

* I had enough trouble entertaining my mom when she visited me at college, so when she joins me on the road, I am generally at a loss for ideas. Fortunately, when she met up with me in Israel, she had her own agenda. Like many travelers, she had studied all the guide books and read all the articles so she knew exactly where she wanted to go, what it would look like, and how she was supposed to feel once she saw it.

The Dead Sea was on the top of her list of places to go. My mother wanted to rent a car and drive there from Jerusalem. I wanted to take the bus, blend in with the locals, and avoid the stress of her driving. We compromised. She rented a car and I drove. It only took us about an hour to drive halfway across Israel—less time than it takes to digest a falafel.

I had been in Israel long enough to know that one of the rules of the road is to pick up hitchhiking Israeli soldiers. (Another rule of the road is not to pick up suicide bombers.) Soldiers often go home to visit their families, and it is common courtesy to give them free rides. My mother was not so fond of this. She doesn't normally pick up hitchhikers—especially ones with large guns. After much persuasion, I convinced her to give it a try and from then on, we had at least three armed soldiers in our backseat at all times.

The conversations usually went something like this:

My mom: Are you boys in the army?

Me: Yes Mom, they're in the army.

My mom: Quiet, Doug. I was asking them.

Army guys: Yes, we're in the army.

We arrived at the Dead Sea in the afternoon, drove past a few ritzy hotels, and parked near a beach. This entire area is well below sea level and I can describe it with one word: EXTREMELYFUCK-INGHOT! Without looking at a thermometer, I'd guess it was about three hundred degrees. It was far too hot to get out of the car, so we just sat there with the air conditioner on full blast for an hour. This was a bit rough on the engine, but what the hell, it was a rental.

We finally decided to try out the Dead Sea, which is very famous because of all the floating dead people. Sorry, I couldn't resist. Actually, they're just tourists and most of them are not dead at all.

I waded into the warm, salty water and walked out until it was too deep to stand. Then, instead of going underwater, my feet just popped up to the surface as if David Copperfield had levitated them with magic, or maybe with some of that stuff he puts in his hair.

After several minutes, I determined this water was not very practical. Swimming was too difficult because my feet just slapped the top of the water. I couldn't get the water anywhere near my eyes because it stung like dandruff shampoo. I couldn't get the water in my mouth because it tasted like dandruff shampoo—not that I go around eating dandruff shampoo or anything. In addition, the water was too warm to be refreshing, and it left a sticky film on my body.

"It's not supposed to be fun. It's supposed to be interesting," said my mother as she watched me spitting up some of the water I had accidentally swallowed.

The Dead Sea seemed better suited for taking snapshots than for swimming, which thrilled my mom, who finally had a chance to try out her new camera. She made me do the standard tourist pose repeated by just about everyone who comes here: pretending to read a magazine while floating. No one actually reads in the Dead Sea. The water and the air are both too hot. This was a bit of a disappointment because I had seen so many photos of people reading, I figured the Dead Sea was adjacent to a library.

No one actually reads in the Dead Sea; it's just some sort of publicity stunt everyone feels the urge to replicate. Including me.

My mother handed me her camera, waded out shin deep, and sat down. I couldn't tell if she was floating or sitting on the bottom, but I took her picture anyway. She was enjoying herself.

When she came out she insisted that I engage in the other traditional Dead Sea photo-appropriate activity: smearing "medicinal" Dead Sea mud all over my body. The guide book said that the Dead Sea is famous for this mud. Strangely, the only mud I could see was in a plastic bucket, guarded by a man who was charging three shekels (one dollar) to let tourists use just enough to cover their bodies. My mom put up the money and I coated myself from head to toe. About ten other tourists were doing the same thing and we looked like a family from the Planet Zwonk. I couldn't stop laughing—until the mud on my face dried like cement and turned me into a Betty Crocker mud biscuit.

In addition to providing numerous highly comical photo opportunities for my mother, this mud bath was supposed to improve my skin. I didn't notice any difference after I washed off the mud, except for the attractive and tenacious sulfur smell. My mom considered it a souvenir.

The Dead Sea seems to be a "must" for every tourist who comes to Israel. And I confess, it's hard to pass up a world-famous natural wonder. But my mother had her own reasoning. "It's important that you experi-enced this," she said as we left, "so you can tell your children about it."

I am covered in a dollar's worth of special Dead Sea mud. They say it's supposed to possess unique powers . . . besides becoming rock hard and making you smell like sulfur for several days.

"But Mom," I protest-ed, "I don't have any chil-dren."

"Don't worry," she confided, "you will."

Bless This Mess

Spending a night on Mount Sinai

The Sinai Peninsula, Egypt

Moses spent forty days and forty nights on top of Mount Sinai. I just wanted one peaceful evening under the stars at this holy site. I wasn't expecting to speak to God or bring back any new laws—I leave that to the televangelists and politicians.

The taxi ride from the Red Sea coastal town of Dahab to the base of Mount Sinai was a bit more expensive than I expected: fifteen dollars. I was trying to negotiate a deal with one driver when I overheard two other travelers bargaining with another driver for a ride to the same place. So much for my perfect solitude, I thought. But, as long as we all were going, we decided to share the cab ride and cut our costs. To my surprise, this nice Danish couple had managed to haggle the price down to thirteen dollars—a feat that took them twenty minutes. We split the cost three ways.

The taxi driver, always on the lookout for an extra buck, picked up two Germans headed for Mount Sinai. The morale in the taxi was a bit low. We were all upset we wouldn't be spending the night on the mountain alone. Only Moses, it seemed, had that privilege.

After driving a few hours through the desert, we arrived at Mount Sinai. If you've been to the Rockies or the Alps, this doesn't look like much of a mountain. In fact, if you piled up all the Mount Sinai hospitals, the result would probably be more impressive than the actual

Mount Sinai . . . provided they don't bill you for the procedure.

Our driver left us at the base of the mountain next to St. Catherine's Monastery, where, according to my guide book, the Sinaiticus Codex, the first bible bound like a book, was found. Unfortunately, the monastery was closed when we arrived so that's all I can tell you about it.

I had heard other travelers say that they "climbed" Mount Sinai. Climb is not exactly the right verb. No ropes or ice axes are involved; the "climb" is a two- or three-hour hike up a gentle incline that can easily be done in sandals. You can even ride up most of the way on a camel if you don't feel like walking. I wasn't in the mood to bargain with the camel jockeys, but the Germans were, so I left them and set out on foot with the Danish couple.

The hike started at St. Catherine's Monastery and went to . . . well . . . the top—past several Bedouin snack vendors in little concession shacks strategically positioned along the trail. That's why the trail was clearly "marked" by empty water bottles, Snickers bar wrappers, and flashlight batteries. (My guide book reminded me that Thou Shall Not Litter was not part of the Big 10 package, hence the trash is not official sacrilege.)

We caught the "holy sunset" just as we reached the top. I was too distracted by the beauty of the moment to notice my surroundings. Once the sun was gone, however, I noticed that the peak, which was about the size of the roof of an apartment building, was also occupied by about thirty Dutch high-school kids, the two German camel riders who had finally reached the top, and two Bedouins, each in his own shack, competing to sell us hot chocolate and lemon wafers.

We were a little disappointed by the crowd. I tried to look on the bright side. This could be fun. A pajama party on Mount Sinai.

No such luck. The Dutch guys, being teenagers, were conducting a pissing contest off to one side of the mountain, while several of the older guys and girls were off to the other side having their own parties in rather crowded sleeping bags. And I am pretty sure they were not wearing pajamas. The Germans were the only ones who brought marijuana this night, but, judging from the amount of discarded rolling paper on the ground, they weren't the first holy trekkers to get high. I suppose some people feel if they can't find a spiritual experience on top of this mountain, they can at least try to chemically induce one.

It was much colder than I had anticipated. I was shivering. The Danish couple sat down next to me with blankets.

"Where did you get those?" I asked.

"Over there," they said casually. The Bedouins were renting blankets for two dollars.

I rented a blanket and leaned back on a rock to take part in the main Mount Sinai activity—star gazing. I had never seen the Milky Way so clearly. There were shooting stars everywhere. And the Dutch group applauded after each one. In between the cheering and clapping, I could hear X-rated sounds coming from several sleeping bags. It felt more like Bob's Youth Hostel in Amsterdam than a sacred mountaintop. I had seen a fantastic sunset and some shooting stars. I didn't feel obligated to suffer through another ten hours of this circus.

I decided to walk down and the Danish couple went with me. Unfortunately, we didn't have a flashlight. The stars were bright, but with no moon we could hardly see the trail. A pleasant and easy ascent had become a dangerous descent. (With all the probable late-night traffic on this trail, I wonder how many tourists have accidentally walked off one of the many ledges.) Luckily, occasional pieces of trash would glimmer and briefly illuminate our trail. It wasn't exactly spiritual guidance, but it did the trick.

I confess, the whole experience didn't give me much faith in the biblical account. Moses never mentioned the trash, or the camel drivers, and he made it down the mountain hernia-free while carrying two massive tablets, tablets he conceivably could have purchased from one of the Bedouins—possibly a two-for-one deal with blanket rental.

Armed to the Teeth

Hanging with the military in the Middle East

Damascus, Syria; Jerusalem, Israel;
Luxor, Egypt; and Amman, Jordan

It's almost impossible to avoid contact with the armed forces in the Middle East, one of the most war-prepared regions in the world. Soldiers are everywhere: manning checkpoints, driving around in long convoys, pointing their guns at you, playing with the safety switch . . . all standard military procedure. My encounters with various "peacekeepers" have always been memorable.

Syrian Secret Police

There are many rumors about the Syrian secret police, and most lead you to believe that they practice a thumb-screws-on-first-ask-questions-later type of law enforcement. This was not the case in Damascus when my girlfriend, Signe, and I asked a man on the street for directions to a museum. He pulled out a gun and told us he was "secret police" (he was, apparently, not very good at keeping secrets) and said he would personally help us get to the museum. We told him it wasn't necessary and he could just point us in the right direction, but he took this to mean "we are terribly thirsty" and immediately insisted on buying us a mango juice, or rather, waving his gun at a mango juice vendor who then graciously offered us some for free.

After refreshments, the not-so-secret agent started waving his gun at oncoming traffic until a uniformed police officer arrived on a moped with the pedals hack-sawed off. Our new friend pulled rank, commandeered the moped, and motioned for the two of us to get on. "You can't be serious," I said. He was. Somehow, we squeezed on and the three of us rode off to the museum at the speed of a riding lawn-mower, where (at gunpoint) the guards decided to let us in for free.

Jordanian Border Patrol

When we arrived at the Jordanian border, a security force was carefully inspecting all luggage, so I decided to voluntarily hand over my pocket-sized canister of mace, lest the customs officials find it during the luggage search.

The customs official I gave it to couldn't speak English and he had no idea what I was giving him, despite my Academy Award-winning pantomime demonstration of the effects of mace on the human eye. The poor guy nearly took himself out while examining the bottle. Everything was finally cleared up after I reexplained it to about eight different, progressively higher-ranking officials, including, I think, the Minister of Defense.

I WISH TO INFORM U.S. MILITARY INTELLIGENCE THAT I KNOW FOR A FACT THAT THE JORDANIAN BORDER PATROL NOW POSSESSES AT LEAST ONE BREATH FRESHENER-SIZED SELF-DEFENSE MACE SPRAYER AND I WAS PERSONALLY INVOLVED IN (AND FINANCED) THIS SHIPMENT OF ARM(S). I SINCERELY HOPE THIS DOES NOT UPSET THE BALANCE OF POWER IN THE REGION. SORRY FOR ANY INCONVENIENCE.

Israeli Soldiers

My first night in Israel, I walked into the Underground, a popu-lar bar and dance club in Jerusalem, with some acquaintances from my youth hostel. After a few minutes of dancing—Whack!—something smacked into my head and knocked me to the floor. I looked up, while rubbing my head, to see that I had been hit by the barrel of an army-issue rifle. It was strapped to the back of a dancing Israeli who had no idea he had nearly cracked my skull. In fact, there were about five Israelis, all with guns on their backs, drinking beer and dancing in a circle.

What did I do? Not much. My mother taught me not to pick fights with well-armed soldiers. The reason for the guns, I learned later, is that if an Israeli soldier loses or misplaces his gun, he goes to jail for seven years. No excuses accepted.

Egyptian Police

I was bargaining for a few scarves in a night market in Luxor, and enjoying the process, when the vendor and I reached an impasse. I said twenty-five Egyptian pounds and he said thirty-five. I knew the local price was thirty, so if I stuck it out a little longer, it seemed we might arrive at thirty-two. Instead, I offered to flip a coin: heads, I buy five scarves for twenty-five pounds each; tails, I buy five scarves for thirty-five pounds each. It was roughly a five-dollar bet. He agreed.

By the time someone had located a coin, a substantial crowd of locals had formed. A neutral party flipped the coin and when it landed on the ground, everyone pushed in to look. I won the toss, but the vendor announced he was only joking and would not sell them for less than thirty-five. We began to argue and this attracted the attention of a nearby police officer, who positioned himself as judge and let us (with the help of a volunteer interpreter from the crowd) argue our points. The officer made his decision by pointing his Uzi at the vendor and giving me a smile. I handed the vendor 125 pounds and took the five scarves I had selected. It was the only time I received a better-than-local price.

Iraqi Military

I wasn't feeling so well when I checked into one of the five-dollar hotels in the center of Amman to take a nap. I woke up sixteen hours later with a fever and, in round numbers, six thousand bedbug bites. I noticed a bottle of aspirin on the table next to me and a wet compress on my throbbing head. The door opened and two men in fatigues came in, introducing themselves as sergeants in the Iraqi military who were staying in the room next door. Even though I was American, they had taken care of me all night. And they continued nursing me back to health for the next two days.

As I got better I was able to join the rest of the hotel guests in the TV room to watch the finals of the French Open. This group of spectators included a Lebanese teenager, a Syrian businessman, an Iraqi engineer, a few Palestinians, and the two Iraqi sergeants. I spent at least half of the tournament trying to explain why tennis players say "love" instead of "zero." We had such a massive pile of *baklava* (honey-soaked pastries) that, after we had stuffed ourselves silly, we began to exchange volleys during commercial breaks.

Perhaps, I thought, we had stumbled upon the road to peace; we simply need to rearm the region with edible munitions.

Rubbed the Wrong Way

Taking a Turkish bath

Bursa, Turkey

 You can't leave Turkey without taking at least one Turkish bath. It would be like going to Belgium and not having a waffle, going to New Zealand and not bungee jumping, or going to France and not getting drunk on cheap red wine.

I visited several Turkish baths *(hamam)* during my two months in Turkey, but the most memorable was my first experience. I traveled four hours south of Istanbul to a town called Bursa especially for this purpose. Bursa's mineral-rich waters are known throughout the Middle East for their curative powers.

In my hostel in Bursa I found two travelers, Phillippe, from France, and Peter, from the Netherlands, who were looking for a similar experience. We shared a taxi to Yeni Kaplica (meaning "new bath"), which was last renovated in 1522 by Sultan Suleyman the Magnificent. For ten dollars each, we purchased the all-inclusive deluxe package, clearly designed for the novice Turkish bather.

We were each given a loincloth and wooden sandals and then led upstairs to some lockers to change. Since this was my first loincloth, I wasn't quite sure how to wear it. There was no label, so I might well have had it on backwards. Either way, I felt like a Christian going to do battle against the lions.

The sandals were half the size of my feet, so I was able to tuck only three toes under the foot strap, leaving my heels firmly on the floor. I didn't want to make a cultural faux pas by not wearing the sandals and I was afraid that exchanging them might be as frustrating as exchanging shoes at an American bowling alley, so I just shuffled along.

The bath area was like nothing I had ever seen at a health club. I had stepped into a steamy Moorish painting. While outside of the baths were tour buses and Coca-Cola vending machines, inside, nothing, save an electric light and some plastic washbowls, had been affected by the last hundred years. The floors and walls were yellow-stained marble and cement. Prominently displayed were a large coal-heated hot tub without the Jacuzzi feature and a smaller tub with burn-your-big-toe hot water. Around the perimeter of the room stood washing stations with faucets, bars of soap, and sitting stools. Half-naked men meandered about, their muffled conversations bouncing off the walls into distortion.

Phillippe, Peter, and I tried to blend in by studying everyone's behavior and attempting to emulate it. (It's not easy to do this casually while wearing a loincloth.) We eventually discovered the basic things to do in a hamam are 1) wash yourself, 2) lie around and sweat, 3) wash again, 4) make idle conversation in Turkish, 5) wash again, 6) repeat cycle.

After forty-five minutes of this (minus the conversation in Turkish), I had sweated out half my body weight and cleaned myself eight or nine times. I also realized we were the only tourists in the hamam so, despite our spectacular blending techniques, we stood out like a bunch of honkies.

A monstrous Turkish man in a white towel came over and asked the three of us to follow him into a steamy side room. We did. He selected Phillippe to be the first massage victim. Phillippe lay belly-down on the massage table and the Turk first buried him in soap suds, then started massaging. Phillippe began screaming and swearing in French. "Should we make him stop?" we asked. "No," Phillippe answered between yelps, "It—ARAAAARAGH— feels good." Peter and I were happy to hear this because we didn't relish the prospect of trying to physically restrain a huge Turkish masseur while wearing our loincloths.

I was next. I lay down on the table and reminded myself I was too old to cry. I told myself it was not as though I was going to have my leg amputated, which, in retrospect, might not have been nearly as painful. My torture began the same way as Phillippe's. The Turk covered me with foam. Then I felt two hands press down on my back and heard a crack along every one of my vertebrae. The pressure knocked most of the wind out of my lungs. My Turkish torturer then went about the business of crushing my bones into a fine powder. I only yelped once, when he squeezed my calf muscle like a lemon.

He covered me with foam again and donned what looked like an oven mitt. It's actually a special bathing brush called a *kese*, which I believe is Turkish for "industrial-strength sandpaper." He scrubbed several layers of skin off my back, flipped me over, and did the same thing to my front. I had thought I was clean but I watched chewing gum-like wads of dead skin go flying off my body. Then he splashed a bucket of hot water on me. Then a bucket of ice water, followed by another bucket of hot water. I was finished. I went over to sit by Phillippe, feeling like a skinned, boneless chicken.

We watched Peter get his "treatment," then all three of us went to the hot tub and melted. After ten minutes we decided that we were completely dehydrated and staggered to the showers. We barely had enough energy to stand.

When we exited the bath area, our wet loincloths were replaced by dry towels. An attendant draped another towel over each of our shoulders and tied smaller ones around our heads so we looked as though we had just walked off the set of "Lawrence of Arabia Goes to the Steam Room." We were led to a small sitting room where a waitress took our drink order. There were only two to choose from: Mineral Water or Disgusting Yogurt Drink. I had one of each.

Every few minutes an attendant would come by and drape a few more towels over us. After twenty minutes, when we finally stopped sweating, we had each accumulated enough towels to dry the entire U.S. water polo team.

An attendant then led us upstairs to a room full of dormitory cots. He told us to sleep and said he would wake us in an hour. We nodded off immediately. When we were gently wakened an hour later and served tea, it felt like the entire experience had been a dream. I felt completely invigorated, relaxed . . . and zestfully clean!

The masseur, waitress, towel drapers, and a few other attendants we had never seen before lined up to say good-bye and collect their gratuities. We walked past them and dropped a few coins into each of their extended hands—probably far too much because they were still smiling after we gave them the money. Or maybe because my wet loincloth was stuck to my shoe.

Dabbling in Socialism

Banana picking on an Israeli kibbutz

Ein Gev, Israel

People come from around the world to volunteer on one of Israel's many self-sufficient farming communities *(kibbutzim)*, and I always assumed they came to get an inside look at Israeli culture and partake in this community lifestyle. I also assumed that kibbutznicks welcomed them wholeheartedly, introduced them to the culture, and let them contribute equally toward the upkeep of the kibbutz. Unfortunately, in my experience, this was about as close to reality as Marilyn Manson winning the Nobel Prize in literature.

I arrived in Israel without a kibbutz reservation and the placement agency in Tel Aviv didn't have any openings, so I decided to find a kibbutz myself. A tip from a traveler in a youth hostel led me to Ein Gev, one of the supposedly volunteer-oriented and affluent kibbutzim (one of the few that didn't completely depend on government support). When I arrived, I noticed a pool and tennis courts on my way to see the volunteer supervisor, who told me the kibbutz really didn't need any more volunteers, but—as a favor—she'd let me stay.

The deal, she explained, is that volunteers get a bed, food, use of the facilities, and enough shekels to buy some ice cream at their little supermarket in return for eight hours of manual labor per day. "And you have to stay a minimum of two months."

"Fine," I said. But before I could start, I had to pay a forty-dollar registration fee, a twenty-five-dollar physical examination (and AIDS test) fee at a nearby clinic, a forty-dollar kibbutz insurance fee (whatever that is), a thirty-dollar security-against-leaving-before-my-two-months-were-up fee, and a five-dollar room key deposit. I never had to pay so much to volunteer before.

After she had her money and test results, I was issued work clothes: a ripped T-shirt, oversized work pants plastered with old paint, transparent plastic sandals, and odoriferous canvas boots. With these clothes, I fit right in. The dress code on the kibbutz was not exactly casual. "Garage Mechanic" would be more accurate.

I was put into a small room with Klas, a German, and Alain, a Frenchman. They explained the basics while I unpacked.

"Zee kibbutznicks, zey are not good managers," said Alain.

"And the food is sucking," added Klas, who managed to use a gerund every time he opened his mouth. Why did they bother to stay?

"Zee drinks air cheap and zee sozial life iz good," offered Alain, who later admitted dating about twenty women on the kibbutz in the span of two months.

"Friday is disco-ing night," said Klas, "so most volunteers are getting drunk."

"Zay also do ziz Zaturday zhrough Zhurzday," added Alain.

The volunteer compound, where we lived, was like an international coed fraternity with an equal sampling from Europe, Australia, and South America. To my surprise, only a few of the volunteers were Jewish, and most attached no religious significance to being on a Jewish kibbutz. For that matter, neither did most of the Jewish kibbutznicks.

I was initiated as a volunteer my first night when fellow volunteers snuck into my room and dumped a bucket of dirt and leaves on my head at three in the morning. This, I was told, was much nicer than the previous month's initiation: shaving off one eyebrow.

I began work the following morning as a dishwasher in the

tourist restaurant (Ein Gev's biggest revenue generator). It's the first job almost every volunteer gets and many develop a nasty habit of "accidentally" breaking about twenty dishes per shift to ensure a quick transfer to another job. But I accepted my task and worked diligently, at least until the supervisor's critique of my washing skills became overbearing, which took about one day. So when Klas (who had been at the kibbutz for four months, but never "graduated" from dishwashing duty) sprayed me, I sprayed back. By the end of the day I was half washing dishes and half dousing fellow dishwashers, who couldn't understand why it had taken me more than five minutes to catch on to their system.

After a week I got transferred to the mango-picking grove. Actually, my transfer was a reward for scoring a goal at an informal kibbutz soccer game. I worked hard at my new job for the first few days; then a combination of getting up at half past four in the morning, pressure from the other volunteers to eat more mangos than I picked, and a domineering boss drove me to become another typical slacker volunteer. About the time I learned to appreciate eating several mangos per day, I learned that if I didn't pick a mango just right, a micro burst of acid from the stem could hit my arms and face and give me an unflattering rash severe enough to get me transferred to my third and final job: banana picker.

This is the career I've always dreamed of, except for the bananas . . . and the lack of pay . . . and the whole manual labor aspect.

The banana bunches

weighed around eighty pounds and, after lifting them for eight hours, my arms felt like garden hoses. Some days weren't as rigorous. I just secured the banana trees to support cables, protected exposed bunches with paper bags, or drove the tractor. A tractor has about six hundred gears and I would usually grind a good number of them to make the thing move, but the banana supervisor didn't seem to mind.

I hated getting teamed up with the few older kibbutznicks (over forty-five and all male). You'd be hard-pressed to find a more domineering group of men who didn't have their own totalitarian regime. If, for example, they wanted us volunteers to follow them, they'd use the Hebrew word *boa,* meaning "come." However, they'd never just say, "Boa." They'd chant it: "Boa! Boa! Boa! Boa! Boa! Boa!" as though they were speaking in tongues, and they wouldn't stop until we were standing right next to them. I repeatedly explained that I wasn't a dog*, and one "boa" would suffice. It never helped.

By far the friendliest and most hardworking members of our group were the Ethiopian Jews. The problem was I didn't speak Ethiopian. And the Israelis didn't speak Ethiopian. And the Ethiopians didn't speak English or Hebrew. So, even though I worked side by side with them all day, we didn't have much in the way of meaningful communication. But they were always smiling. I never saw anyone have so much fun farming. They were probably just happy to see actual food coming out of the ground.

Meeting Israelis outside of work was frustrating because of the disconnected social structure of the kibbutz. Actually, it was more like segregation. We volunteers had our bar and the kibbutznicks had theirs. In the cafeteria, we had our own separate eating area. My first day, I scorned my fellow volunteers for not making an effort to

---

*The kibbutznicks often confused "dog" with "Doug." And in Hebrew, "doug" means "fish." So, in their minds, they were treating me like a fish, not a dog, which may have accounted for some of the confusion.

integrate with the kibbutznicks and learn the language and culture.

"Go sitting with them," Klas told me.

So I walked over and joined some elderly Israelis. They told me I was in someone's chair and asked me to move. I scooted down a little to where a younger Israeli was sitting. We started a conversation, but when a few more kibbutznicks showed up, he switched back to Hebrew and completely ignored me. Defeated, I returned to the volunteer table, where I discovered many others had had a similar experience.

There were surprisingly few opportunities to make contact with the kibbutznicks, and the handful of conversations I had never lasted longer than a drive-thru fast-food order. Ein Gev used to have an Adopt-a-Volunteer program until a few male volunteers had affairs with the women in their Adopt-a-Families while the Adopt-a-Husbands and Adopt-a Boyfriends were away on military service. One kibbutznick confided, "It's just easier to stay distant. Most volunteers don't really care about the kibbutz anyway. They just want to party." During my stay, I did meet a few friendly kibbutznicks—roughly the same number as volunteers who were genuinely interested in working.

Several kibbutznicks admitted to me that they unloaded some of the most menial jobs on volunteers and didn't make much effort to get to know them because they were "lazy" and would "leave before you had a chance to become friends." On the other hand, most volunteers came because they wanted a relatively cheap holiday and their interest in Israeli culture didn't seem to extend much beyond drinking Israeli beer (which, by the way, was not bad). It seemed to me that the whole volunteer program had gone astray.

As someone who arrived anxious to work, interested in meeting kibbutznicks and learning about their way of life, I suppose I was a misfit. It took about a month for me to finally give up and move on, having paid over a hundred dollars to work about 160 hours. If this is socialism, I think I'd prefer minimum wage at a kosher deli.

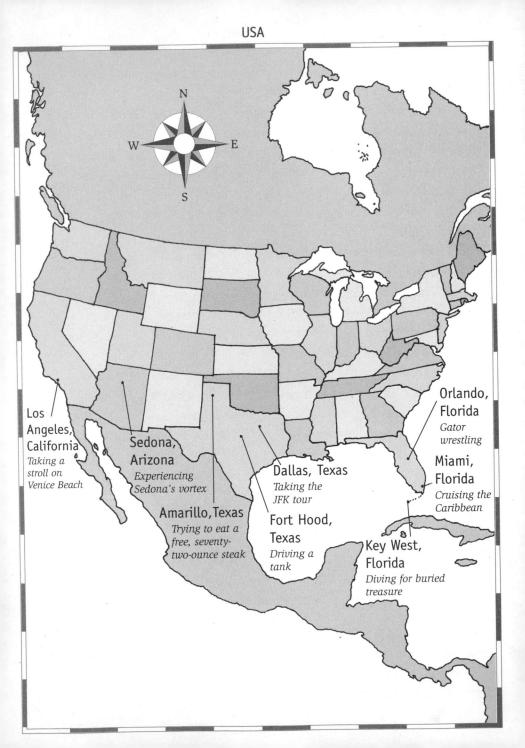

USA

N
W E
S

Los Angeles, California
Taking a stroll on Venice Beach

Sedona, Arizona
Experiencing Sedona's vortex

Amarillo, Texas
Trying to eat a free, seventy-two-ounce steak

Dallas, Texas
Taking the JFK tour

Fort Hood, Texas
Driving a tank

Orlando, Florida
Gator wrestling

Miami, Florida
Cruising the Caribbean

Key West, Florida
Diving for buried treasure

USA

The land of the free and the home of TV shopping. If Francis Scott Key were alive today, what kind of national anthem would he write? Would it have a grunge sound? Would there be "smart bombs bursting in air"? "O'er pay-per-view Rams game we watched"? When you spend a few years on the road, you get an odd view of your own country, clear in some ways, yet warped in others.

Walking through the market in, say, Istanbul, no less than twenty people (mostly carpet sellers) will ask me which nationality I am. As I say "American," I wonder what that tells them. That I have money? That I may be concealing a handgun? That at this very moment my VCR back in the States is automatically taping every episode of Oprah that I'm missing? Naturally, I try to separate myself from these stereotypes. But when you spend years divorcing yourself from your country's stereotypes, you end up feeling divorced from the entire country, and you feel a little guilty about it—as though you should pay alimony (or taxes). The only real cure is to return home for a while and have a look around. Which is exactly what I did.

Alligator Wrestling Made Easy

Gator wrestling in Florida

Orlando, Florida

 Alligator wrestling? In civilized society? Absolutely. And I'm not talking about ripping the label off a Lacoste tennis shirt. This is the real thing. Well, sort of.

Mike, a veteran alligator wrestler at Gatorland, an alligator theme park located about twenty minutes and three dollars in toll-road charges from Walt Disney World, will be the first to tell you he's more of a handler than a wrestler. Still, thirty-four of the last thirty-five gator wrestlers have been bitten, most more than once.

The alligators they wrestle aren't the 1,500-pound monsters that swim around Gatorland's pools and eat prepaid fish tossed to them by tourists, though this distinction meant little to me when I foolishly agreed to feed one a frozen chicken from the "Gator Jumping Booth." Before I was allowed to dangle over the rail with a chicken in my hand, however, Mike put a secured "safety belt" around my waist in case a jumping gator tried to take more than my entire upper torso!

I was supposed to wait for a gator to jump out of the water and then, as a reward, toss the chicken into his mouth. What actually happened was that when a gator leaped at me, I got so nervous I tossed the chicken in the direction of Cuba, missing the gator's mouth by as much as forty feet.

I continued in that vein until I emptied my poultry pail; then it was time to move on to the wrestling. I watched Mike's twenty-minute wrestling show. He didn't wear a spandex jumpsuit. He didn't do any power slams off the third rope. He didn't have a bikini-clad manager yelling at the officials. In fact, there were no officials. What Mike did do, however, was nearly as impressive. Placing just his chin on the gator's snout, Mike held its jaws open for several seconds and then put the gator into a "sleeper hold" by flipping it over. He was able to maneuver the gator with the ease of a Democratic fundraiser working a room of celebrity whale-huggers.

Then it was my turn. I suddenly felt unwell. The gators were all seven-foot-long five- and six-year-olds that weighed about 130 pounds. One hundred and thirty pounds may not sound like much, but 90 percent of their body weight is muscle and their jaws are strong enough to bite through your arm or leg if you don't know what you're doing . . . and I didn't.

I jumped across the yard-wide moat, where about ten gators were swimming, and landed in the wrestling ring, a square sand pit about five yards across. The ring and moat were surrounded by enough bleachers to seat three hundred tourists.

A surprising number of the tourists who had attended the real show stuck around to watch me go a few rounds with the gator. Perhaps the announcement of Tim Williams, the media coordinator, caught their interest. "This is Doug Lansky. He's a travel writer, and he's going to try to wrestle an alligator. You can watch if you want." The audience understood this as "This is wacko writer Doug Lansky. There is going to be blood. Lots of blood. And missing fingers. Feel free to stick around."

Mike picked out Jughead, the meanest-looking gator, and taped his mouth shut with packing tape so that he looked like a UPS nightmare. Then he let the gator back into the moat so I could fish him out.

The first trick was to find Jughead. This wasn't easy, because I was up to my thighs in water, sneaking up on a pack of gators from the rear, while glancing behind me, like a pitcher trying to keep a man on second, to see if another gator (one without packing tape) is creeping up on me.

Mike and Tim helped me locate the right tail. I grabbed it firmly as directed, and the midsized reptile started to fight. I struggled to keep my grip on the tail as he thrashed it in my face, spraying the water and making it impossible to keep an eye on the rest of the pack.

Between bursts, I hopped up into the ring and, using my weight, pulled Jughead up with me. Then, as instructed, I jumped on his back and placed both my hands firmly in the "safety position" on his neck, which was about twice the width of Roseanne Barr's.

Jughead was breathing only once every thirty seconds or so, and each breath came as a bit of a surprise. I was very conscious of not making the gator uncomfortable in the slightest, yet I definitely

Alligator wrestling is up there with the career choices my mother does not approve of. I believe punt returner, rodeo clown, and infomerical host are the others.

wanted to do my best to convince him that I was The Boss. (Though he'd probably not think twice about biting Bruce Springsteen's fingers off either.)

I was starting to get the hang of it, just sitting there on the back of a taped alligator posing for photos. Jughead seemed as happy as could be expected under the humiliating circumstances. Then Mike stepped up, put one hand on Jughead's snout, and removed the tape with the other. Jughead opened his mouth and everyone was suddenly much more serious, especially me. "Whatever happens," said Tim, "don't let go of the neck." With that, Tim gave Jughead a kick in the belly. Off he went to the other side of the ring with me riding on his back.

After that joyride, which lasted from about ten seconds to about ten years, I carefully dismounted and let Jughead scurry back into the water. More pictures were taken, hands were shaken, backs were patted, and I was told that I had wrestled a gator and could still play the piano. Which I was very glad to hear, because I couldn't play the piano before.

Available for Purchase at Gatorland:

Alligator Skin Football: $875
Lacquered Alligator Head: $595
Sunglasses with Alligator Skin Rims: $256
Alligator Skin Lipstick Holder: $39

Tanks for the Ride

Taking an M1A1 for a joy ride

Fort Hood, Texas

 I don't want you to lose faith in our armed forces when I tell you that the army just let me—a guy whose only military experience was watching reruns of *M*A*S*H*—spin around in a top-of-the-line, $2.2 million, sixty-seven-ton M1A1 Abrams tank. What should alarm you is that they let me fire it.

Frankly, I was more surprised than you. I simply rang up Cecil Green, the Fort Hood public affairs coordinator, and asked if I could learn how to drive and fire a tank. "Roger that," he replied casually, as though I had just asked for permission to come over and mow his lawn.

I arrived at oh-eight-hundred the next morning and met Cecil, an extremely obliging retired officer who certainly rolled out the camouflage carpet for me, though he had developed this funny military habit of "Roger-ing" almost everything I said.

First, he gave me a tour of Fort Hood's motor pool, which houses a third of America's ground forces and looks like the Christmas wish list for the Branch Davidians. The 2,433 tanks, 2,935 fighting vehicles, and 190 attack helicopters make Fort Hood the world's largest artillery post. ("It's not a base," Cecil often corrected me gently. "This is the army. It's a post.")

Then, Cecil introduced me to Bert Chole, the civilian simulator chief, who was extremely gracious, even if he did tell me about 600 percent more than I ever thought I wanted to know about military simulators. I eventually got the feeling he was hoping I would buy one for my personal use.

What I can tell you about his lecture is that the simulator system is called the CCTT (Close Combat Tactical Trainer) and it's for armored cavalry and mechanized infantry and should definitely not be confused with SIMET (the old system). I also learned about AAR, JANOS, UCOFT, IVIS, CID, UMCP, CES, FSE, FABTOC, and if I could remember what any of it stood for, I would gladly tell you. Apparently, the military has an AFE.*

On the outside the simulators look just like giant refrigerator units. And on the inside they look exactly like the vehicles they're supposed to simulate, which makes sense. I spent time in all the simulators, often firing at or driving into our own troops because— as in real life—it's hard to tell them apart from the bad guys; after all, they drive vehicles and wear outfits that we sold them.

After the simulator, First Lt. Walter Richter provided me with a Nomex, a green fire-retardant jumpsuit that's standard issue for tank personnel. The idea was that I should look like one of "the guys," except I had about five inches more hair on my head than any of "the guys," and everywhere I went "the guys" all stared at me and my hair as if we were the advance team for the military's first tribute to Bob Marley.

We were driven out to the tank range by our own staff sergeant in our own HUMVEE (High Mobility Multi-Wheel Vehicle), which is the modern version of the Jeep; it tips over less but breaks down more.

First Lt. Richter introduced Cecil and me to Captain Tram, a North Korean who fled to the U.S. via Vietnam and somehow ended up as a tank company commander for the U.S. Army. Our

---

*Acronym for Everything

First Lt. Walter Richter is asking me if the Army could use my large hair for target practice.

meeting went something like this:

    Tram: "This must be the journalist."

    Green: "Roger that."

    Tram: "Welcome Mr. . . ."

    Me: "Lansky."

    Tram: "Pardon me?"

    Me: "Sir, Lansky!"

    Tram: "Sir Lansky?"

    Me: "Err, I mean, Lansky Sir . . . Sir!"

    Tram: "Sir Sir?"

    Me: "Sir, yes Sir."

After we cleared up the introductions, Captain Tram fed us lunch, or in this case an MRE (Meal Ready to Eat), which is basically what you would get if you let the Pentagon get involved in the school lunch program. MREs come in twelve unsavory, high-calorie versions, and each is served in its own hermetically sealed pack. I managed to eat most of my technologically advanced corned beef hash, and I think my digestive system will be chipping away at it for weeks.

It was time to take a ride in what the U.S. Army calls "the best tank in the world." An Abrams M1A1 is the size of a two car garage, yet has the interior space of a Volkswagen Beetle. The driver is relegated to steer from a tiny space under the hood and peer through a scope that provides the sort of visibility you might get by looking through a bar straw. The Abrams M1A1 breaks down more often than a PC laptop, and it doesn't come equipped with items you'd find on most midsized rental cars: no glove compartment, no makeup mirror, no power windows. In fact, no windows at all. How's the mileage? It takes ten gallons of jet fuel just to start it up, and the 1,500 horsepower engine gulps two gallons per mile. Seems a lot for a vehicle with a top speed of just forty five miles per hour*—especially since there's no air conditioning, which makes things a bit sticky when it's 120 degrees inside and you're wearing a Nomex and a helmet and there's no place to put a cold drink. War really is hell.

But boy an Abrams M1A1 is fun to take for a spin! I was sitting at the helm of a vehicle with enough fire power to merge onto a Los Angeles freeway . . . during rush hour!

The tank rode like a Land Rover, sounded like squeaky baggage carousel, and kicked up so much dust, breathing could be better described as sucking dirt. From a distance, we looked like a moving, brown dust cloud. Perhaps this is part of the stealth technology.

It occurred to me as I was driving around in the tank, looking very much like Michael Dukakis during his famed tank ride, that quite a few people were now involved in my tanking experience. I had a driver, a gunner, and a gun loader with me in the tank, plus

---

*This is the official speed. The actual speed, I was told, is top secret.

Captain Tram, First Lt. Richter, Cecil Green, and our staff sergeant HUMVEE driver standing in the hundred-degree heat watching with binoculars. I felt I had commandeered half of Fort Hood.

I heard on the radio headset mounted in the helmet that the control tower was now giving us permission to fire at some targets with our machine gun. (Now the control tower was getting in on the act!) I switched places with

I'm seated here in the gunner's position in the world's most lethal tank. I have been sitting at the controls for a whole thirty seconds and have not killed anyone. As far as I know.

the gunner and, as I had been trained on the simulator, adjusted the magnification on the viewfinder, switched to machine guns, engaged the gun maneuvering system, and scanned for the targets.

I couldn't find the targets.

"They're right in front of you," someone from the control tower said, trying to be helpful. I couldn't, for the life of me, see them. And it didn't help that I had no idea what sort of targets I was supposed to be looking for.

After five frustrating minutes, I spotted some cutout soldiers about a half a mile closer than I had been looking. I swung the gun around, positioned the first target in the red crosshairs, and let loose a few rounds. I hit the first faux soldier and the second, but the rest of the platoon popped back down before I had a chance to fire at them. The officers in the control tower, probably the same people who counted all our SCUD "hits" in the Gulf War, told me "you got them all."

"Roger that," I replied.

As we drove back to meet my entourage, I realized that this is exactly the sort of experience wealthy Americans without press passes might be willing to pay a lot of money for. Fort Hood could be the next major adventure-travel destination: Tank Driving Fantasy Camp. Fun for the whole family! The fort already has tennis courts, swimming pools, and fast-food chains. Kids would love it.

And best of all, it would be a great way for the Pentagon to defray the defense budget. Don't be surprised if you see the brochure on the next visit to your travel agent.

Conquering the Cow

Trying to eat a free, seventy-two-ounce steak

Amarillo, Texas

This is Steak Country. Cows outnumber the trees. Vegetarians are fictional characters in books. And Hamburger Helper is considered a subversive plot by the United Nations.

It's also the home of The Big Texan Ranch Restaurant, where brave souls regularly come to beat the meat: a challenge posted by the owners to eat a seventy-two-ounce steak, a baked potato, salad, shrimp cocktail, and dinner roll in just one hour. In this Iron Man Triathlon of the culinary world, those who finish under the guidelines don't have to pay the normal fifty-dollar fee. Hence, The Big Texan prefers to call it their Free Steak Meal.

The contest dates back to 1960, when a cowboy, or perhaps a sumo wrestler, walked into The Big Texan looking hungry enough to eat a cow. Bob Lee, then the owner, fed him one . . . seventy-two ounces worth, anyway.

Roughly twenty-five thousand people have attempted this feat since, and about five thousand have succeeded, including a sixty-three-year-old woman and an eleven-year-old boy. The week before I arrived, a fourteen-year-old boy licked his plate, although it's worth noting that the lad weighed 238 pounds.

"If you finish it, you're going to puke," one of the women at the gift shop told me. "The question is: Will you puke at the table, or will you make it to the bathroom?"

One of the articles posted on the wall of the eatery came from Men's Fitness magazine, wherein two doctors explained the health risks of attempting this feat. One said it was harmful to swallow that much food, and the other agreed, adding it was particularly harmful with red meat. Nonetheless, I signed the waiver relieving The Big Texan of responsibility in case, I suppose, I were to explode.

I had a few strategic decisions to make. Did I want to slide the meat down with steak sauce or eat it dry and save the vital space? Did I want the steak cooked "well" so it would be smaller, or leave it "medium" so it would be more tender, but larger? I asked Rhonda, my waitress, for guidance, but she wasn't much help. Another waiter recommended the Taco Method. "How does it work?" I asked, eager for a hot tip. "Take the salad, the bread, the shrimp cocktail, and the potato and dump it on the center of the steak, fold the steak over it, pick it up with your hands and start chomping."

Rhonda made an announcement to the forty or so diners: "This is Doug Lansky from Minnesota and he is going to attempt the seventy-two-ounce steak. He has one hour to finish it." The crowd applauded, which just made me more nervous. Not only would failure involve getting violently sick and having to pay fifty dollars, I would also be publicly humiliated. And there was no place to hide. According to the rules, I had to sit at my own table in front of the stage.

After fifty minutes of cooking, the meat arrived. It was the size of a phone book. Seventy-two ounces translates to four and a half pounds. Or twenty-two Big Macs. I wasn't sure if I could bench press it, much less consume it.

"The Lord may forgive you," said one passerby, "but your colon never will."

I took my first bite. The meat was tender and delicious. I started cutting the monster to pieces and chewing, trying to keep up a steady, relaxed pace. Suddenly, I noticed I was the main attraction

Photo by Signe Mattsson

I suppose this is what Texans call a Happy Meal.

in the restaurant. People started taking pictures of me and everyone began taking a route to the restroom that brought them past my table. Granted, as entertainment, my only competition was an amateur singer performing some nauseating country western music and enough animal heads mounted on the walls to send a humane society member into catatonic shock.

Under the rules of the challenge, I couldn't leave the table or even stand up. I had to cut everything myself. And if I got sick, I'd lose—not to mention the embarrassment. Or the very real possibility of provoking some kind of domino puke effect.

They said I could cut away the fat and gristle, but—God knows I searched—there wasn't any to cut away. Fortunately, I didn't have to eat the garnish, the saltine cracker, the potato peel, and the two small tomatoes on the salad.

After thirty minutes using my Cut Everything into Small Pieces Method, my jaw began to cramp. I had to cut the meat into yet smaller pieces. Then my fingers started to cramp from cutting. I switched hands continuously before I finally gave up and began shoveling food in with my fingers.

I had eaten half the steak, all the salad, all the shrimp (the spicy cocktail sauce nearly made me toss up the whole shebang), and the bread with twenty minutes to go. I was on pace. But with each bite, the steak tasted less like steak and more like the flesh of a cow.

My digestive tract was clogging faster than the arteries of a chain-smoking mayonnaise tester. I began wondering how much it would cost to have my stomach pumped . . . and if all the servers had been well trained in the Heimlich maneuver.

With five minutes left, my face was green. Or maybe purple. I had consumed double or triple my biggest Thanksgiving meal and still had ten ounces of meat left, which, at most restaurants, is the amount of steak you get when you start eating. Rhonda saw I wasn't going to make it and threw in the towel, or in this case, the doggie bag.

I had made a respectable showing by all accounts, but I couldn't conquer the cow. I pushed back and noticed that, if my table was a trailer park, I could have applied for tornado disaster relief funds. I moved my debris aside and put my head down.

"Want some dessert?" asked Rhonda with a perky smile. Under Texas state law (Statute 322A: Poorly Timed Humor), I was permitted to shoot her.

Home, Home of the Strange

Taking a stroll on Venice Beach

Los Angeles, California

Are you a chainsaw juggler looking for your first big break? An unappreciated Rollerblading balloon-animal twister? A lonely, geriatric breakdancer? A militant, vegan fire-breather who can't get on *Jerry Springer*? Come and join your brothers and sisters here in Venice Beach, America's smorgasbord of the rationally challenged.

Strolling down the beach, Signe, my girlfriend, and I stopped first for a chat with Bobby Brown, a fifty-something-year-old man lying comfortably on a cushion next to a sign that read: "WORLD'S GREATEST WINO!! TRAINED IN JOKES, SONGS, AND SEXUAL COUNSELING."

Bobby, whose sign used to read "SUPPORT YOUR LOCAL WINO!" said he had been a surgical nurse in Georgia and a caddy on the PGA before losing most of his eyesight.

After an obscene joke involving Bill, Hillary, and Newt, Bobby moved on to some sexual counseling. "Foreplay, foreplay, foreplay," Bobby advised me. "Start by sucking on her ear, then work your way down." He didn't hold back on the details, demonstrating as best he could without disturbing his comfortable position. I thanked him for the advice, gave him a dollar, and moved on.

Venice Beach has no shortage of psychics and fortunetellers. All you need, it seems, is a card table and a few chairs. The first one to catch my eye was an astrologist who looked more like an IBM sales rep. He was sitting at a table with a laptop running off a Die Hard battery next to his feet. The only mystical element to his setup was his tablecloth, which was covered with little stars and crescent moons as though someone had spilled a box of Lucky Charms on it.

For five bucks, Dennis (psychic name: "Denn") typed in my birthdate and place of birth, then let his laptop plot the data. He interpreted my chart and told me that I would be "accident prone" for a week and might become "obscene with desire, perhaps even experimental and kinky."

Midway through the reading, Denn's computer crashed, which I immediately took as a bad omen. "Don't worry about it," said Denn, kicking the battery and restarting the computer, "my other computer—with a Pentium processor—works much better."

I moved down to Luann Hughes (psychic name: "Luna") for a tarot card reading. Luna looked as mystic as anyone on the beach. She had blond hair extensions down to her waist, faux fingernails long enough to take soil samples from the Earth's core, and more crystals on her table than you'd find on planet Krypton.

I shuffled the cards three times, then said my name aloud three times and handed the cards back to Luna. She fanned them and instructed me to pick several.

After examining the cards, she told me just about every cliché that came to mind: "The world is your oyster." "Your cup of life is overflowing." "Don't worry, be happy." Then, with a totally straight face, she said, "You are spending money on silly things with very little return." Hmmmmm.

Next to Luna was George French (psychic name: "Mad George"), a "Master Palm Reader." He wore a *Jurassic Park* wrist-watch and the only thing on his table was a Diet Coke.

Mad George studied both my palms with jewelers' magnifying

glasses for several minutes before he said a word. And when he finally did speak, he was confident and specific. "One thing is certain," he began, "you are a hammer, not a plow."

He told me I would live to be eighty-three. I would become rich at age thirty-five. If I had been alive two hundred years ago, I would have had two sons and three daughters.

"What about in this century?" I asked.

"With birth control and all that, who knows," he replied.

The only thing all three soothsayers had in common was that they had something to say about my relationship with my car. Denn said I was a reckless driver. Mad George told me I drove decisively. And Luna warned me of an impending breakdown. She even counseled me on getting my tires and fluids checked. I believe this says more about the traffic in Los Angeles than anything else.

Photo by Signe Mattsson

In case there's any confusion, I'm the one laying on my back.

It's hard to miss the most famous site in Venice: Muscle Beach, the outdoor weight-training facility where Arnold Schwarzenegger used to train. For three dollars, I bought a day pass, swallowed my pride, and stepped into the "Pit," as it is known by the regulars.

Almost immediately, I met Espen Tompter, a Norwegian trainer, and Stratos (no last name), a model/actor. They offered to show me the ropes.

"First," said Stratos, "you

have to take off your shirt." I reluctantly doffed my top in front of about thirty spectators. "Try not to be self-conscious," added Stratos, whose tanned pectoral muscles were each the size of a radial tire.

Espen and Stratos helped me through a series of lifting maneuvers. At one point, a young woman called Stratos and me over for a photo. This is the glamour of Muscle Beach, I thought. Then she handed me the camera and asked me to take a picture of her and Stratos. I should have guessed.

After several more strenuous acts, I said good-bye to my newfound friends and headed down the beach with my puny muscles screaming in agony.

Fortunately, about fifty masseuses offered their services right on the sidewalk. I picked one named "Shabba: Hands of Fire," who gave me the most painful, yet effective, massage of my life for four dollars plus a roll of film. Shabba wrenched from my body every Bobby Brownism, every contradictory fortune, and every muscular deficiency—I guess you could call it a true out-of-body experience.

Meditation for Dummies

Experiencing Sedona's vortex

Sedona, Arizona

☆ One look at the bulletin board outside the Eye of the Vortex Book Shop tells you they're unlikely to hold the next Republican National Convention here—unless the Republicans suddenly get an urge for colon hydrotherapy, ear coning, internal organ rejuvenation, and galactic healing.

Sedona, aside from being one of the most beautiful towns on this planet, is also the capital of all things celestial. They say that the earth's "power lines" form a vortex here, whatever that means.

Jackie, the owner of the Eye of the Vortex, advised me to try meditating on my own before I went under the guidance of a "facilitator." She mapped out a route to Rachel's Knoll, a popular local meditation spot. How do I meditate?

"It's like the reverse of praying," Jackie said. "Instead of sending messages out, open yourself to receive them. If you need to touch a rock or a tree to get in touch with nature, then do it. And if you want to lay down and fall asleep, that's okay too."

"It's okay to go to sleep?"

"Sure, but it's better to stay awake. You may have a sighting."

"A sighting?"

"See a UFO," she clarified, finally realizing she was dealing with a total moron.

The sun was setting and neither Signe, my girlfriend, nor I had eaten since breakfast, so I stuck a granola bar in my pocket before we started our hike up the knoll. My first sighting was of a bull running towards me. I started running from it, wondering if this was a sign and how I should interpret it. A charging bull reminded me of the Running of the Bulls, which reminded me of eating paella in Spain. Then, when Signe pointed out it was a cow, I thought maybe it could be a symbol for Ben and Jerry's ice cream.

Five minutes later, a giggly woman came down the hill in tight shorts and a jogging bra, holding a glass of champagne.

"Is this the way to the meditation hill?" I asked.

She paused reflectively for several awkward moments, then replied, "Yes, I am," and walked off.

I had no idea what to make of this, though it vaguely reminded me of the kind of answers I regularly receive from my parents.

Not much later we arrived at the meditation spot. The focal point was a medicine wheel: small stones placed in a circle the size of a plastic, kiddy swimming pool with another circle of stones the size of a large pizza placed in the center. Four lines of stones connected the smaller circle to the larger one. Signe, a med student, had no idea what to do with it, so we just sat on these uncomfortable rocks and stared at it.

The entire valley was lit up under the full moon. The canyon's silhouette was stunning—dark turrets, spires, and crevasses surrounded us. The atmosphere was as perfect for meditation as I could imagine, so I decided to dive right in.

I took off my shoes and socks, as Jackie instructed, and put my feet on the ground. It was immediately apparent that my feet really stunk and I hoped the smell wasn't disrupting the vortex or its power lines, perhaps causing a spiritual blackout across the globe.

My concentration wasn't very good because I kept thinking about the granola bar in my pocket. Imagine Bill Clinton trying to

Photo by Signe Mattsson

Here I am summoning all the primeval powers of nature, commanding the sun to set in the West.

meditate with a Big Mac in his pants.

I tried to sleep, but the stones were so uncomfortable, the only thing I could meditate about was the size of the chiropractor bill I would have to pay if I stayed there any longer.

In the silence of the valley, I heard what I thought was an airplane, but when I looked into the clear night sky, I couldn't see any planes. The noise sounded a bit odd as it bounced off the canyon walls. Signe heard it too. A "sighting"? No. As I said, I couldn't see a thing. It was just a "hearing," which, even among UFO aficionados, qualifies you as a loon.

No trees or stones called out to me to go over and touch them. I felt kind of bad about it. I was really trying to open myself to this sort of thing. I opened my eyes and spotted a bush that looked, in the darkness, vaguely like a bush in my mother's front yard, so I decided to initiate contact. I went over and touched the bush. But nothing much happened, so I gave it a hug. I really did. And it didn't feel all that bad. Signe fought back her laughter and—"just for fun"—joined me. Just then, as we were hugging this bush on the top of a hill under a full moon, a couple came walking up the trail. Of course, we didn't hear them until they were right next to us, which was quite embarrassing.

So we left.

I returned the next morning with a "facilitator." Raheilio, a thirty-something-year-old descendant of Mexico's Aztecs, brought me back to Rachel's Knoll to help me meditate. He had me lie down in the shade of a tree on a beach towel placed over a large, flat rock. Sitting near my head, he instructed me to close my eyes. Then he lit a small sprig from a juniper tree for incense purposes; however, I didn't know he was doing this. It sounded like he was lighting my hair on fire.

Then he took a rattle made from goats' toenails* (what else!) and rattled it for quite some time, which helped distract me from the helicopter flying overhead giving scenic tours of the area.

What, I wondered during something I suppose you could describe as my first induced meditation, is the helicopter pilot saying? ("And over there is the famous Raheilio. He's rattling the toenails now over that man's feet. Raheilio appears to be smiling—no wait, he's not smiling, he's wincing, possibly from some kind of pungent odor. Maybe once that guy's hair starts burning, we'll be able to see more clearly.")

Then Raheilio played a cedar flute above my head and followed this by beating a Native American drum. I could feel the drum's vibration as he hovered over me with it. Then he began chanting until I suppose I passed out.

When I came to an hour later, I didn't see any auras or spirits, but I felt very relaxed and refreshed—about how I imagine I would feel after a massage, if I could ever convince Signe to give me one. Maybe after she's finished rubbing the tree.

---

*Goats do not actually have toenails, they have cloven feet. But the cloven feet have cornified keratin, the same protein found in human toenails, so it's close enough for me, if that was what Rahelio was actually waving about. I didn't press him on the issue or take a sample back to the lab for testing.

Full Feed Ahead

Cruising the Caribbean

Caribbean Cruise

 Five million people will take a cruise in the coming year. They will eat Thanksgiving-sized meals for breakfast, lunch, brunch, dinner, and again at midnight—on the same day!—just to "get their money's worth." They will purchase expensive cocktails with very little alcohol in gigantic souvenir glasses that they have no intention of keeping. And they will attempt (in public) the Electric Slide, a line dance choreographed by people who were unable to handle the complex butt-wiggling of the Macarena.

I know this because I did it myself. I survived three days aboard the Sovereign of the Seas, a mega-liner cruise ship the size of Afghanistan.

Getting on Board

Three-day cruises usually leave Miami on Friday at 5 P.M. At 4:30 P.M. Signe, my girlfriend, and I still did not have tickets for a cruise—all the ships were sold out. We jogged back and forth between Norwegian Cruise Lines, Carnival Cruise Lines, and Royal Caribbean Lines, hoping for a last-minute cancellation . . . which is typically how I buy bus tickets in developing countries.

It doesn't quite work this way with cruise ships. No one seems to board these vessels on stand—I mean—tread-by. Each port agent was just as perplexed by our request as the next, especially Royal Caribbean, which, after our second inquiry, had the only empty cabin of the bunch. "We're not set up to sell tickets here," the manager on duty explained. "I wouldn't even know what to charge you." Apparently, cruise fares are set using the airline school of pricing, which holds that no two passengers may be charged the same rate.

There was much pleading, making of puppy dog eyes, and waving of credit cards, and at one point, I nearly blew the whole deal by calling the boat a boat. "It is not a boat, it is a ship!" she corrected me. Of course, we all know this isn't true. It's an entire island-nation.

We managed to convince her that we were from Florida (by saying: "We're from Florida.") so we could get the Florida resident discount. She called the ticket office, got the tickets printed up, extracted an enormous amount from my credit card (which was less than half the brochure-listed price), checked our passports, then realized we were not, in fact, from Florida. "You don't live in Florida!" she exclaimed. It was 4:58 P.M. The crew was starting to release the lines, so we just smiled and jogged for the ship. She didn't try to stop us.

The Cabin

Our cabin was huge. We thought perhaps we had ended up in a suite, especially after hearing most passengers gripe about how small their rooms were, but later we learned we were in the same size room as everyone else. I guess it depends where you're coming from. We were coming from camping in our rental station wagon. Everyone else, I presume, was coming from someplace with indoor plumbing.

My favorite part of the room—by far—was the toilet. I think if this were a seven-day cruise I would have wanted to spend half a day playing with it. Unlike most toilets that swirl water around, the ship's toilets were hooked to a vacuum strong enough to suck a

Bratwurst through a swizzle stick. I used larger and larger discretionary cabin items to test its suction capacity, until Signe stopped me when I reached for a pillow.

The first order of business was to do some laundry, since we hadn't come prepared with a fresh wardrobe. The ship washes laundry for what they call a "reasonable" rate. I suppose that depends on your definition of reasonable. The laundry list read more like a menu, and everything was à la carte. T-shirt: $2.50. Pants: $3.50. Swimsuit: $2. Socks: $1. Bandanna: $.75. To wash one load would have cost $25. Without dry cleaning! We did our laundry in the sink and then decorated the cabin with it, hoping it would dry before the end of the cruise.

Entertainment at Sea

Ken the Cruise Director was the sort of person who required a rim shot with each joke. If there was no drummer around, he could be counted on to follow his jokes with: "Ba-da-bing, Ba-da-bang."

At first I thought Ken was some kind of hypnotist. He'd say things like: "Everyone hold hands." (Everyone would hold hands.) "Now ask the person on your left for their room key." (And people would do it.) "Gotcha! Ba-da-bing, Ba-da-bang."

Then I realized that the audience was prehypnotized—perhaps it was the brochure or something they ate on the way to Miami—because when Ken wasn't around, some passengers would parade around holding hands (often in white loafers without socks) and carry on about "What if the person on my left had actually given me their room key?"

But Ken was always around. He made almost-hourly announcements over the PA and he was featured on the ship's closed circuit television channel. I remember one moment watching Ken on TV while listening to him make an announcement over the PA just as we were getting ready to go to an event hosted by Ken.

Everything that happened on board, even when Ken was not present, was complemented with a special drink, and you could bet your cocktail umbrella a ship's photographer would be on hand to take a picture of you drinking it. There was a

During our journalistic investigation, Signe and I moved about the ship in disguise. Captain Gunnar has no idea who we are.

"Welcome on Board" drink, a "Love Connection" drink served during the "Not-so-Newlywed" game, a "Sex on the Beach" drink served during Karaoke, and a "Save the Waves Shooter" to emphasize the cruise line's dedication to the environment.

I noticed in our cruise literature that we had an art auctioneer, Coleen Colby, on board, but I never made it to the art auction. I also skipped the "Learn-How-to-Be-100%-Happy-with-Your-Skin Clinic." Nor did I sit in on the "Friends of Bill W. Meeting," whatever that was. But I did go to "Final Bingorama," where I was surrounded by people who monitor ten cards simultaneously and play with the same neurotic behavior normally reserved for the stock market.

The final round of Final Bingorama for $1,500 was particularly memorable because this very large woman yelled out "BINGO!" and jumped up and down and exclaimed "SHOW ME THE MONEY!" several times. Then, when we discovered she had missed a number, we all—out of civic duty—booed her longer than we'd boo an NFL referee for making a horrendous call in the play-offs, and a few irate players even stood up and mocked: "Show me the Bingo! Ha, ha!*"

*I will neither confirm nor deny participation in this chanting.

Eating on Board

Breakfast wasn't easy. If you wanted to eat you had to make a decision: the continental breakfast delivered to your room, the Gigi dining room breakfast, the Kismet dining room breakfast, or the breakfast buffet in the Windjammer lounge by the pool. There was also the late breakfast that ran up until lunch.

Lunch was a bit easier. It was served as a buffet in the Gigi and the Kismet dining rooms. (There were also some organized afternoon snacks, though I never managed to find them.)

Dinner was a no-brainer. It was served in two seatings in the Gigi and the Kismet, one at 6 P.M. and one at 8:30 P.M.

Naturally, by midnight, half the ship was starving again, so the ship offered a midnight buffet.

At each of these meals, even the ones that were not buffets, you could eat as much as you wanted for no extra charge. If you wanted three of everything on the menu, all you had to do was ask for it. Eating was just about the only activity included in the price of the cruise, so people seemed determined to get their money's worth by eating every organic morsel they could get their hands on. Some passengers got so much of their money's worth that they had to go to the ship's doctor, who looked vaguely like the doctor on *The Love Boat*, except that she was not a man—but don't hold me to that.

Dinner was the only meal that had assigned seating. We were seated with a friendly group, most of whom were in the navy. (Strange, I thought, they would take their vacation on a boat.) Our table was assigned a Turkish waiter who provided impeccable service and a Portuguese busboy who looked as lost as a politician in an empty room.

I created quite a disturbance the first evening, the effects of which are still sending shock waves through the cruise-line industry. You see, I requested a glass of carbonated mineral water. This, I eventually learned, was not a drink on the complimentary drink list.

Our Portuguese busboy, who looked painfully confused by the order, brought me both water and Sprite, just to cover his bases, or maybe he thought I could mix them. I clarified as best I could using my hands as visual aids to simulate rising bubbles while saying "water." He came back with a bottle of Peregrino, imported from Italy (for an additional cost of six bucks), which I did not want. I tried to explain that I did not want to pay for it. "But you must," he implored.

Since I refused, he sought the help of the headwaiter, another Portuguese man with a better grasp of English. I told him to forget the whole thing and bring me a Coke, but he wouldn't hear of it. He wanted to show off his customer service training. I told him that the Coke is free and the Sprite is free. I would just like some generic mineral water for free. "But Peregrino is not free," he explained, "you must pay for it." The maitre d' spotted the commotion and came over to clear things up, which didn't help in the slightest.

I decided to concede defeat (and six bucks) before the captain of the ship became personally involved.

Into the Bahamas

At which island did we stop in the Bahamas? Good question. None of the fourteen passengers nor the seven crew members I asked could tell me. One woman, who had been there three times before, assured me it was called "Nassau," which is the name of the town, but not the island. The assistant cruise director told me: "It doesn't have a name. It's just 'The Bahamas.'" I learned later from a map that the island is New Providence.

What did the passengers do when they got off the ship? I followed a few into Wendy's. Yes, Wendy's! Apparently six all-you-can-eat meals per day and twenty-four-hour room service was not enough. Or perhaps, having been outside the United States for nearly ten hours, they were longing for a reminder of home.

Most passengers disembarked to buy the big three: Jewelry,

Perfume, and Booze. The jewelry, I discovered, is imported from Mexico and Italy. I asked one saleswoman why tourists buy it.

"Because it's better than the jewelry you get in the States," she assured me.

"Surely America can import jewelry as well?" I wondered.

"Yes, but it's not as good," she insisted. "Why else would all the Americans come here to buy our jewelry?"

I pointed to a silver necklace with a pendant the size of a motorcycle license plate that read "NIKE." "Who buys that?" I asked.

"Everyone. That's one of our most popular pieces."

In the "Legendary Straw Market" I saw coconuts painted like American footballs and straw hats with Tickle Me Elmos beautifully stitched onto them. This is one of the odd things about mass tourism: tourists want to find something traditional, and locals want to fabricate something they think the tourists will like. So tourists usually end up buying some kind of bizarre cultural crossbreed.

The woman at the Nassau tourist office told me that several of the tourist beaches were completely off-limits to the locals. I asked her how it felt to be banned from a place in your own country. "No one cares," she said, "because locals don't go to the beach." What's the most common question at the Nassau tourist office? "Where's the bathroom?" (It's just behind the tourist office.) And what do the locals on New Providence do when they have a vacation? "They fly to Miami and go shopping."

The Private Island

The second day, the ship anchored just off Coco Cay, a tiny island owned by Royal Caribbean Cruise Lines. It was about as private as you can imagine a tiny Caribbean island could be with two thousand cruise passengers and their kids roaming all over it.

The first thing we did upon landing on Coco Cay was—you'll never guess—eat. A gargantuan buffet was waiting for us.

I didn't want to shell out thirty bucks to snorkel, so I just waited around until all the snorkelers got third-degree sunburns, then I asked one if I could borrow his snorkeling gear. In addition to the gear, this kind man also gave me a roll to feed the fish with. I thanked him and stuck it in my pocket.

The cruise people running the island mandated that every snorkeler wear a special scuba life vest, just so—I presume—they could charge anyone who tried to save money by bringing their own snorkeling gear. As a scuba diver and decent swimmer, I refused to wear this life vest while swimming in seven feet of water, especially since a life vest was not required for swimming in the same area. So I took off my snorkeling gear and stuck it in my swimsuit and pretended to be a swimmer, although this was not a very effective way to view the fish. I swam like this most of the way out to the underwater plane wreck (an old Cessna planted there by the cruise line so they could rent out snorkel equipment—since most of the bottom was covered with sea grass, which looks nearly as exciting as your front lawn would look under seven feet of water).

Once I put the snorkel on, I spent so much time avoiding the snorkel instructors that I forgot to take the roll out of my pocket. I only became aware of the soggy bread lump as I began wading out of the water, so I dredged up the roll (the major pieces of it, anyway) and tossed it into the ocean. Almost immediately, an eight-year-old kid came up for air and accidentally swallowed half of it, started coughing violently, and—thank God—spit it up before I had to perform the Heimlich maneuver.

Two Thumbs Up

Cruising is a 60-billion-dollar industry. And for good reason. The people I saw on board just love to cruise; they ate, gambled, danced, and applauded at all the right times and usually with a smile. When our Norwegian captain, Gunnar Oien, announced that a new ship was being built at this very moment that would be *twice* as big, everyone clapped so loud it sounded like they were ready to sign up for the inaugural ride. This new ship, Captain Oien went on to tell us, will have an *ice skating rink* on board. And apparently this was not a joke, because Ken was right there and we didn't hear the slightest peep out of him.

Ken did eventually take the microphone (surprise) and point out that there were upwards of fifty nationalities working and vacationing on the ship and wouldn't it be great if the world could get along as well as we had for three days. Of course, what Ken forgot to mention is this would only work if we could put the whole world on a cruise ship and set it up so that all the people from undeveloped and underdeveloped nations had to pamper the people from developed nations. And the only thing the people from the developed nations had to do was promise to pay for their mineral water. Ba-da-bing, Ba-da-bang!

Top Ten Dumbest Passenger Questions
(as told by Ken and the cruise-directing staff)

10) Do these stairs go up or down?

9) Do we need to go ashore for an excursion?

8) Which elevator goes to the front of the ship?

7) What's the altitude here?

6) What time is the Midnight Buffet?

5) Is the water in the toilet fresh water or salt water?

4) Do they play music in the disco?

3) Does the crew sleep on board?

2) Does snorkeling necessitate getting wet?

1) If the photos aren't marked, how do I know which ones are mine? (The ones with you on them are yours.)

A Killer Ride

Taking the JFK tour in Dallas

Dallas, Texas

 You've seen *JFK*, the movie. You've probably read one of the eight jillion JFK books. Perhaps you've even gone to a school called JFK. Well, now there's JFK: The Ride.

It seemed morbid at first, but as my girlfriend, Signe, and I boarded the black 1962 Lincoln Continental convertible just behind the grassy knoll outside the Texas School Book Depository, Signe remarked that—with the chauffeur and convertible and all—it felt, oddly enough, a lot like going to the prom. And it did feel like going to the prom, but not mine. I took my date in a Toyota hatchback.

The car was one of three replicas of the car that took JFK down the road on November 22, 1963. Signe sat in the rear left where Jackie O. sat. I sat in the rear right where JFK sat . . . and was shot—since I figured the odds were pretty slim of it happening twice in the exact same place.

Once at Love Field, Paul (the chauffeur, guide, and JFK-mobile owner) started the tape of the actual radio announcement of Kennedy's arrival and drive into town. We followed his exact route (nearly) while we heard it described by the announcer in "real time." Paul stopped the tape occasionally to point out which buildings were there in 1963 and which were new. Some places, such as the "I Can't Believe It's Yogurt" shop, didn't require explanation.

We went down Turtle Creek Road, down Main Street, where the clock on the Old Mercantile Building still remains stopped at 1 P.M. We couldn't go up Houston street because— possibly to prevent others from making that ill-fated ninety-degree turn—it has

Signe's trying out JFK's seat and I'm checking out Jackie's perspective. During the ride, I opted for JFK's place, figuring the odds were pretty slim that it would happen twice to someone in the exact same seat.

been made into a one-way road going the opposite direction. Then, we moved slowly down Elm past the old Texas School Book Depository, thinking the tour was going to end in Dealy Plaza.

Suddenly, shots rang out*, catching us both off guard. Who fired the shots? I don't think anyone really knows. The sound, however, came from a tape recording Paul played from the driver's seat.

Paul then stomped on the accelerator. All 320 horsepower came to life, jerking our heads back and to the right. We sped off with tape-recorded sirens blaring, leaving several tourists standing in Dealy Plaza in total confusion.

This unique vantage point was surprisingly affecting, but was I supposed to act shot? Was Signe supposed to cradle my head? We weren't sure as the car picked up speed and we raced down the freeway to Parkland Hospital at seventy miles per hour. With the recorded sirens still blaring, we pulled into the emergency entrance, where we were met with strange looks from the hospital staff.

It took the entire drive back to Dealy Plaza for the effect of the

---

*I'm not sure how many.

ride to sink in. And for my wind-blown hair to settle down. I wasn't moved to tears, but I was definitely moved. Paul had made the tour about as tasteful and educational as could possibly be expected.

However, a story about the JFK assassination wouldn't be complete without a little controversy, and there just so happens to be some. The Sixth Floor Museum, located in the old Texas School Book Depository (which houses the window the Warren Commission claims Oswald fired the shots from) and the self-appointed "guides" who roam Dealy Plaza (most of whom are conspiracy theorists who started guiding during the tourist rush that followed the Oliver Stone movie release of *JFK* in 1991) are duking it out over Dealy Plaza's two million annual visitors. The museum wants to kick out the entrepreneurial "guides" and replace them with their own "guides," who would be less likely to discuss conspiracy theory and more likely to send people up to the Sixth Floor Museum. The entrepreneurial "guides" claim that this is another attempt by Warren Commission conspirators (who they believe are linked to the Sixth Floor Museum) to squelch the facts.

The conspiracy theorists, as you may have heard, believe that Lee Harvey Oswald may have been set up by any of a number of people, including a faction of the CIA, the mob, Vice-President Johnson, the local Dallas security forces, Oliver North, Deep Throat, Kato Kaelin, and someone named "Patsy." This is perhaps best summed up in the 108-foot abstract mural in the basement of the nearby Conspiracy Museum, which you can see for just five dollars. The museum owner will explain with a straight face how JFK—just before the fatal gun shot—was actually pierced through the neck with a poison dart fired from an umbrella . . . but I digress.

The most noteworthy thing about the Warren Commission's findings is that less than 11 percent of Americans believe them. However, 69 percent don't want the case reopened, so JFK, the tourist industry, will undoubtedly continue to flourish.

Looking for Mr. Gold Bar

Diving for buried treasure off Key West

Key West, Florida

You should know a few things about modern-day treasure hunting: "X" never marks the spot; treasure hunters don't have names like Eyepatch or Two Fingers or Bullet Wound anymore—they're named Mel and Pat and Kim; and if you can't find any treasure yourself, you just get a lawyer and sue someone who can.

The treasure-hunting capital of America is Key West, home of key lime pie*, Ernest Hemingway's cats, and Mel Fisher, the guy who found $500 million worth of loot twenty miles off the coast. Mel has shown that treasure hunting can be more lucrative than opening a Christian theme park or launching a new cruise ship and schlepping sunburnt, liver-spotted tourists around on the gentle sea.

Now seventy two, Mel Fisher mostly hangs out in his Key West office, which is attached to the Mel Fisher Maritime Museum and the Mel Fisher Treasure Restoration Project, where he keeps an eye on his salvage operation and signs copies of his book, *The Dreamweaver* ("The most action-packed, true-life adventure of our time!!!"), with Mel Fisher pens** engraved with Mel Fisher's famous quote, "Today's the Day!"—a quote Mel has been using for

---

*Now served on a stick!
**That work underwater!

twenty years.

I received permission to join Mel's salvage operation from Mel's amicable associate Pat, who has been working with Mel since well before 1985, when they hit the "mother lode": the cargo hold of the Atosha, a Spanish galleon that was believed to have sunk in 1622 during a storm while carrying riches from South America back to Spain.

Today, they're looking for what they believe still remains of the Atosha cargo: eight bronze cannons, sixty pounds of emeralds, thirty boxes of gold bullion, a hundred and twenty thousand stray Pieces of Eight (encrusted silver coins the size of rolled condoms), and silver bars the size of bread loaves, which, after three hundred years, will look as fungal as a real three-hundred-year-old bread loaf would look. They believe it's all down there. Most of it, however, is buried between three and ten feet under the muddy ocean floor.

I got a ride to the wreck site in a speed boat with Kim Fisher, Mel Fisher's son, who explained that the Fishers have been battling to keep their treasure ever since they found it. Everyone, it seems, wants a piece of the action. They've been to court 112 times, with a record of 111-1. You'd think after you'd won a hundred court cases, people would leave you alone. Normally, yes. But we're talking about $500 million here. The real pirates in this modern-day treasure-hunting scenario seem to be the lawyers.

Flying the Jolly Roger, Dauntless, Mel's principal salvage boat, houses a captain and four twentysomething divers, mostly from New Jersey. All four were commercial divers or scuba instructors who were looking for a change of pace; not even one was a beachcomber who made a jump to the next level. It's actually not so strange that they all came from scuba backgrounds. Mel was one of the scuba pioneers; treasure hunting used to be his hobby.

"Once you find something," Mark, one of the divers, told me, "you're hooked." I asked if he got to keep it. "No, but the boat gets a bonus." It sounded to me more like underwater gambling, but they all quickly assured me that there are plenty of casinos they'd rather visit than spend the day on the mucky ocean bottom with no visibility. The biggest frustration on the job seemed to be that the Key West video rental shop wouldn't let them check videos out for their five-day stints at sea.

Because the Atosha drifted as it sank, the treasure has been scattered along the bottom. Now that the mother lode has been found, finding the bits and pieces is a painfully arduous process. First, Mel's other son, Kane, tows a sonar behind his speed boat, and uses buoys to mark the places that get "hits." Then Dauntless comes around and the divers drop down to the muddy bottom fifty feet below with $1,500 hand-held metal detectors, clip on to the base of the buoys, and swim in continually wider circles until they find what set off the radar and record its location with a digital global-positioning system. If they can't find it that way, they've got to dig . . . or in this case, suck.

Kim and his wife, Sue, took me down to the wreck site to show me how to operate the airlift. The airlift is a massive underwater vacuum that could suck a bowling ball through an IV drip. It spits the debris about ten yards up into the water. The silt drifts off, and the chunks of shell, rock, and—hopefully—jewels come raining down.

Most commonly, the airlift uncovers metal fragments from targets destroyed by the U.S. Navy—a tad ironic since the U.S. government has been pursuing Mel in court to stop him from messing up the ocean floor during his treasure hunt. (I can't comment on the effect of stirring up the silt in a plant-free and coral-free section of ocean, but they are certainly cleaning up the Navy's mess.)

When the airlift is working, unless you happen to be right next to it, or in the one magic spot where the debris comes raining down, it feels like you're diving in dirt. Kim's wife was holding my hand so we wouldn't get separated, and when I'd look over at her, I could only see as far as my elbow. The only way you knew you were on the bottom was to keep one hand on it. Kim passed me the airlift and turned it on, but I didn't have my feet set on the bottom and the vacuum just started sucking downward into the muck and taking me with it. By the time Kim helped me straighten things out, I had sucked myself into a refrigerator-sized hole.

After I recovered from that little adventure, I searched the airlifted area with Mark. The metal detector, which clicks more frequently when it gets closer to metal, started going off like a woodpecker on Viagra. We dug a hole about a foot deep, I reached down into the muck and wrapped my hand around a metal object. A sword, perhaps? I pulled up an encrusted chunk the size of my forearm and held it up. Mark put his metal detector over it and it went off. With our adrenaline pumping, we surfaced to get a better look.

"You found part of the Atosha wreck!" Mark told me. It was the rim of a barrel.

"What's it worth?" I asked eagerly.

"Nothing. We find those all the time."

I didn't manage to find any treasure despite two days of searching. Guess I'll need a lawyer.

Epilogue:
It's a Disney World after All!

Epcot may be coming to a country near you

Orlando, Florida

If you want to travel around the world, you basically have two options: one involves careful planning, continuous hassles, and occasional dysentery; the other requires going to Orlando and buying a ticket to Epcot Center. After spending several years doing it the first way, I figured it was time to try Walt Disney's version.

So I called the Disney publicity office and told a high-ranking publicist that I was doing an in-depth profile of Epcot's World Showcase and that hundreds of millions of people might read it. Or they might not. Either way, he made two tickets available (one for Signe) and even provided us with a guide, probably to make sure we wouldn't spend the entire day drinking beer in Disney Germany. This was my first planned media-related freebie and I felt kind of, well, goofy about it. But I figured, hey, travel writers do this sort of thing all the time and as long as I informed *you* that I was sucking up to Disney for free tickets, it wouldn't be a problem.

Signe and I met our guide, Mark, in the morning. We thanked him for the tickets and his time. "Don't worry about it," Mark said, "it's on the Mouse." Mark, aside from being one of the finest human beings on planet Earth, is surely one of the most loyal workers in Michael Eisner's employ and is definitely deserving of a huge raise.

First things first. We picked up our Epcot Passports (twelve bucks), which were also "on the Mouse"—no mug-shot passport photos necessary—and I was guaranteed that no pesky customs officials would hassel us at the borders. Plus the passports came with a complete set of colorful "exotic" decals to help fill up any blank spaces that might be left over after our world tour.

We started walking clockwise around the eleven Disney countries, which were evenly spaced around a 1.2-mile man-made lake. First stop: Mexico. Disney Mexico is set behind a four-story papier-mâché (or maybe Styrofoam) Mayan Pyramid. We entered the pyramid, which was—surprise!—a gift shop, and browsed through sombreros and maracas. Then we made our way twenty meters to Disney Norway, where we took a boat ride past a polar bear (though I never saw one while I was in Norway) and a few papier-mâché fjords.

I began thinking the whole thing was shallow, but then, I figured, it can't be much more shallow than the view people get when they try to see all of Europe in three weeks. The general effect is the same: you get your stereotypes fulfilled and buy some postcards and tacky souvenirs. Only instead of, "It's Thursday, so this must be Rome," you say "It's 2 P.M., so this must be Rome, and look, there's Mickey Mouse now!"

Are the countries accurately depicted? I asked one of the Germans working at Disney Germany what the people thought about their pavilion, and she said just about everyone liked it except the German tourists. I asked if the German tourists enjoyed the other countries. "Oh, yes, they love Epcot." This proved to be true with all the pavilions: foreign tourists enjoyed all Disney countries except the "inauthentic" one that represented their own.

By the time I got to China, I had to go to the bathroom. Would they replicate the squat toilets of China? No. In fact they ducked the entire issue. There are no toilets at all in Disney China.

It wasn't until we arrived in Disney Italy that I really began to appreciate this cultural biosphere. Disney Italy was basically a Venetian backdrop. When I was in Italy recently, Venice was filled with just as many English-speaking, video-camera-toting tourists as Disney Italy and, in fact, it felt more like Disney World than Disney did—more tourists, longer lines, and more souvenirs.

I realized that Walt Disney was a visionary. Some people have said that Epcot Center pavilions do not reflect the countries they're supposed to represent. This might be true—for now. But they will soon. And it's not going to happen by redesigning or reforming Epcot; the world is what's going to change. As twisted as this sounds, the world is already changing to fit Disney's crafted version of it. The Epcot Center is, unlike Tomorrowland or Future World, a self-fulfilling prophecy.

Countries around the world are now calling their historic treasures "attractions"; they make you buy a ticket and stand in line to see everything; nearly everyone speaks English (in order to sell the postcards, T-shirts, and trinkets); and one person in every tour group I've ever seen, from the Great Pyramids to the Great Palace in Bangkok, wears a Mickey Mouse T-shirt.

Tourists, in their search to see sights and cultures around the world, have beaten down a path. So, to avoid disappointing us, many countries seemingly took a page out of Disney's replication handbook. But—and here's the catch—Disney is better at providing a glossed-over version of the country than the actual country is. They have the budget to hire better singers, better dancers, better costume makers, better sound engineers and light technicians. And Disney entertains you while you stand in line to see something. If you go to Mexico, you'll find a mariachi band playing by the pool of a five-star American hotel. Disney Mexico, at least, gives them a Mexican backdrop. Why visit Morocco and pay to watch belly dancers with a bunch of tourists in a Western restaurant when you can watch better dancers perform in Disney Morocco inside a genuine-looking Casbah?

Is there any real culture in Epcot? No, not in the theme park. But I thought I might find some among the twenty-five hundred workers, mostly young people from the eleven different countries, living together in a Disneyfied United Nations. I asked several of these foreign employees what it's like to live there. Epcot to some of them meant "Every Paycheck Comes on Thursday," but the general consensus was that it's one big party. Many think the French stick together too much, as do the Moroccans. The Chinese are lacking in English skills, and the Brits, Canadians, and Norwegians have formed something of a social club. But everyone agrees the Mexicans are the most outgoing and the Japanese are the nicest.

All in all I'd give Epcot a thumbs up. And this has nothing to do with the expensive lunch Mark bought us at Disney Japan. Naturally, it's not a place for hardened travelers who enjoy the arduous aspects of a journey or for people who are ready to spend some quality time getting to know a country. But for a large number of people who lack the deep-down urge and simply feel obligated to travel (or who lack the time and money), this is the perfect place. Where else can you walk from Norway to Morocco before lunch and still have enough energy to go water sliding in the afternoon? Disney pulled out all the stops: Morocco was clean, the Mexican water was drinkable, the British food was edible, and even the French were friendly.

And because Epcot attracts people who would otherwise water down the cultures in the actual countries, I suppose—and I never thought I'd hear myself say this—Disney is true eco-tourism!

Order Form

Qty.	Title	Author	Order No.	Unit Cost (U.S. $)	Total
	Age Happens	Lansky, B.	4025	$7.00	
	European Customs and Manners	Braganti/Devine	5080	$10.00	
	Familiarity Breeds Children	Lansky, B.	4015	$7.00	
	For Better And For Worse	Lansky, B.	4000	$7.00	
	Golf: It's Just a Game!	Lansky, B.	4035	$7.00	
	How to Line Up Your Fourth Putt	Rusher, B.	4075	$7.00	
	Italian without Words	Cangelosi/Carpini	5100	$5.00	
	Laugh Twice & Call Me in the Morning	Lansky, B.	4065	$7.00	
	Lighten Up!	Lansky, B.	3514	$5.95	
	Lovesick	Lansky, B.	4045	$7.00	
	Up the Amazon without a Paddle	Lansky, D.	5095	$10.00	
	Work & Other Occupational Hazards	Lansky, B.	4016	$7.00	
				Subtotal	
			Shipping and Handling (see below)		
			MN residents add 6.5% sales tax		
				Total	

YES! Please send me the books indicated above. Add $2.00 shipping and handling for the first book with a retail price up to $9.99. or $3.00 for the first book with a retail price of over $9.99. Add $1.00 shipping and handling for each additional book. All orders must be prepaid. Most orders are shipped within two days by U.S. Mail (7–9 delivery days). Rush shipping is available for an extra charge. Overseas postage will be billed. **Quantity discounts available upon request.**

Send book(s) to:

Name _____ Address _____

City _____ State _____ Zip _____

Telephone (_____)_____

Payment via:

❑ Check or money order payable to Meadowbrook Press (No cash or COD's please)

❑ Visa (for orders over $10.00 only)   ❑ MasterCard (for orders over $10.00 only)

Account # _____ Signature _____

Exp. Date _____

A *FREE* Meadowbrook Press catalog is available upon request.
You can also phone or fax us with a credit card order.

Mail to: Meadowbrook Press
5451 Smetana Drive, Minnetonka, MN 55343
Phone (612) 930-1100   Toll -Free 1-800-338-2232   Fax (612) 930-1940
www.meadowbrookpress.com

2065